RESOLVING COUNTER-RESISTANCES IN PSYCHOTHERAPY

RESOLVING COUNTER-RESISTANCES IN PSYCHOTHERAPY

Herbert S. Strean, D.S.W.

BRUNNER/MAZEL *Publishers* • NEW YORK

Library of Congress Cataloging-in-Publication Data
Strean, Herbert S.
Resolving counterresistances in psychotherapy/Herbert S. Strean
    p. cm.
  Includes bibliographical references and index.
  ISBN 0-87630-713-6
  1. Countertransference (Psychology) 2. Resistance
(Psychoanalysis) 3. Psychotherapist and patient. I. Title
  [DNLM: 1. Countertransference (Psychology)
2. Physician-Patient Relations. 3. Psychotherapy—methods. WM 420 S91ra]
  RC489.C68S77 1993
  616.89'14—dc20
  DNLM/DLC
  for Library of Congress   92-49095
                                                    CIP

Published by
BRUNNER/MAZEL, INC.
19 Union Square West
New York, New York 10003

Manufactured in the United States of America

10 9 8 7 6 5 4 3 2 1

To Marcia
my best friend

Contents

Preface

During the course of my work as a practitioner and teacher of psychotherapy, I have noted repeatedly that one of the most neglected dimensions in the study of the therapeutic process is how the clinician's personal dynamics can impede therapeutic progress. Although considerable attention has been given in the professional literature to how and why the patient or client resists facing himself or herself, only limited consideration has been given to how the therapist's fantasies, defenses, superego injunctions, ideals, neurotic symptoms, and other personality factors can contribute toward therapeutic stalemates and to negative therapeutic results.

Particularly since the publication of my book *Resolving Resistances in Psychotherapy* (Strean, 1985/1990), many of my colleagues and students have reiterated that it is one thing to understand the meaning of the client's resistances, but it is difficult to help the client resolve them unless therapists can face their *own* issues: for example, their boredom or excessive enthusiasm in the therapy sessions, their overtalkativeness or verbal inhibitions, and their latenesses to interviews or beginning the interviews too early. This book is written with the aim of trying to help therapists face and resolve the counterresistances that continually appear in the therapeutic process.

It is only in recent years that the psychotherapeutic literature has been acknowledging the fact that therapy is an ever-present interaction between two individuals whose dynamics constantly affect each other. Unfortunately, and for too long a time, therapy has been misconceptualized and misrepresented as a process in which a healthy, mature clinician ministers to an unhealthy, immature patient. This is a residue of the outmoded medical model, which frequently has had a most deleterious effect on the human partnership between two imperfect human beings.

It was not until the 1980s that the *Journal of the American Psychoanalytic Association* devoted a complete issue to countertransference, and it was not until the 1990s that an article on the personality of the psychoanalyst appeared in the same journal. An examination of other psychoanalytic and psychotherapeutic journals reveals that the subject of the practitioner's counterresistances essentially has been shrouded in secrecy (Abend, 1989; Boesky, 1990).

Just as there is no such thing as psychotherapy without resistance by the client, it is equally true that there can be no treatment conducted by any practitioner without counterresistance. Practitioners are increasingly recognizing that the idea of a therapy in which all of the resistances are created by the client is a serious distortion of the therapeutic process. Just as clients sooner or later create obstacles to therapeutic progress that they do not consciously intend, it is inevitable that practitioners will do the same. Practitioners are vulnerable human beings very similar to their clients.

As I have been studying counterresistances with my colleagues and students, we have learned that the counterresistances of the therapist are frequently similar to and as intense as the resistances of the client. For example, when a client is inclined to project his or her therapy-induced anxieties onto the therapist and aver, "You are an incompetent therapist," the therapist will be very inclined to respond, "You are an incompetent patient." Often, the therapist will not state his or her sentiment openly but will imply it through his "objective interpretation" (Glover, 1955).

In focusing this book on the clinician's counterresistances, I want to try to help the therapist genuinely accept the fact that it is no sin to counterresist; it is par for the course of treatment. When we act in a mechanical, rotelike manner, we can infer that some counterresistance is at work. Also, when we find ourselves responding to our patients or clients without thinking through in advance what we are trying to achieve, we are probably resisting dimensions of the therapeutic process. When we feel strong and consistent doses of hatred or erotic passion toward our therapeutic partner, but do not know from whence it comes, we can first tell ourselves that these reactions are inevitable and then begin to ask, "What bothers me about *treating* this person?"

One of the by-products of accepting and understanding our counterresistances with compassion and without self-denigration is that we will become more accepting and more understanding of our clients'resistances. As we comprehend the dynamics behind our own lateness to interviews and accept our own intermittent opposition to doing therapy, we will become more empathetic when our clients do the same. Similarly, as we accept and understand our own envy of clients when they possess something we don't have, our competition when we aspire to their status, or admit to our injured narcissism when they justifiably criticize us, eventually we will be able to help our clients resolve these issues within a safer and more benign therapeutic environment.

In *Resolving Resistances in Psychotherapy,* I stated:

> Although the term *counterresistance* is not foreign to most therapists, there have been few systematic attempts in the literature to discuss the therapist's contribution to the evolution, maintenance, and intractability of client resistances. From the moment the client calls on the phone for a consultation to the termination of the contact, the therapist has fantasies and feelings toward the client that strongly influence the client's activity and inactivity in the therapy. (p. xi)

I am more convinced of the validity of the above statement than when it was written close to a decade ago. In this book, I want to try to demonstrate that just as clients use their habitual defensive maneuvers to protect themselves from anxiety in the therapy, clinicians do the same. However, therapists can more easily justify their resistances to the therapeutic process than clients are permitted to do. For example, a client's prolonged silence in the therapy is frequently regarded as an opposition to the treatment; a therapist's prolonged silence is frequently regarded as a sound therapeutic technique. A client's monotone is frequently viewed as a sign of resisting spontaneity; a therapist's monotone is frequently regarded as neutrality. A client's wish to make a phone call during a session is frequently regarded as acting out; a therapist's answering the phone is frequently interpreted as the practitioner making himself or herself available to clients.

In this book, I also want to demonstrate that therapist and client, in the words of Harry Stack Sullivan, are both "more human than otherwise." Although they have different roles, therapist and client are equal partners who affect each other profoundly. I hope I will be able to help the reader become convinced of the fact that the client's resolution of his or her resistances depends in many ways on the therapist's resolution of his or her counterresistances. When therapists can accept their own errors as being human, they can help their clients do the same. As Albert Rothenberg (1988) said in *The Creative Process of Psychotherapy*:

> It is not only that erring is human and that artists assert their humanness or individuality in the errors they make, but error itself and a special orientation to error are intrinisic to the creative process. Both commission of errors and handling of errors are important and special matters in creative processes. (p. 150)

Dale Boesky (1990) has proposed that the patient's resistance is a mutual creation of patient and analyst. He said, "If the analyst does not get emotionally involved sooner or later in a manner that he had not intended, the analysis will not proceed to a successful conclusion" (p. 573). Boesky also pointed out that of the numerous problems that await future research, the nature of the manner in which the analyst participates in the analytic process especially deserves intensive further clarification.

In Chapter 1, I would like to define and clarify the concept of counterresistance and discuss several types of counterresistances as they emerge in the therapeutic process. Starting with Chapter 2 and through the final Chapter 7, we will follow the therapist from the first session to termination, focusing on him or her as a major actor in the psychotherapeutic drama. Each chapter will contain case illustrations that focus largely on the therapist. In Chapter 2 we will discuss typical counterresistances that emerge in the initial sessions of therapy. The therapist's resistance to getting data, setting fees, and defining the parameters of therapy will be discussed and accompanied by case illustrations.

In Chapter 3 we will present case illustrations depicting counterresistances to the therapeutic honeymoon—a typical phenomenon in most treatments whereby the patient feels a temporary euphoria and the therapist experiences something similar. During the course of psychotherapy, the client, after the honeymoon, experiences "the first treatment crisis" (Fine, 1982). He or she feels discouraged, disappointed, and often wants to flee from the treatment.

In Chapter 4 we will discuss and demonstrate through case illustrations phenomena such as the therapist resisting an awareness of the client's resentment, the therapist's reluctance to accept the client's criticism, or the therapist's excessive need to accept too much responsiblilty for the client's dissatisfactions.

Most clients are asked to comply with specific requests such as coming to sessions at certain fixed times and days, paying a fee, and discussing certain issues. Some therapists resist making requests of clients. In Chapter 5 we will present illustrations of therapists who feel uncomfortable about making requests of clients and will try to explain why they are uncomfortable. We will also address how and why therapists resist helping clients to continue to comply with requests and, in certain cases, how therapists encourage clients to rebel against therapeutic rules and regulations.

Although overt resistances and overt counterresistances such as lateness or forgetting an appointment are usually not too difficult to detect, subtle resistances such as not facing certain topics, intellectualizing emotionally laden issues, or mild seduction between therapist and patient are not always easy to spot. In Chapter 6 we will discuss and present examples of how therapists can collude with clients to oppose, albeit subtly, the therapeutic process.

Finally, in Chapter 7 we will discuss how the therapist can create roadblocks to termination and how he or she can avoid facing and avoid helping the client to face the inevitable anger and sadness that accompanies the termination process.

In writing this book, several individuals were indispensable in helping me make this a finished product. I am very grateful to Mark Tracten, President of Brunner/Mazel, and Natalie Gilman, Editorial Vice President, for their splendid cooperation and generous support. My wife, Marcia, edited and typed every page with her characteristic devotion. Finally, to the many patients, clients, students, and colleagues who fed me ideas, experiences, and cases, I am deeply indebted.

RESOLVING COUNTER-RESISTANCES IN PSYCHOTHERAPY

1

What Is Counterresistance?

Psychotherapy is an intense, anxiety-producing experience for both of the participants. Although the difficulties for the client have been well documented in the literature, it is only in recent years that the therapist's personal dynamics as a crucial variable in the process and in the outcome of therapy have been addressed (Viederman, 1991). Inasmuch as psychotherapy is now being conceptualized as an interactional event with two vulnerable, imperfect human beings constantly influencing each other (Boesky, 1990), the therapist's role in both enhancing therapeutic progress and in retarding it is being more carefully considered.

A crucial feature of psychotherapy that has received scant attention is how and why the therapist resists participating constructively in the therapeutic process. Although it is widely accepted among mental health professionals that all clients sooner or later will stop producing material and cease to examine themselves because they sense dangers in revealing themselves, professionals have not given sufficient time and attention to what dangers are at work for themselves as they interact with their clients.

When clients face forbidden fantasies, memories, and superego injunctions in therapy, they tend to move away from this unbearable material by utilizing their habitual defensive maneuvers. Inasmuch as therapists are not less human than their clients, when their clients' productions stir up anxiety-provoking thoughts and feelings in themselves, therapists become as equally defensive as their therapeutic partners. For example, when a client who habitually represses sexual and aggressive thoughts enters therapy, he or she will consciously or unconsciously try to avoid examination and discussion with the therapist of sexual and aggressive themes. Similarly, many a therapist in his or her daily life represses sexual and aggressive fantasies. However, what has not been documented in the literature are how, when, and where in the therapeutic process therapists steer away from material that is expe-

1

rienced as dangerous for them and how their own resistances affect their clients' therapeutic progress.

Mental health professionals, regardless of the setting in which they work and regardless of which theoretical perspective they prefer, need to face more diligently how they impede the course of therapeutic work. Concomitant with their careful scrutiny of how their clients subtly and/or overtly oppose therapeutic progress, that is, *resist* the therapy, practitioners need to observe and resolve those actions and attitudes of their own that block the forward movement of treatment. When clients are late for sessions, avoid them, or belittle them, practitioners of diverse persuasions are usually quite ready to assess the dynamic, genetic, structural, and topographic meaning of these resistances. However, they are frequently loathe to devote the same kind of examination to discover the unique meaning of the same kinds of behavior in themselves. When therapists cease to examine their own behavior in relation to their clients and/or demonstrate attitudes or behavior that impede therapeutic progress, we refer to this kind of activity as *counterresistance*.

Resistance is considered to be a universal phenomenon in all therapy, and all clients, despite their suffering, want to preserve the status quo. Similarly, counterresistance is a universal phenomenon and all therapists want to preserve their own psychological status quo. Just as many clients resist facing their wishes to merge with their therapists, have sex with them, marry them or kill them, many therapists resist facing these fantasies in themselves and, therefore, become oblivious to how their counterresistances affect the therapy. Baranger and his colleagues (1983), in examining the role of the patient in the psychoanalytic process averred, "He who doesn't cry doesn't get cured" (p. 10). It might also be suggested that he who doesn't cry doesn't cure (Boesky, 1990).

Although psychotherapists consider themselves, at least in part, as scientists, they are also artists. Consequently, different therapists, even if they subscribe to the same theoretical perspective, behave differently with the same client, depending upon their own dynamics, defenses, and values (Compton, 1990). Therefore, when therapy does not progress, it is usually a function of both the client's resistance and the therapist's counterresistance. Therapeutic stalemates, in effect, are a mutual creation of client and therapist (Boesky, 1990). If the relationship between any two mates goes stale, both of them can claim some responsibility for the happenstance! Successful therapy, therefore, requires the effective resolution of the resistances of both therapist and client (Weinshel, 1990).

When psychotherapy is conceptualized as a constant interaction between two vulnerable human beings, each resisting the process at crucial times, the notion of "therapeutic collusion" becomes pertinent. Just as marital partners select each other to preserve certain defenses, gratify specific wishes, and submit to a cluster of superego injunctions, therapists and clients do the same. And just as spouses preserve and defend certain types of dysfunctional role interactions such as sadomasochistic orgies, sexual abstinence, or emotional distance, therapists and clients also do the same. Two people have to be present and interacting for psychotherapy to take place (Compton, 1988; Weinshel, 1990); when the psychotherapeutic relationship is not working well, like all relationships, the two people are colluding, albeit unconsciously, to preserve the dysfunctional equilibrium.

CLASSIFYING COUNTERRESISTANCES

Perhaps the most thorough classification of resistances that clients in therapy pose was presented by the founder of modern psychotherapy, Sigmund Freud. In his book, *Inhibitions, Symptoms, and Anxiety* (1926), Freud discussed five types of resistance: (1) repression and other defenses; (2) transference resistance; (3) epinosic gain; (4) superego resistance; and (5) id resistance. All of these forms of resistance are shown by therapists as they interact with their clients but have not been sufficiently appreciated as ubiquitous counterresistances that very much influence the therapeutic process. Let us see how Freud's classification of resistances can be transposed to therapists.

(1) Repression and Other Defenses

All human beings are constantly bombarded by forbidden wishes, by commands from the superego that activate guilt, and by threats from the environment; all are difficult to cope with. These events create anxiety to warn us that a danger is impending. To cope with the danger, we use defense mechanisms such as repression, regression, reaction formation, isolation, undoing, denial, projection, introjection, and turning against the self (A. Freud, 1946).

Although these mechanisms are apparent in our clients as we observe them in treatment, therapists have not given their own defense mechanisms that they use in treatment the attention they deserve. Let us consider a few common examples of how therapists defend themselves in the treatment situation.

No therapist who has practiced psychotherapy has been exempt from feelings of boredom. A client's productions can seem routine after a while, his affect blunted, and his way of relating to the therapist cold, aloof, and uninterested. In response, the therapist finds his or her mind wandering to issues away from the therapy, and looks at the clock constantly, counting the minutes until the session ends.

All too often the therapist, when exhibiting the above behavior, will say to himself or herself, "I have a boring client," and not pursue the matter any further. However, if the same therapist heard that the client found the therapeutic sessions dull and monotonous, watched the clock constantly, and found the therapist to be a boring person, the therapist would probably not let the matter rest. The therapist would investigate with the client what wishes, superego commands, and external threats of the client were being warded off in the therapy that were creating anxiety and causing the client's boredom.

BOREDOM IN THE THERAPIST

When any individual is feeling bored, wishes and fantasies are being repressed at the behest of his or her superego because the wishes and fantasies create anxiety. The person then feels empty and lethargic (Greenson, 1978).

> John Alexander, a therapist in a mental health clinic, was treating Ms. Z., a single woman in her early thirties who was very depressed. After just a few sessions with her, John shared with his supervisor that he found Ms. Z. "to be a very boring lady." John lamented, "She keeps talking about how lonely she is, never examines herself, never has anything to do with me, and keeps on feeling sorry for herself."
>
> Ms. Z. was doing in the therapy with her therapist what she did with every man—creating distance and desexualizing the relationship—and John Alexander was doing with Ms. Z. what he did with every woman who did not love or find him appealing—he subtly rejected her and removed himself from her in anger.
>
> John Alexander's boredom was a defense against the anger that he felt toward his client for not loving him, a defense against the sexual fantasies that he had to repress, and a defense against the recognition that he was suffering from injured narcissism.
>
> Through supervisory discussions, John could accept his own anger and was able to admit that he felt like a frustrated and rejected lover. By doing this, he eventually was able to help Ms. Z. face her fears about being intimate with John, her therapist, and all men in general. However, had he not faced the reasons for his boredom, that is, his counterresistance, he would have continued to reject Ms. Z., albeit subtly, and she probably would have discontinued therapy.

All of us form impressions of other human beings and invariably these impressions are based partly on objective reality and partly on distortions made by the observer. Although there is some variation among individuals, most of us welcome positive assessments of our character and want to discount statements that reveal our neurotic propensities, childish yearnings, and irrational beliefs. That is because most men, women, and children want to think well of themselves and hope that others will do the same regarding them. Thus clients in psychotherapy resist facing the truth, opposing the therapist's assessments and interpretations of their attitudes and behavior.

Therapists can easily rationalize their clients' impressions of them and of their therapeutic activity, ascribing the client's assessment, particularly when it is an unflattering one, to transference reactions. However, transference interpretations can be used by the therapist to protect him or her from anxiety (Szasz, 1957).

ANGER IN THE THERAPIST

Sarah Bell, a therapist in private practice, was treating Mr. Y., a married man in his forties, for sexual problems and marital conflicts. Mr. Y. felt constantly attacked by his wife, referring to her as a "castrator." He felt that his sexual dysfunctions and marital unhappiness were due to his wife's "belligerent" attitudes.

In the early stage of therapy, Mr. Y. formed a positive transference to Sarah Bell, as he did toward his wife during their courtship and the first several months of their marriage. However, after a few months of twice a week psychotherapy, Mr. Y. began arriving late to his therapy sessions and had a combative attitude toward Ms. Bell. He began to tell her that she was very critical, "belligerent," and that when she made interpretations, she was really trying "to cut me down."

Just as Mr. Y felt attacked by Sarah Bell's observations of him, Ms. Bell felt attacked by Mr. Y.'s observations of her. However, the therapist was able to use transference interpretations as armor and told Mr. Y. that he was "distorting" her aims, seeing her "objective interpretations" as castrating remarks, and much the same way as he "distorted" his wife, he was "distorting" her. Mr. Y. experienced his therapist's transference interpretations as further attacks on himself and soon left treatment.

When Sarah Bell reflected on her own activity in the therapy after her work with Mr. Y. terminated, she realized how vulnerable and angry she was feeling when Mr. Y. experienced her the same way he viewed his "castrating" wife. She also realized that she had enjoyed the initial stage of the therapy with Mr. Y. because she was being positively contrasted to Mrs. Y. and felt affirmed as a sexual, loving woman. However, when Mr. Y. considered her to be quite similar to Mrs. Y., Sarah Bell felt hurt and unappreciated.

Crucial to understanding the therapist's defensive behavior with her client is that what she did say to Mr. Y. about himself was essentially true. The client did have an unconscious wish to be demeaned by women and inevitably would have the same complaints about his female therapist that he had about his wife. Most practitioners who work with men and women who have difficulties in their marriages realize that behind every chronic marital complaint is an unconscious wish (Strean, 1985). However, to help Mr. Y. have some conviction about his own distortions and neurotic contributions to his marriage, he needed to have a therapist who would *listen* to his complaints about her without censure or retaliation. Although Sarah's comments were correct, they were made prematurely and her tone revealed anger rather than understanding. Mr. Y.'s premature and hostile termination of treatment in many ways mirrored his therapist's premature and hostile transference interpretations.

When therapists make "correct" transference interpretations but are using them defensively to discharge their own anger and protect themselves from feeling vulnerable in the treatment situation, they put themselves in the same position as those spouses who make valid criticisms about their marital partners, but use these criticisms to avoid facing their own anxiety, fear of intimacy, and competition. The "truth" can be used as a defense in many interpersonal conflicts.

THE THERAPIST PROHIBITS SEXUAL FANTASIES

One of the frequent, if not universal, phenomenon in psychotherapy is that clients and therapists have sexual fantasies about each other. Just as clients frequently have difficulty acknowledging their sexual and loving feelings toward their therapists, practitioners often have the same difficulty with their clients. One way that therapists can defend against their own sexual excitement is to prohibit the client from overtly or covertly experiencing sexual fantasies in the therapy.

Ed Crane was a psychotherapist in private practice treating an attractive married woman in her forties, Ms. X., for low self-esteem, depression, and sexual inhibitions. Ed, a man who was a few years older than Ms. X., was enjoying his work with this client. Ms. X., after a few months of therapy, was feeling better and functioning better as she, too, was enjoying a positive feeling toward her partner in therapy.

As the mutually warm feeling between Ed Crane and Ms. X. strengthened, the latter began to express sexual interest in her therapist. She wanted to dine with him and eventually go to bed with him. When Ms. X. became more explicit about her sexual fantasies, talking about titillating foreplay and exciting positions she would like to have in love-making with Ed, he told his client that he could not help her therapeutically if they became sexual partners. Ms. X. soon left therapy.

In the above vignette, the therapist again made a "correct" statement when he said that the therapy would not work if he and the client became lovers. However, the statement was made prematurely and used to protect the therapist from experiencing the client's, as well as his own, sexual excitement. Rather than *listening* to Ms. X.'s verbalization of her erotic fantasies and learn what propelled them, the therapist instead tried to reduce his own discomfort by rejecting his client's efforts to be a sexual woman with him.

In most cases, therapists usually do not prohibit the client from verbalizing sexual fantasies toward them. However, many practitioners protect themselves from being an object of their clients' sexual fantasies by making a premature transference interpretation. This type of "intervention," nonetheless, is also a rejection of the client as a sexual person because the therapist is saying, "Don't love me. I'm just a figment of your imagination." Although the statement may be true, it is frequently used in the service of the therapist's counterresistance.

Therapists are often made uncomfortable by their clients' homosexual fantasies toward them. Instead of listening to these fantasies and encouraging their elaboration, practitioners often quickly inform their clients that homosexual urges are "normal and universal." When clients are reassured too quickly by their therapists that their homosexual desires are "normal," in lieu of feeling better, frequently they begin to wonder, and with good reason, how really comfortable their therapists are with their own homosexual desires.

REASSURING CLIENTS EXCESSIVELY

When therapists try to reassure their clients that an emotion, a lifestyle, or a character trait is "normal," they are usually trying to reassure themselves of their own "normality." When therapists have their own anxiety about a particular emotion or wish in themselves, they can try to reduce their anxiety by reassuring clients that what they show in the sessions that parallels their own emotional life is normal.

Reassuring clients is probably the most popular device used by therapists to protect themselves. Listening to clients' self-doubts; hearing clients' obsessive ruminations, wondering about whether they will lose their job or spouse; all of this, and more, can create anxiety in the therapist. Clinicians want to help their clients and, instead, the clients feel worse. Therapists want their clients to take action and, instead, the clients can feel helpless. Consequently, therapists in these situations not only begin to question their own ability, but also they feel as if they are on an emotional seesaw in their identification with the client. To diminish their own self-doubts, to increase their own self-confidence, to lessen their own hopelessness and helplessness, therapists offer reassurance.

Helen Diamond, a social worker, was seeing Ms. W. in a mental health center twice a week in psychotherapy. Ms. W., a single woman in her early thirties, sought treatment because she was constantly being rejected by men and was worried that "time was running out" and that she would "never get married."

In her therapy, Ms. W. would spend of lot of time talking about her dates with men, wondering what the "correct" responses to men should be. Ms. W. often asked her therapist if she should have sex on her first date, whether she should invite the man to her home for dinner, or if Ms. Diamond could provide an opinion on whether a particular relationship with a man was going poorly or well.

During the initial phases of the therapy, Helen Diamond tried to help Ms. W. explore her own questions and doubts. Sometimes Ms. W. would try to understand her anxiety about "conquering a man," but most of the time she wanted reassurance and advice from her therapist. Slowly Helen capitulated. From being a neutral therapist who explored her client's dilemmas with her, she became an advice giver and a reassurer. On realizing how much she was departing from her usual role as a therapist, Helen brought the case of Ms. W. to supervision.

In supervision, Helen was able to recognize that she was overidentifying with Ms. W.'s plight of "conquering men." She recalled during the discussions with her supervisor several times in her own life when she felt that she would be left "manless." Despite the fact that she was now happily married, Helen realized that the emotional state of being "manless" was one that she had not fully resolved. By reassuring Ms. W. that the latter would get a man, and by providing her client with advice on how to do so, she was, in effect, reassuring herself that she was not lacking a male partner. Concomitantly, she was stopping herself from recalling difficult times in her own life similar to those that Ms. W. was now having to endure.

When therapists reassure, give advice, make premature transference interpretations, or repress their own feelings toward their clients and become bored, they are demonstrating that, like their clients, "they are more human than otherwise" (Sullivan, 1953). To defend oneself from anxiety is a universal phenomenon and therefore all clients and all therapists will do so in their sessions with each other. Defenses are like skin—they protect the human being from danger and therefore are not relinquished readily.

Practitioners of psychotherapy can enjoy their work more and be more empathetic toward their clients when they can accept the fact that they, like their clients, will be using habitual defenses throughout the course of their therapeutic work. And, rather than reject their similarity to their clients, they will be more able to understand how their own defensive maneuvers affect the therapy.

(2) The Countertransference Counterresistance

Although Freud and many of his followers tended to separate transference and resistance as two distinct phenomena, transference must be viewed as a resistance because it preserves the status quo and protects the client against danger. When Freud initially conceptualized transference as a resistance (1912), he pointed out that patients in psychoanalysis wish to perceive the analyst as if he were a figure of the past so that they can avoid facing unpleasant emotions and unpleasant memories in the present. Rather than recognize their own wishes to continue a battle with parents or other family members, analysands can frequently ascribe parental qualities to the analyst and then feel that the analyst is provocative, rejecting, or manipulative.

Countertransference is nothing more and nothing less than the therapist's transference reactions to his or her client (Brenner, 1985). Because transference is a universal phenomenon of the mind, dominates each person's relationships to his environment, and exists in all relationships (Freud, 1912), therapists are no less exempt from transference reactions toward their clients than the rest of the human race is as they interact with others.

Just as practitioners in all helping professions need to be very aware of how they are being experienced by clients in order to evaluate the effects of their work, they also need to be quite sensitive to how they are experiencing their clients. If Jane Smith experiences her therapist as a lovable mother, she will probably take in the latter's interpretations as "good milk." If Jane Smith has a negative transference toward her therapist, she will, in all probability, experience the latter's interventions as unpalatable food which will have to be "thrown up." And, if the client has an ambivalent transference toward her therapist, she will accept some of her helper's comments, reject others, and feel ambivalent toward most of them. A therapist's countertransference toward a client may be viewed similarly.

If Jerry Jones, a therapist, experiences his client as a lovable son, he will probably respond to most of his client's productions benignly and formulate more of his interventions with warm affect. However, if Jerry Jones experiences his client as a hated brother or hated father, he will, no doubt, experience his client's productions with resentment and formulate his comments with a certain coldness or arrogance. And, if the therapist has an ambivalent countertransference toward his client, he will alternate in his responses to his client's productions, feeling warmly on occasion, hostile on other occasions, and ambivalent on most. Fenichel (1945) noted that "different analysts act differently and these differences influence the behavior of patients, and the personality of the therapist influences the transference" (p. 72). Hurwitz (1986) made the same point in describing his own personal therapy with two different analysts.

In all relationships, the transference response induces another so that sadists can induce masochistic responses in their role-partners, submissive individuals can provoke aggression in their role-partners, and anxious individuals can induce controlling responses in their role network. In psychotherapy, both therapist and client bring a cluster of transference wishes and responses to the encounter and each unconsciously attempts to induce the therapy partner to assume complementary roles (Sandler, 1976). For example, many a self-effacing client or therapist unconsciously invites his or her counterpart to assume a critical or reassuring transference response to him or her, and many a sexually inhibited client or therapist wants to turn his therapeutic collaborator into a celibate or a rapist.

Just as transference reactions are always traceable to childhood, so, of course, are countertransference reactions. However, clients and clinicians can have "compensatory fantasies" to make up for what was lacking in their childhoods (Fine, 1982). That is, the client fantasies that the therapist and/or the therapist fantasies that the client is somebody that his mother, father, sibling or the spouse should have been. "At last, I have found her (him)," joyfully avers the client and/or the therapist.

ACTING OUT BY THE THERAPIST

Mutual compensatory fantasies are probably a major variable when therapist and client fall in love and have an affair. Although the affair is usually rationalized by both partners, each of the actors in the drama believes, for a while at least, that he or she has found the "perfect" partner.

> Tony Efros, a psychiatrist in private practice, was treating Ms. V., a married woman in her thirties with two young children. She entered treatment because of her inability to discipline her children, intense hatred toward her husband with whom she had little sexual or emotional satisfaction, frequent arguments with aged parents, conflicts with friends and an aimless searching for a good job.
>
> Within a few months of her three times a week therapy, Ms. V. found that from feeling dejected and lacking in self-confidence, she became confident, assertive, and began to feel more self-esteem than she could ever recall enjoying. It soon dawned on her that she was "in love" and Tony Efros had become her "rescuer." His understanding demeanor, his unwavering empathy, and his keen insight made her feel "wanted and appreciated."
>
> As Ms. V. shared her enthusiasm with Tony and told him how grateful she felt toward him because of his outstanding help, Tony felt grateful to Ms. V. for appreciating his skills and talents as a psychiatrist. During the sixth month of therapy, at the end of a session, Ms. V. warmly and gratefully hugged Tony and with some awkwardness, he returned the hug. Tony justified his response to Ms. V. by telling himself that he was offering her a corrective emotional experience by helping her like herself more as a woman. "Being appreciated by a man she held in high esteem," Tony reasoned, "will help her appreciate herself more and raise her self-esteem."
>
> The hugs between therapist and client became more than momentary and their physical communication became more animated and less confined to hugs. Soon they were in bed having sexual intercourse on a regular basis.
>
> Although Tony was very eager to continue his affair with Ms. V., he felt uncomfortable as he concomitantly treated her in psychotherapy. Eventually he referred her to another therapist and went into treatment to try to help himself.
>
> In his treatment Tony learned that he was just as depressed as his client and was turning Ms. V. into the mother he had never had. He also learned in therapy that he was not facing his own marital conflicts and was using his relationship with Ms. V. to escape from looking at them.

As Tony studied his own countertransference reactions to Ms. V., he realized that her transference reaction to him was similar, that is, he was being experienced by her as a mother as well. Their affair, in effect, expressed a strong mutual yearning to be children and to be nurtured by a mother—a mother-child symbiosis.

Dahlberg (1970) studied nine cases in which the practitioner had sex with his patients. The practitioners were all middle-aged male psychoanalysts in a depressive period who let themselves be convinced by their patients' fantasies that they might be able to recapture a fantasied youth. Fine (1985), who studied a sample of therapists from his own caseload who had sex with their patients, concluded from his sample that the male analysts were invariably acting out some foreplay fantasy that resulted from their own inadequate sex life. "In one case the patient was being seen four times a week, two of the sessions the usual ones on the couch, and two in bed. Both analyst and patient were completely nude in bed, but while the patient was quite willing, the analyst refused to have sex with her. . . . The whole countertransference acting out was only foreplay for him" (p. 13).

It has often been recognized that a very common use of the transference is the client's projecting onto the therapist unacceptable parts of his own psychic structure—id wishes, ego defenses, superego mandates—but it has been underestimated how frequently the same phenomenon occurs with therapists who project onto clients parts of themselves. When clients project their unacceptable id impulses onto the therapist, the latter may be called by them "a dirty old man" or "a seductive wench." Clinicians can use a different type of verbiage, but when they speak with only thinly veiled contempt about a client who is "an impulse-ridden psychopath with no superego," they are frequently projecting their own unacceptable id wishes onto the client.

Very often when practitioners use pejorative diagnostic labels, aver that their clients are untreatable or need a different therapeutic modality from the one being used, and find reasons to come late or absent themselves from sessions, they are probably perceiving in the client parts of themselves that they resist confronting. Like their clients, their perceptions may be based partly on fantasy and partly on reality.

Rather early in his career Freud recognized that if the analyst did not master his own id wishes, become aware of his own defensive maneuvers, and overcome his punitive superego mandates, he could not help his patients to do the same. Said Freud, "We have noticed that no psychoanalyst goes further than his own complexes and internal resistances permit, and we consequently require that he shall begin his activity with a self-analysis and continually carry it deeper while he is making his observations on his patient" (1910, p. 145).

Freud modified his position about self-analysis and recognized that it was very difficult to be analyst and analysand simultaneously. Contemporary therapists often joke about this issue and say, "Self-analysis is impossible because the countertransference gets in the way!"

Actually, in contrast to his comprehensive and meticulous discussions of transference (1912, 1914a, 1915, 1926), Freud wrote very little on the subject of countertransference. He did point out that "the countertransference arises (in the analyst) as a result of the patient's influence on his unconscious feelings, and we are almost inclined to insist that he shall recognize this countertransference in himself and overcome it" (1919, pp. 144–145). As Abend (1989) pointed out, "Freud's original idea that countertransference means unconscious interference with an analyst's ability to understand patients has been broadened during the past forty years: current usage often includes all of the emotional reactions at work" (p. 374). This view has received much support in psychotherapeutic and psychoanalytic literature. Slakter (1987) referred to countertransference as all "those reactions . . . to the patient that may help or hinder treatment" (p. 3).

There is now a rather large body of literature on countertransference, with most authors acknowledging that it is as ever-present as transference and must be constantly studied by all therapists from the neophyte to the very experienced (Abend, 1982, 1989; Arlow, 1985; Brenner, 1985; Fine, 1982; Heimann, 1950; Kernberg, 1965; Little, 1951; Reich, 1951; Sandler, 1976; Strean, 1988). Virtually all authors agree that countertransference, like transference, can be subtle but is very influential on the therapeutic outcome (Moore & Fine, 1990). Furthermore, most writers concur that analyzing countertransference, although a constant task, is difficult for even the most experienced practitioner. Like any self-exploration, one is too easily satisfied with what Freud called "a part explanation."

In recent years, those writers who have explored countertransference phenomena have demonstrated how the client is exquisitely sensitive to and influenced by the therapist's countertransferences (Epstein & Feiner, 1979; Langs, 1976; Searles, 1978). However, as early as 1951, the psychoanalyst Margaret Little, in demonstrating the universality of transference in all relationships, pointed out that not only does the therapist hold up a "mirror" to the patient, but the patient in turn holds one up to the therapist. She also suggested that the patient can often become aware of real feelings in the therapist even before the therapist himself is fully aware of them. Concluded Little, "What comes (from the patient) may on occasion be a piece of real countertransference interpretation for the analyst" (1951, p. 39). Racker (1968) suggested that just as a patient can direct many of his neurotic tendencies toward the therapist and form a transference neurosis, the therapist can do likewise and relate to the patient with a whole array of neurotic symptoms.

Winnicott (1949) suggested that one of the most overlooked dimensions of the therapist's countertransference is hatred of the patient. And in his discussion of the therapeutic function of hate, Epstein (1979) suggests that many individuals do not resolve their problems in therapy because their hatred of the therapist is not confronted. Often this is the consequence of the therapist being out of tune with his own hatred.

> . . . Why do the destructive tendencies of the patient not enter into the transference neurosis? I would suggest that the major reason is that the patient's hate and destructiveness as they emerge in the analysis, beget the analyst's hate and destructiveness and that for most analysts, it is their own hatred more than the patient's that is abhorred. (p. 219)

Although the subject of countertransference has been receiving more attention by clinicians, it needs constant examination and reexamination. Like clients, with their strong resistance to becoming aware of their powerful transference reactions, practitioners of psychotherapy require a constant reawakening of interest in observing their countertransference reactions (Issacharoff, 1976). As Racker (1953) suggested four decades ago:

> The lack of scientific investigation of countertransference must be due to rejection by analysts of their own countertransferences—a rejection that represents unresolved struggles with their own primitive anxiety and guilt. These struggles are closely connected with those infantile ideals that survive because of deficiencies in the personal analysis of just those transference problems that later affect the analyst's countertransferences. (p. 130)

As Reuben Fine (1985) concluded in his article, "Countertransference and the Pleasures of Being an Analyst," that by facing and examining countertransference responses consistently, doing clinical work with finesse and enjoyment becomes much more possible.

COUNTERTRANSFERENCE, CHOICE OF THERAPEUTIC MODELS, AND THEORETICAL ORIENTATION OF THE PRACTITIONER

Before taking leave of the subject of countertransference in this chapter, it is important to note an issue that has received limited attention in the professional literature, namely, the practitioner's theoretical perspective, choice of therapeutic models and their relation to countertransference issues.

It is a truism that a psychotherapist's view of the human being, particularly the human being with conflicts, and what the therapist thinks will help the individual resolve conflicts, relates very much to the story of the practitioner's life. For example, Karen Horney had a very conflicted relationship with her father, a sea captain. She yearned to be with him on his voyages, but most of the time she was left to be on her own without him. It would appear that her definition of neurosis—"loneliness in a hostile world"—is an autobiographical statement. Her strong denunciation and abandonment, eventually, of Freud and Freudian theory is most probably an expression of her revenge and retaliation toward her father (Kelman & Vollmerhausen, 1967).

Similarly, Harry Stack Sullivan's notion that every child, in order to grow into a healthy, mature adult, needs "a chum" probably is related to the fact that Sullivan spent much of his childhood alone on a farm (Perry, 1982). Alfred Adler as a young boy suffered from rickets and many other diseases. He was much smaller in height than his contemporaries and resented them as well as his older brother. It is probably much more than a coincidence that Adler explained human suffering on the basis of "organ inferiority" and the "ordinal position" in the family. The discoverer of "the Oedipus complex," Sigmund Freud, may have come upon his research findings, as a child, when he tried to fall asleep in the parental bedroom (Jones, 1953).

It is helpful for practitioners to study carefully their affinity to a particular theoretical perspective or therapeutic model as well as their abhorrence of other perspectives and models. When our clients idealize and/or denounce certain individuals, or certain "isms" with a great deal of affect, we try to help them resolve their infantile attachments and overdetermined hatred. Yet, therapists, perhaps more than many professional groups, have their esteemed gurus and professional enemies. What this tells us about therapists is "the child" in them is very much alive and needs to be confronted constantly to ascertain how this "child" is affecting clients and other individuals in their professional lives.

The competition among therapists and the hatred they direct toward each other as they differ about theories, therapeutic practices, training and supervision often has little to do with the theoretical perspectives or treatment models themselves. Rather, envy, feelings of vulnerability, unresolved childhood conflicts, and unresolved transferences are influential factors that are not being confronted or evaluated by clinicians. Freudians and non-Freudians fight with a bitterness that is reminiscent of civil disorders, if not wars! Even among one "school," there are prolonged fracases. Consider the vendettas among the self-psychologists, object relations specialists, and classical Freudians. If any practitioner in any one of these "subgroups" had a client who was as rejecting of colleagues as therapists are inclined to be, the practitioner would study the phenomenon and find that many reasonable explanations evolve. However, there are few explanations available about why clinicians carry on unproductive wars with each other and therefore the battles continue.

Resolving these battles is much more than a didactic exercise. It is no different from trying to resolve other countertransference problems. We try to master countertransference problems so as to overcome biases, hatreds, maladaptive defenses, punitive superego mandates, and other immature parts of ourselves so that we can use ourselves, as best we can, to help our clients. We can help our clients much more when we hate our colleagues less, try to understand their points of view, and tone down our rigid championing of certain tenets and therapeutic practices as if they were prescribed religious rituals.

Sigmund Freud said that he always had "a beloved friend and a hated enemy"

(Jones, 1953). Many, if not most, psychotherapists have emulated the master! Had Freud somewhere in his 24 volumes of work tried to write about his ambivalence toward his parents, his sibling rivalry and consequent inability to cope with dissent, his sexual conflicts, and some of his paranoia, he would have provided a needed model for practitioners to confront and eventually resolve their countertransference problems.

(3) Epinosic Gain

A resistance in psychotherapy that is frequent, if not universal, is epinosic gain or what is sometimes referred to as "secondary gain" (Greenson, 1967). The "gain" that the client derives is unconscious gratification and protection from neurotic symptoms. Although there is much suffering from compulsions, obsessions, phobias, or psychosomatic symptoms such as ulcers or asthma, clients can nonetheless enjoy the benefit of being relieved from responsibilities in work, marriage, and other areas of living while being incapacitated. Consequently, they cling to symptoms.

Mental health workers now recognize that behind every client's chronic complaint is an unconscious wish. The husband who constantly complains that his wife is cold and critical unconsciously wants such a wife; a warm and encouraging mate would create too much anxiety for him to bear. Similarly, the wife who constantly complains that her husband is weak and passive unconsciously wants such a husband; a strong and active mate would create too much anxiety for her. Parents and children derive much epinosic gain as they "collect injustices" (Bergler, 1969) and spend hours in therapy castigating each other.

Although the gratifications that clients derive in maintaining their symptoms is an accepted truism, little consideration has been given to the gratification that clinicians derive when clients maintain their symptoms. In addition, it may be asked, "What do clinicians do and not do in the treatment situation that maintains and sustains the client's conflicts?"

In order to appreciate better the epinosic gains that practitioners derive from unconsciously aiding and abetting clients not to improve from therapy, we should consider some of the reasons that individuals choose psychotherapy as a career. If listening to clients daily reveal their innermost secrets is routine in therapeutic work, it would be reasonable to infer that therapists are unconsciously seeking some, perhaps a great deal of, voyeuristic pleasure. Second, if men, women, and children, in order to be helped therapeutically, need to depend on a helper with a sustained interpersonal relationship, it would follow that those who become psychotherapists derive some pleasure in being depended upon and gain pleasure from an ongoing interpersonal relationship. Related to their gratification from relationships in which clients are dependent on them, many clinicians unconsciously gratify rescue fantasies (Fine, 1982).

If one becomes a psychotherapist, it can also be assumed that mental conflict interests him or her (Brenner, 1982, 1985). Not only may the therapist, like the surgeon, be fascinated by observing another human being suffer, but also therapists may view the psychotherapeutic encounter as one where they may be able to learn more about their own psychodynamics. Finally, those doing psychotherapeutic work may be able to deny and defend against their own pathology by daily saying to themselves, "It is they, the patients and clients, who are emotionally disturbed; we, the experts, are not!"

There are many other epinosic gains that clinicians can derive as they perform their therapeutic tasks; however, like many other counterresistances, it is a dimension of clinical work that needs more research. Let us discuss a few examples of therapists deriving epinosic gains from their clinical work.

THE PRACTITIONER AS A VOYEUR

If gratifying voyeuristic wishes is an issue for practitioners, they should have sufficient understanding and mastery over their wishes so that they do not hamper the client's therapeutic progress.

> Mary Ferguson, a psychologist, was treating a 21-year-old college student in a counselling center of a major university. The student, Ms. U., sought help because she was not able to get involved in relationships with men. However, as she discussed her sexual and social inhibitions with her therapist, Ms. U. began to feel less anxiety. Within a few weeks after the onset of therapy, she was actively dating men.
>
> Mary Ferguson and Ms. U., as a consequence of the client's quick progress in therapy, drew closer to each other and looked forward to their weekly sessions. The interviews became animated and stimulating for both client and therapist as Ms. U. discussed and described in detail her many sexual encounters with men.
>
> After about five months of therapy, Ms. U. began to express concern about what she felt was her "continuing promiscuous behavior with men" and felt that she should "try to achieve a monogamous relationship with one man." Her therapist, however, told her that after living a long time as "a celibate," Ms. U. "needed" to enjoy being "a free spirit" for a while longer. The more Ms. U. championed monogamy, the more Mary Ferguson tried to convince her client that she should maintain her new "lifestyle." The differences between client and therapist grew into a power struggle, and Ms. U. left treatment prematurely and in anger.
>
> On reviewing the case of Ms. U. in a training seminar, Mary Ferguson gradually realized that she misdiagnosed the meaning of her client's active sexual behavior. Although it did reflect an overcoming of some of her inhibitions and resistances, the sexual behavior was really more of an expression of Ms. U.'s homoerotic transference to her therapist. By telling Mary Ferguson

of her sexual encounters, Ms. U. was unconsciously trying to "turn on" her therapist. It was really her growing homosexual transference that was creating anxiety for the client, and her therapist was not aware of this.

As Mary Ferguson reflected more on her counterresistance with Ms. U., she further realized that she derived a great deal of vicarious pleasure in identifying with her client's sexual activity. Consequently, she encouraged it rather than reflect with her client on its meaning. Rather than help Ms. U. gain insight into the defensive and transferential aspects of her sexual activity, the therapist encouraged it.

Practitioners can be alerted to the possibility that they are deriving epinosic or secondary gain from the therapy when they find themselves encouraging the client's behavior and attitudes rather than trying to understand with the client the meaning of the latter's behavior and attitudes.

EXCESSIVE SUPPORT BY THE THERAPIST

A popular criticism of psychotherapy is that it encourages the client's dependence and hinders the growth of autonomous problem solving. Although practitioners have been inclined to become defensive when confronted with this type of accusation, contending that for an individual to be helped in a meaningful way, he or she needs to confide in another trustworthy human being who will listen empathically and nonjudgmentally. Just as criticisms may be made for a variety of reasons and defending against them may serve myriad purposes, the idea that therapy for some clients may sustain their regressive attitudes and lower their self-confidence may have some merit.

Jack Gold, a social worker in a family agency, was treating Mr. T., a senior citizen 74 years old. Mr. T. was referred to the agency by his clergyman because he was continually arguing with his wife since the onset of his retirement from work at age 72. Mr. T., at intake, jocularly noted that as an attorney he enjoyed debating with his adversaries, but now that he was no longer engaged in legal work, he was possibly turning his wife into an adversary!

In his once-a-week treatment with Jack Gold, Mr. T. initially derived much pleasure in discussing the "old times" with his therapist. He reminisced, boasting of winning cases in court, being admired by colleagues, friends, and family, and emerging as a prominent member and leader of his community. As Mr. T. talked of his past, Jack Gold expressed admiration to him and respect for him. When the client told his social worker how aggravating his wife constantly was, Jack Gold offered sympathy and kindness. However, Mr. T. continued to yearn for and mourn the past, and his fracases with Mrs. T. continued to mount. After several months of work with Jack Gold, the client's marital and other difficulties were exacerbated.

In discussing the case of Mr. T. in peer supervision, Jack Gold and his colleagues eventually realized that by his offering constant support to his client, the latter had to inhibit any expressions of hostility toward the therapist because Jack Gold appeared to be not the neutral clinician but a doting parent. What Jack Gold did not realize was that Mr. T, who felt very unhappy about being retired, envied his therapist and felt anger toward him. However, the latent negative transference of Mr. T. could not be expressed in the treatment encounter because the therapist was overly benign, offering excessive support but limited understanding.

At no point did Jack Gold question what his client realized early, which was the obvious fact that Mr. T. was using his wife as a scapegoat. By forming and encouraging a love-and-be-loved relationship with his client, Jack Gold deflected expressions of aggression toward himself and subtly promoted Mr. T.'s marital woes.

Jack Gold derived epinosic gain from the case of Mr. T. because he had made Mr. T. a father figure with whom he could not tolerate any hostility. Not only did Jack Gold unconsciously block Mr. T.'s expressions of hostility and competition toward him, but he did not want to feel anything but kindness toward his client. In effect, he treated Mr. T. as if the latter were a helpless little boy, frightened to let him be an aggressive, assertive man in the treatment encounter.

If therapists are too friendly and supportive, they can deprive the client of the opportunity to dissent. It seems quite apparent that a very protective and strong supportive approach, frequently advocated by many therapists (Adler, 1967; Blanck & Blanck, 1979), turns the practitioner into a gratifying parent, something for which the patient is probably still looking. However, the result is that the client is forced to idealize the therapist. This offers both client and therapist a passive form of narcissistic joy, but the client's aggression goes underground only to appear in the form of increased marital conflict and other kinds of neurotic symptomatology (Nagelberg, 1959; Strean, 1985/1990).

When the client is psychologically required to suppress and disguise hostile reactions to frustration, the resistance against feelings and expressing the hateful parts of the psyche is, of course, maintained. Yet when the client is helped to discharge hostile fantasies, the ego is freed of its excessive destructiveness and the creative parts of the personality are made available for healthier productivity (Nagelberg, 1959).

THE NEGATIVE THERAPEUTIC REACTION AS AN EPINOSIC GAIN

One form of epinosic gain that Freud discovered toward the end of his career is the *negative therapeutic reaction* (1926). By this term, Freud referred to the many patients who could verbalize all the interpretations given to them but still maintained their symptoms. He reasoned that there must be some force within these patients that prevents them from using the insights that they derived from treatment. Freud identified this force as the superego.

When clients resist getting better, their superegos are restraining them from enjoying pleasure. The superego, which houses the internalized voices of important authorities in the individual's history, forbids the client to extract too much joy from life.

Concomitant with experiencing superego pressure, the client with the negative reaction to therapy is also trying to defeat the therapist—albeit in a subtle manner. By constantly calling attention to the fact that he never improves from therapy, the client is demeaning the therapist and not permitting the latter to have any meaningful impact on him. When clients insist that they are not getting better and never will, they are unconsciously discharging anger toward their helpers (Fine, 1982).

There are many possible sources for the negative therapeutic reaction. Clients may be acting out childish competition with their therapist. They may be furious that their infantile fantasies of omnipotence are not being gratified by the practitioner or that the practitioner is not an omnipotent parental figure. Clients can react negatively to denial of dependency gratification, to sexual frustration, or to the therapist's neutrality and relative anonymity (Moore & Fine, 1990).

What has to be considered as a very real possibility in the treatment encounter is that practitioners can have a negative reaction to the therapy of one or more of their clients. Clinicians are not exempt from competitive fantasies toward their clients and may unconsciously interfere with their clients achieving success in and out of the therapy. Many therapists, if not all, have omnipotent fantasies and therefore, can have negative reactions to those clients who love and/or idealize individuals other than themselves, particularly if those individuals turn out to be helpers of some kind. Being human, clinicians from time to time may want some appreciation and recognition for their hard work, but many clients do not feel ready to provide them with this form of gratification. Clinicians can then resent their clients for being too withholding. Finally, the therapist may want to be viewed as a desirable sexual man or woman and the client may not have any conscious sexual fantasies toward the therapist. Hence, the therapist can feel angry and revengeful for not appearing sexually desirable to the client.

Although feeling angry when frustrated is quite appropriate, many clinicians have such punitive superegos that they cannot allow themselves, for even a moment, to harbor angry feelings toward their clients, particularly when they have the strong conviction that they are being deprived of gratifications that are not the client's responsibility to supply. However, as we have already implied, it is precisely the client with the negative therapeutic reaction who says to the therapist, "You are a professional helper and I should not resent you for not letting me be your perfect lover, son, or daughter. Neither should I resent you for not making me feel like Superman or Superwoman—that is not your role." But, acute resentment is what the client feels, despite his or her disclaimers, and despite his or her dim recognition that it is sparked by unrealistic fantasies and expectations. And although these clients' fury is unconscious, it is nonetheless alive and is used to sabotage the therapy.

HOSTILITY IN THE PRACTITIONER

Just as there are clients who are not aware of the childish gratifications that they are seeking from the therapy, there are many therapists who are unaware of their own childish strivings in the treatment encounter. Like their counterparts, these practitioners are also unaware of their hostility toward their clients, but their unconscious hostility serves as a force to sabotage their client's growth.

Shirley Hart was a psychiatrist in private practice, treating Mr. S., a single man in his thirties who sought help for many reasons. Mr. S. was unable to sustain intimate relationships with women; he was not moving ahead in his firm where he was employed as an industrial psychologist; he was frequently depressed; and during his depressions he was sexually impotent and had suicidal thoughts.

During the first several months of the treatment, Shirley Hart and Mr. S. developed a good working relationship. Mr. S. found his therapist to be "warm, engaging, and quite sexual." During his "therapeutic honeymoon," Mr. S. began to date a woman whom he described in much the same way as his therapist. As the relationship between Mr. S. and his girlfriend deepened, the two of them thought seriously of getting married.

When Mr. S. shared his thoughts about marriage with Shirley Hart, she, without first exploring her client's fantasies, thoughts and feelings, declared, "It is against the rules of therapy to make any major decisions while you are are in the middle of it." Mr. S., taken by surprise, asked for a rationale for this rule, and when no rationale was forthcoming from Dr. Hart, he became despondent, turned the anger he had toward his therapist against himself, and kept saying, "I'm not a very good patient. I don't know how to obey the rules and I don't even know what they are all about."

Because his therapeutic experience was still very important to him and because he still had many warm feelings toward his therapist, Mr. S. compliantly explored his wishes to marry. A few times during the exploration, he had thoughts about his own mother and Shirley Hart was quick to point out, "You are acting out your childish wishes to have a perfect mother figure. Your plans to marry are self-destructive."

Mr. S., although hurt and angry again, nonetheless continued to examine his fantasies about getting married. However, while doing so, his girlfriend, a psychotherapist, started to encourage Mr. S. to become a therapist himself. Mr. S. welcomed this and told his therapist how pleased he was to think of becoming a therapist and to join his girlfriend in a mutual venture. Again, without much exploration, Shirley Hart told Mr. S. that he needed a great deal of training and supervision before going into private practice. It was shortly after these admonishing statements that Mr. S. left treatment. His girlfriend referred him to another therapist who turned out to be very much to his liking.

When Shirley Hart studied her countertransference reactions to Mr. S., she realized that her own competitive wishes interfered with helping her client move forward. She was jealous of his relationship with his girlfriend and felt displaced by her. She was also threatened by Mr. S. becoming a therapist because he would be assuming a status similar to her own. Unaware of her competition both with Mr. S. and with his girlfriend, Shirley Hart had a negative reaction to her client's growth and unconsciously aided and abetted his leaving treatment.

THE CLIENT'S STRENGTH CAN ACTIVATE ANXIETY IN THE THERAPIST

An issue that may often be a part of the therapist's negative therapeutic reaction is that the client may have conflict-free issues that activate conflict for the therapist. Consequently, the therapist, like an envious child rather than as a mature therapist, interferes with the client's growth and development. There are clients whose sexual problems, interpersonal conflicts, anxiety about dependency or aggression, or issues around self-esteem and gender identity may be less than their therapist's. However, clients, like dependent children, may have to deny that their helpers are less mature in some areas than they are and then make some kind of dysfunctional adaptation to this disparity.

Sam Isaacs was a psychologist in his middle seventies who had recently suffered a stroke. In sessions with his clients, he often became inattentive and from time to time fell asleep. His concentration being poor, he often repeated the same question or statement several times, completely unaware that he was doing so. One of his clients, Mr. R., a man in his forties who was very attached to Sam Isaacs, for months denied that anything was happening to his therapist. He referred to the therapist's sleeping as "heavy breathing," his repeated questions and statements as "emphasizing things to show concern," and his inattentiveness as an attempt to encourage Mr. R.'s assertiveness.

When clients have negative therapeutic reactions, they need therapists who can confront them with their wishes to defeat the treatment. However, when practitioners react negatively to the therapy, their clients are usually not aware of it and rarely can help them resolve it. This is why a therapist's negative reaction is much more serious. The client usually has to adapt to it, and usually the adaptation is a neurotic, masochistic one. Clients frequently rationalize their therapists' latenesses, sleepiness, irritability, sadism, masochism, and other negative contributions to the treatment.

Sometimes they do such a good job of rationalizing away their therapists' neurotic problems that they convince themselves and their therapists that the latter "have it together."

(4) Superego Resistance

Superego resistance emerges when one or more of the following conditions take place: (1) clients unconsciously obey a parental mandate to deny themselves pleasure; (2) clients unconsciously battle with their parents and significant others, and by getting better, they feel hostilely triumphant and then punish themselves by getting worse. As we saw from our review of the "negative therapeutic reaction," by feeling worse and functioning poorly, clients are unconsciously releasing anger toward their therapists and covertly trying to defeat them.

Many clients in therapy have internalized images of parents who constantly admonish them that they will never amount to anything. These internalized images are part of the client's superego, and every time the client moves forward in life and/or in treatment, he or she feels obligated to acquiesce to parental dictates.

Many individuals who practice psychotherapy have punitive superegos and therefore cannot permit themselves or their clients to derive much pleasure from life and/or from doing therapy. Practitioners of psychotherapy have been known to spend day and night for many years training to become master clinicians only to force themselves later to work day and night for many years after completing their training.

The founder of dynamic psychotherapy, Sigmund Freud, obviously suffered from a severely punitive superego. In one of his letters to Jung, Freud (Freud & Jung, 1974) wrote of the "grim necessities weighing on my work" (p. 230), and of "the thick skin we need to dominate countertransference, which is after all a permanent problem for us . . ." (p. 231). After a summer vacation in 1940, Freud lamented:

> Today I resumed my practice and saw my first batch of nuts again. I must now transmute the nervous energy gained during my holiday into money to fill my depleted purse. It always takes a week or two before they all turn up, and for a while there is enough resilience and alertness left for scientific work. Later on one is content with sheer survival (p. 359).

Tacitly acknowledging that he was a masochistic workaholic, Freud wrote to Jung in 1911: "I am delighted with your decision not to let yourself be enslaved by your practice in the future. If I do so, I must be forgiven because of my age, my complexes, and the numerous offspring I have to provide for" (p. 435).

Freud seems to serve as a paradigm for many therapists and has become the source of what Reuben Fine (1985) has aptly termed the "analytic superego," which dominates the professional lifestyles of many practitioners. Summarizing Freud, and the superego attitude of many psychoanalysts, Fine's poignant statement can probably be applied to all psychotherapists:

> Analysis is hard work, you deal with nutty people who try to drive you crazy, yet it is absolutely necessary to earn money . . . . You must never admit that you enjoy your work; always put up a grim front and complain of all the hardships (pp. 4–5).

Other writers have demonstrated that the "analytic superego" which is punitive and rigid, is not a mere fiction. Greenson (1967) wrote that the practice of psychotherapy was a lonely one and Janet Malcolm (1981) tended to imply that those who practice psychotherapy and psychoanalysis were doing something close to "the impossible."

In trying to appreciate how the therapist's superego influences his or her clinical practice, it is helpful to take a closer look at just what the superego is. Succinctly, it is that part of the human psyche consisting of the conscience and of the ego ideal. The conscience embraces that part of the superego that forbids and punishes. The ego ideal represents the part of the superego that consists of the positive, life-affirming ethical imperatives which exist in all human beings.

If a clinician's superego consists of voices that condemn human desires, then the therapist will not be able to be nonjudgmental and empathetic with his clients. He will tacitly criticize them instead, and if his ego ideals consist of notions like "perfectibility" and "superior performance at all times," he will impose too much pressure on his clients to produce and their resistances to therapy will be compounded.

THE PRACTITIONER IS JUDGMENTAL

To do effective therapy, practitioners have to provide a safe environment for their clients to be themselves and to report whatever ails them. If the client is an addict, he needs a therapist who will not condemn the addiction but will try to understand it with the client. The same nonjudgmental attitude should apply to extramarital sex, perversions, murderous wishes, and so on. Very often the clinician's condemning superego can hurt the client and the therapy.

> Mabel Josephs, a psychologist working in a clinic for clients of low socio-economic status was treating Mr. Q., a married man in his forties who came for treatment because of chronic unemployment, alcoholism, and severe marital problems. In a drunken rage, Mr. Q. would physically attack his wife from time to time.
>
> Mr. Q. responded well to his therapist's understanding attitude toward his drinking and other problems. When Mabel Josephs told Mr. Q. that he had suffered a great deal as a child and therefore found it difficult to trust others,

Mr. Q. thanked her "for pointing out something that makes me feel more like a human being." And when Mabel Josephs told Mr. Q. that he used alcohol as a substitute because he felt that not much warmth was available from human relationships, Mr. Q. told her that she was "a kind woman—the woman I should have had for a mother or a wife."

As Mr. Q.'s self-esteem rose, he drank less, worked more, and continued to derive a great deal of satisfaction from therapy. As his relationship with Mabel Josephs developed, he started to admire her clothing, her figure, and her "warm words." Shortly after expressing his words of adulation to Mabel Josephs, Mr. Q. began an extramarital affair with a woman at the factory where he worked. At first, Mabel Josephs just listened to Mr. Q. boast about the details of his sexual escapades. However, as the escapades became more frequent and the descriptions of them more colorful, Mabel Josephs began to have some question about her client's affair. As she asked him more about his motives for the affair and tried to explore his fantasies toward his partner, her tone clearly reflected disapproval.

Although Mr. Q. did not acknowledge his anger and disappointment with his therapist, after being questioned about his affair, he discontinued treatment, blaming it on inconvenient working hours.

Reflecting on the premature termination of the case of Mr. Q., Mabel Josephs was able to recognize that her own punitive superego was at work in exploring her client's extramarital affair. Her warm understanding toward Mr. Q.'s alcoholism contrasted strongly with her cold explorations of his extramarital life. Furthermore, Mabel Josephs was not sensitive to the fact that Mr. Q. was in love with her and needed help in expressing his erotic transference fantasies toward his therapist. Mabel Josephs, a married woman, eventually realized that she would have liked to have had an affair with her client, but feeling too critical of herself for just fantasying an affair with Mr. Q., she induced her client to displace his feelings onto an extramarital partner. Then she tacitly condemned his behavior rather than understand it.

FEES

An aspect of clinical practice in which the practitioner's punitive superego often expresses itself is in the area of fees. Practitioners often find it difficult to take money from clients, even if the money is given to an agency or clinic and is not handed to them directly. Some therapists believe they are hurting and even depleting their clients when they charge a high fee. Other clinicians feel guilty about arranging to have "the good life," while their "unfortunate" clients suffer. And still other practitioners contend that their limited skills and talents do not warrant their charging substantial fees.

In trying to understand the severity of any individual superego's punitive dictates, we always have to relate the dictates to that person's forbidden id wishes.

Consequently, when therapists castigate themselves for depleting their clients financially, in order to resolve their counterresistances, they have to confront their own wishes to deplete someone. If they do allow themselves to explore their acquisitive fantasies, invariably they learn that they have felt depleted by their own therapist or analyst when they were patients or clients, and are seeking revenge. Projecting onto their clients that the latter are being depleted in the same way they were when they were clients, therapists have to maintain low fees so that they won't take advantage of their clients as they themselves felt exploited in treatment.

Very often recipients of therapy sarcastically gossip about their therapists taking prolonged vacations, purchasing luxurious homes, and buying expensive clothes "on their patients' money." Many therapists, themselves, share this attitude with their clients. As this conviction is subjected to analysis, we usually find that it derives from a wish "to identify with the aggressor" (A. Freud, 1946). When children feel mistreated, exploited, and used, they often bellow, "Wait 'til I'm a mother (father, doctor, teacher)! I'll show them who's boss!" Men and women who become clinicians often have had some painful life experiences and therefore have a strong desire to demonstrate aggressively who is boss. When they achieve their goals and become "boss," they can also become frightened of their coveted positions, abdicate their authority, and charge low fees.

When practitioners have the conviction that they should not be permitted to charge substantial fees because they lack the appropriate clinical skills, usually they are beating themselves up for being in a position that they fantasy as "too powerful." Feeling like some sons or daughters who reached or surpassed the status of their parents, they feel so guilty about their power that they have to relinquish it. The realistic power is confused with omnipotent power. Therefore, one way to rid themselves of something that feels too dangerous to own is to take a vow of poverty.

Laura Klein, a clinical social worker, was working in a family agency treating Ms. P., a married woman in her forties, for depression, problems on the job at which she did not advance, and difficulties in disciplining her children.

During the first four months of her weekly treatment, Ms. P. made great strides. She began to assert herself more on the job, limited her children without feeling too much guilt, and experienced her self-esteem rise immeasurably. Having repressed much of her aggression for years, Ms. P., with her therapist's encouragement and direction, resolved many of her resistances to feeling and expressing aggression. Inasmuch as Laura Klein was experienced as a benign superego in the transference relationship, Ms. P. felt that she was being given permission to be herself and to like herself with her newly found assertive capacities.

Because the client was so pleased with her treatment, she offered to pay a higher fee for the service rendered. Laura Klein, instead of exploring her client's wish, made several interpretations: "You are feeling guilty for feeling better," she blurted out right after Ms. P.'s offer. After Ms. P. explored the possibility of feeling guilty, Laura Klein told her client that the latter was "manipulating" her. And still later, Ms. P. was told that she was turning the therapist into a prostitute.

It was clear that Laura Klein felt degraded and demeaned by the client's wish to pay a higher fee. Apparently, as a therapist Laura Klein felt like a "call girl" and money contaminated the therapy. As Laura explored her strong overreaction to her client, she realized that she stayed away from the private practice of psychotherapy because she wanted to avoid discussions of money. She had distorted the meaning of money, seeing it almost exclusively as a tool to attain power and gratify sexual and aggressive fantasies.

Very often superego resistances are difficult to resolve because the therapist feels so justified, so moral, so righteous for having them. Obeying the voices of the superego as it condemns making money, having extramarital sex, renouncing id pleasures, and so on can help the therapist feel like a desirable child. Nonetheless, feeling like a desirable child does not necessarily make one a competent therapist.

(5) Id Resistance

The term *id resistance* was used by Freud in referring to individuals in psychotherapy who continue to seek gratification of unrealistic childish wishes, such as the wish to be omnipotent infants and have all desires gratified immediately. Clinicians have learned that id resistances are ever-present in psychotherapy. Many clients want to be the therapist's favorite child and to be adopted by him or her. Often the client's fantasy of having a sexual affair with the helper masks the infantile wish to merge with him or her and never part.

Although the id resistances of clients have been accepted as a clinical reality by most practitioners of different persuasions, id resistances of therapists have received limited attention in the professional literature and in other professional circles. Yet, therapists also have wishes to be their clients' one and only. They, too, want to be loved and admired. Most practitioners may not voice their id wishes in sessions directly, but many counterresistances are id resistances. For example, some practitioners have to make themselves feel indispensable to their clients and "help" them to make calls in between sessions, chat with them after sessions, and under the guise of "support," really gratify their own dependency wishes by making their clients depend on them.

A subtle form of an id resistance may be seen in the way practitioners can couch their verbal interventions. Interventions can be made seductively, sadistically, pleadingly, masochistically, and in a variety of other ways that offer the therapist gratification. Often the response to an id resistance of the therapist is met with another id resistance of the client. Therapist and client can behave seductively with each other, can engage in sadomasochistic battles, and can promote, albeit unconsciously, power struggles with neither consciously aware of what is transpiring between them.

SEDUCTIVENESS IN THE PRACTITIONER

Although acting out sexual fantasies and having affairs is probably limited to a small percentage of therapist-client dyads, muffled sexuality that interferes with the forward movement of the treatment occurs frequently.

Michael Lyons, a psychologist in private practice, was treating Ms. O., a 19-year-old college student. Ms. O. was having difficulty concentrating on her studies, was very depressed, and though an attractive young woman, she did not seem able to meet men and have dates.

In her initial sessions with her therapist, Ms. O. told him that it was difficult for her to be going to college in New York City. Living in a big city after having resided in a small town in the Midwest seemed like a "shock" to her. She found people unfriendly and was "yearning for some warmth and understanding." Michael Lyons commiserated with his client's plight, telling her he realized "how much pain" she was in and how "lonely" she felt. Ms. O. welcomed her therapist's warm and understanding remarks and slowly but surely started to feel much better. Said Ms. O., "I was lonely and depressed and your soft, warm, understanding tone has given me the lift I needed."

The more Ms. O. lauded Michael Lyons for his soft, warm, understanding, the softer, warmer, and more understanding became his tone. And the more compassionate the therapist's tone was, the more "wonderful" Ms. O. felt. A mutual admiration society developed between client and therapist. In effect, he became her boyfriend.

Although at first Ms. O.'s self-esteem and confidence rose, when she realized in later months that Michael Lyons was only behaving like a boyfriend, but was not going to gratify her wishes except by his "soft, warm, understanding" tone in the interviews, Ms. O. became more and more depressed. Without therapist or client realizing why, Ms. O. began to feel worse after her sessions with Michael Lyons and had to be transferred to another therapist.

When Ms. O. went to another practitioner, she soon realized that she felt like a woman scorned. Underneath her depression was a strong rage because she felt teased by Michael Lyons. "He seemed to promise so much, yet did not deliver," claimed Ms. O.

Although most, if not all, clients want the therapist to be an omnipotent parent and love them as much as possible, this id resistance of the client's can only be overcome if the therapist is neutral, nonseductive, quiet, but interested. Otherwise, the client has the right to feel that her infantile yearnings will eventually be gratified.

By his seductive manner, the practitioner can induce false hopes in the client. Feeling her wishes are being alternately stimulated and frustrated, unable to release her rage toward someone she loves, a client can become depressed and even suicidal when her hopes are raised only to be dashed.

The iatrogenic effect of therapy, that is, the client gets worse from the treatment, is seen most often when the client's fantasies are not examined, not understood, not clarified, and not interpreted. Instead they are stimulated, soothed, and supported as the therapist speaks in a seductive tone while "helping" the client. In the case of Ms. O., she needed an experience wherein she could explore her conflicts in separating from home, talk about her wishes to be a young child, though being 19 years old, and examine her fears of growing up. Although Michael Lyons probably was sensitive to these issues in Ms. O., by being preoccupied with his own id wishes for closeness and intimacy in the therapy, he helped his client maintain a regressed childlike position in and out of treatment through his seductive manner. His stimulating manner fostered in Ms. O. the fantasy that he would become her rescuer and her boyfriend. When these wishes were not fulfilled, her mental health became worse than it was when she initially sought out a therapist.

Clinicians Who Show Off

A common id resistance that particularly emerges among beginning practitioners, but also among many clinicians who are not neophytes, is the wish to show the client how much they, the therapists, know and how competent they are. When clients have a strong desire to "show off," their wish to exhibit is usually addressed. Consequently, when clinicians need to exhibit themselves to their clients, some of the motives for this behavior have to be confronted as well.

The pleasure usually connected with exhibitionism is that it increases self-esteem and diminishes self-doubts (Fenichel, 1945). Similar to men or women who have to show off their genitals because they have doubts regarding the adequacy of their own sexuality, clinicians who constantly exhibit their knowledge and who have to make constant interpretations and/or offer loads of advice to their clients need to reassure *themselves* that they are competent professionals. Professionals who have sufficient self-esteem, sufficient confidence about what they are doing, and sufficient self-awareness, can like themselves as they keep quiet for long periods of time, empathically listening to their clients as the latter make many of their own clarifications and interpretations. Clinicians who doubt themselves and doubt their ability to do therapeutic work compulsively work laboriously to prove otherwise. Paradoxically, the self-doubting, anxious therapist who works very hard is often the least effective with his client. He has too much to prove to be helpful.

Frances MacIntyre, a social worker in a child guidance clinic, was working with Mr. and Mrs. N., parents of eight-year-old Jonathan, who was in treatment with another therapist. Jonathan was a very inhibited youngster, a scapegoat in his class at school, and was functioning below his capacity in his schoolwork. Mr. and Mrs. N. were both educators who were very intellectual as they related to the world, showed little spontaneity in their own relationship with each other, and behaved in a similar manner with Jonathan.

Although it was recommended after the intake interviews that what both Mr. and Mrs. N. needed was "an affective experience" in their therapeutic work—one in which feelings were championed while concepts were stressed less—Frances MacIntyre found it difficult to follow the treatment plan. Instead of helping Mr. and Mrs. N. express their anxieties, irritation, and doubts when they asked her questions about child development, child pathology, and the rationale of play therapy, Frances MacIntyre answered their questions. She explained how Jonathan's inhibitions "were part of a neurotic syndrome emerging from anxiety." The anxiety evolved "because he was frightened of asserting himself because he was frightened of his aggression." His aggression "had to do with his sibling rivalry and some oedipal rivalry," as well. The N.'s were impressed with Frances MacIntyre's brilliance, commended her frequently for "having so much insight," and were hopeful that she could come and lecture at the university where they were employed.

Although Frances MacIntyre and the N.'s had an enjoyable intellectual dialogue, they were not helped to feel more assertive and more self-confident as parents. The problems that Jonathan showed—inhibitions, fears of asserting himself, and fears of aggression—which the therapist pointed out, were also problems of Mr. and Mrs. N. To have the "affective experience" that was prescribed for them, they needed a therapist who would *not* answer their questions but would ask instead what they were feeling. In this way, the N.'s might have discovered for themselves what they were feeling, or perhaps they would have felt some irritation with Frances MacIntyre for not gratifying their requests. Either way, they would have been helped to be more spontaneous and to become aware of their feelings.

When practitioners respond to queries with answers, they are often frightened to deal with their clients' possible aggressive response. Taking their clients' aggression as a personal rebuke for their own therapeutic transgressions and limitations, they would rather impress their clients with professional knowledge. For a little while, they will feel less like a reprimanded child and more like an expert.

When practitioners find themselves trying to impress their clients, this can serve as an excellent clue that they are feeling vulnerable about something, and they should investigate what this is about. Frances MacIntyre learned that she felt threatened next to two intellectually gifted clients. Rather than use her expertise to elicit their feelings and to explore their uncertainties, she tried to impress her clients with her intellectual gifts.

In reviewing Freud's writings on the definitions and dynamics of resistance, we realize that Freud first viewed resistance essentially as an obstacle to therapeutic work; later he realized it was an inevitable reality. Until very recently, practitioners have tended to view counterresistances as obstacles to therapeutic work, rather than as the inevitable realities that they are. I should reiterate that all individuals, therapists and clients alike, have to protect themselves against danger. Just as resistances have been accepted as phenomena to investigate and understand, not to judge or deplore, counterresistances, if viewed similarly, can be assets to the therapist and to the therapy he or she conducts.

OBVIOUS RESISTANCES AND UNOBTRUSIVE COUNTERRESISTANCES

Edward Glover, the British psychiatrist and psychoanalyst, divides resistances into two groups: *obvious* and *unobtrusive*. Obvious resistances are "crass" and difficult to overlook, such as a client terminating treatment, being absent from therapy sessions, getting to the sessions late, lagging on the way to the therapist's office, and delaying departure from the consultation room. Glover also refers to other obvious resistances such as prolonged silences, "pedantic circumstantiality," and "trivial garrulousness" (1955, p. 54).

Regarding unobtrusive resistances, Glover refers to minor pauses, slips, inattentions, and circumlocutions in the sessions. Other examples of unobtrusive resistances are excessive compliance, somatization, constant self-demeaning, and subtle attempts at seduction. Unobtrusive resistances are frequently silent and most of the time we detect them in retrospect. One of their major characteristics is that they are subtle, not apparent or "obvious"(Glover, 1955).

Although resistances of the client may be "obvious" to the therapist but not to the client, we can say something similar about the practitioner's counterresistances: they may be "obvious" to the client but not to the practitioner. For example, many therapists have made the decision to terminate treatment without being aware of the fact that they really want to get rid of the client. Just as it is not always "obvious" to therapists when they prolong the course of the treatment out of their own needs, and not by the dictates of the therapeutic situation, they can also terminate treatment mainly to protect or to enhance themselves.

Practitioners can feel obliged to attend professional conferences and find other ways to absent themselves from sessions but not see that their resistance to therapeutic work is obvious. They can be late for sessions because of "important phone calls," a counterresistance that may be obvious to others, but not to them. Therapists can prolong sessions, talk excessively, remain silent for prolonged periods, become very pedantic or excessively friendly, and not be able to see these obvious counterresistances. Even when clients show them over and over what they are doing, practitioners can resist their clients' clear interpretations and clarifications and contend that these "accusations" are transference distortions.

Most of the time unobtrusive counterresistances, being subtle and silent, are easily rationalized away. As we have suggested earlier in this chapter, it is relatively easy for therapists to ascribe their inattention in sessions to a boring client, their circumlocutions to the client's need for more clarity, and their excessive compliance to and intimidation by the client to the client's need for a nonjudgmental parental figure.

Very often practitioners rationalize their counterresistive behavior the way some parents do. Parents, under the guise of meeting the child's need for limits, can be quite punitive, and under the guise of providing tender love and care they can be too indulgent and permissive. And just as there are parents who aver that their youngster is "giving me a headache," clinicians are prone to make it the client's responsibility when they suffer from somatic symptoms in the therapy sessions.

Glover believed that psychotherapists have difficulty coping with their sadistic fantasies toward their clients. Being in a helping profession in which they are expected to be understanding and empathetic can make it difficult for them to acknowledge their sadism. Glover (1955) contended that when practitioners find themselves unclear about their clients' dynamics, unsure about how the treatment is progressing, and undecided about their feelings toward clients, they should think first of their own repressed sadism.

The client's resistances often frustrate the clinician's wish to heal and, therefore, can weaken the practitioner's reaction formation defenses against sadism. Glover also suggested that nowhere is psychological viewing more complete than in the therapeutic situation, and nothing is more calculated to arouse clinician's sadism than the exasperating frustration of his or her curiosity induced by the client's resistance.

There are many examples of the therapist acting out sadism. Every therapist during his or her professional career has behaved in the following manner from time to time: browbeating the client into accepting an interpretation (rather than empathizing with his or her resistance to facing and accepting it); siding with the client against one of his or her real or imagined enemies (rather than helping the client understand the feelings of vulnerability and threat that activate his or her hostility); siding with a real or imagined enemy against the client (rather than the therapist facing his or her own fight with the client); and using pejorative diagnostic labels (Fine, 1982) such as "psychopath" or "borderline" (rather than the therapist facing his or her frustration with the client for not getting better).

More common among practitioners than overt expressions of sadism are counterresistances used to defend against their sadism. Possible forms that this can take are: oversolicitousness; unnecessary reassurances; assisting the client out of a difficulty before the client is aware of any difficulty; postponing confrontations, questions, or interpretations regarding a client's acting out; defending against the client's negative transference; and denying the existence of pathology, conflict, or resistance in the client.

THE PAST AND PRESENT AS COUNTERRESISTANCES

A phenomenon noted by many clinicians is that type of resistance where the client talks only about the present because examining the past is too painful; conversely, the client will talk only about childhood memories and refuse to see their representations in reality because talking about the present is too uncomfortable (Fenichel, 1945).

Clinicians in the therapy situation may find that the client's renditions of the past will evoke anxiety for them. In order to protect themselves, they will subtly guide the client into a discussion of present-day topics. Similarly, a client may discuss a current feeling, current event, or current thought that will disturb the therapist. To escape anxiety, the therapist will guide the client into a discussion of the past.

THE "CRITICAL" CLIENT

One of the most ubiquitous counterresistances observed in therapy is when the client has criticisms of the practitioner about the latter's *current* activity or *current* inactivity, and the therapist, in response, guides the client into a discussion of the past.

Lester North, a psychiatrist in private practice, was treating a single young woman of 22 years, Ms. M., who sought therapy because of sexual inhibitions, inability to sustain relationships with men, and constant arguments with them. After a month of once-a-week treatment in which Ms. M. spent most of her time lamenting about her poor social and sexual life, she told Lester North that she wanted to quit treatment because she found him "too cold." Berating him, she went on to tell him that he never smiled, never complimented her, and "seemed like a drag."

The therapist asked Ms. M. "to free-associate to all of the men in your past who were cold and unfriendly." Ms. M. initially complied with her therapist's request and spent a few sessions talking about her "cold" father, "unfriendly" brother, and "unresponsive" male teachers, but she soon terminated treatment, feeling "misunderstood."

Although Ms. M. certainly had wishes to sabotage her therapy and unconsciously may have maneuvered the therapy to feel misunderstood, Lester North's counterresistance probably compounded the client's resistance. Not wanting to subject himself to criticism, and therefore not wanting to help Ms. M. ventilate her doubts about and irritations with him, Lester North prematurely turned the criticisms levelled against him into her total responsibility. In this respect, he did not appear very warm and empathetic. This left Ms. M. feeling too vulnerable to continue the therapy.

When clients feel critical toward their therapists in the present, the criticisms should be aired and discussed. Feeling they are not being condemned for their hostility, clients are then much readier to recall memories of the past.

AVOIDING THE CLIENT'S SEXUALITY

Just as practitioners ward off anger directed toward themselves in the present by focusing on the client's past, they do the same with sexuality. Many practitioners feel uncomfortable in being the object of the client's sexual fantasies and change the subject, rather than help the client see what he or she wants in the present. If the client is helped to air sexual fantasies and they are accepted by the therapist, as with anger, the client will feel more enabled to enter into a spontaneous discussion of his or her infantile sexual yearnings.

As has been implied, from the inception of formal psychotherapy at the turn of the twentieth century until the present, the client's sexuality has often turned out to be "too hot to handle" for many practitioners. A good example of a therapist resisting the client's sexuality was the activity of Josef Breuer, Freud's esteemed colleague. Between December 1880 and June 1882, Breuer treated a 21-year-old woman, Anna O., who had a severe paralysis and suffered from other symptoms, including hallucinations. She was able to rid herself of her symptoms when she followed Breuer's injunction to say whatever was on her mind (Breuer & Freud, 1893–1895).

Anna O. referred to her successful treatment as "a talking cure." However, as she continued to work with Breuer, she developed an intense sexual transference toward him that was in part manifested by a false pregnancy. Breuer felt helpless in the face of Anna O.'s adoration, broke off treatment with her, and went on a vacation with his wife to have a baby with her. Here, Breuer's counterresistance to being a sexual object of his patient in the present interfered with his helping her to explore her infantile sexuality, an oversight that affected the rest of her life in a deleterious way.

Therapists can also resist facing their clients' homosexual transference wishes by encouraging them to talk about their pasts, so that they, the therapists, will be able to avoid facing their own homosexual fantasies in the present. The following are two typical examples:

Roslyn Oliver, a young social worker in a hospital outpatient clinic, was treating a 15-year-old girl, Leslie L. Leslie was referred for treatment because she was having academic difficulties, was quite depressed, and often argued with her mother with whom she lived alone. Her father left the family permanently when Leslie was eight years old.

After a period of about three months of weekly therapy from which Leslie profited a great deal—her schoolwork improved, she became more cheerful, and she began to cope with her mother with less vituperation—Leslie began to prolong the therapy hours, lingering in the therapist's office instead of leaving, called Roslyn Oliver on the phone in between sessions quite frequently, and clearly showed a desire for more contact with her therapist.

When Roslyn Oliver brought Leslie's wish for increased contact to her attention and suggested that it be discussed in the sessions, Leslie told her therapist that she was "in love" with her, would like to spend more time with her, and that she had been having fantasies of Roslyn Oliver kissing and hugging her. The therapist told Leslie that her wishes were "normal" but that Leslie really wanted to hug and kiss her mother more than she did when she was a little girl, and that was why she was having these fantasies now.

Leslie acknowledged that her therapist's remarks were probably true but that she really liked Roslyn "as a person." The more the client wished to discuss her "crush" in the present, the more the therapist wanted to discuss the client's past deprivations of maternal warmth. When Leslie asked Roslyn Oliver if she ever had feelings like Leslie was having right now, Roslyn avoided the question. In response, Leslie resumed feeling depressed, her academic work began to deteriorate, and her overall condition became even worse than it was at the beginning of treatment.

In supervision, Roslyn Oliver was able to recognize that her client's homosexual fantasies stirred up similar wishes in herself. She became increasingly uncomfortable with her own wishes to hug and kiss her client; consequently, she had to keep trying to move her client's attention away from the present and focus on the past.

Jerry Peters was a psychologist in private practice treating Mr. K., a man in his early twenties, who came for treatment because he was frequently in conflict with authorities both in the graduate school where he was studying and on his job as an accountant. Mr. K. was the oldest of seven children. He was a "father figure" to all of his younger siblings ever since his father died when Mr. K. was 13 years old.

In treatment Mr. K. talked a great deal about how much he missed having a father in his life. Said Mr. K., "I've spent so much time fathering others, I'd like one for myself." Mr. K. had continual dreams of being a little boy sitting on a father's lap, and it became quite clear that Mr. K. wanted his therapist, Jerry Peters, to be his father.

Jerry Peters never seemed to be aware of how much Mr. K. yearned for him and kept focusing on his client's "sad past." When Mr. K. asked Jerry if he had a son of his own, if he ever took him to a ball game, again Jerry Peters did not see the transference implications of these questions and ignored them. Eventually, Mr. K. left treatment, offering all kinds of rationalizations. It was quite apparent, however, that he felt like a dejected son who was not helped to face and resolve his deep yearnings for a loving father.

Jerry Peters, like Roslyn Oliver, was eventually able to face his own homosexual yearnings toward his client, but only after the client had broken off contact. By not letting themselves become aware of their feelings in the treatment situation, both of these therapists could face themselves when they felt they were not in as much danger. Like Breuer, Jerry Peters and Roslyn Oliver had to arrange for the therapeutic contact to be broken off before they could face their own sexual feelings toward their clients.

NOT TALKING TO THE CLIENT

Very often events in the client's past can activate anxiety-provoking thoughts, feelings, and memories in the therapist. The therapist, usually unwittingly, tries to change the course of therapeutic discussion and talk about the client's present exclusively. A client's experience of abandonment, rejection, seduction, or abuse can recall for the therapist similar experiences in his or her life, or through identification, the therapist can feel the same kind of unbearable anguish that the client has undergone. To rid themselves of unbearable feelings, thoughts, or memories, therapists try to rid themselves of the responsibility of talking with the client about the salient issue that the client wants and needs to discuss.

> Marjorie Quinone, a psychiatrist in a mental hospital, was working with a woman in her early forties, Ms. J., who had been diagnosed as paranoid schizophrenic. In therapy, Ms. J. talked about her early history in which she was sexually seduced on many occasions by older male relatives, including an uncle and a cousin. At first, the therapist found herself feeling very indignant toward the men who sexually abused her patient, but later on when Ms. J. talked about her feelings of helplessness in the face of being abused, Marjorie Quinone started feeling helpless herself. Slowly but surely she began to change the subject in the sessions, moving from the client's past to her current functioning in the hospital. As Ms. J. was encouraged to talk about "the here and now," she became more paranoid and also became convinced that her therapist, along with other hospital staff members, was trying to seduce her.

One of Otto Fenichel's formulas was, "Work always where the patient's affect lies at the moment" (1954). Few practitioners would disagree with the wisdom of this proposition, but it is sometimes difficult to effect in practice. When therapists find they are moving away from where the client is at the moment—whether it be away from the client's affect, fantasies, or resistances, present or past—this should serve as a clue that they may be counterresisting in order to protect themselves. Practitioners have to face the fact that their client's past or present circumstances can be as upsetting—or even more upsetting—for the therapist as it is for the client.

ACTING OUT

Acting out is the tendency to substitute an act or series of acts for issues that the client is too frightened to discuss with the therapist. In the early days of psychotherapy it was assumed that this type of resistance occurred more often with severely disturbed clients. It is now recognized that acting out can occur with almost any client and usually does occur, at some time, in virtually every treatment encounter (Greenson, 1967; Menninger, 1973; Stone, 1973). Many clients would rather have an affair than deal with sexual fantasies toward the therapist. Many would rather provoke a fight with a boss than examine sadistic fantasies toward the practitioner, and many clients would rather rescue other people than face their own dependency wishes in the treatment.

Clients can act out in the therapy sessions, as well. They can have acute temper tantrums rather than face the feelings, thoughts, and memories that propel their rage. They can flirt or try without disguise to seduce the therapist rather than face the fact that their "erotization resistance" usually covers up hidden aggression (Menninger, 1973).

It is now well accepted that clinicians can act out in or out of the therapy situation and usually do from time to time during the life of a case. We have already discussed several forms of acting out by therapists: for example, arriving late for sessions; having phone conversations during sessions; making slips of the tongue and seductive and manipulative remarks; and prematurely terminating treatment. What has not been carefully considered by sufficient numbers of practitioners is how certain therapeutic procedures of clinicians can muffle uncomfortable feelings, thoughts, and memories of their own. For example, for many decades psychiatrists have prescribed shock therapy and other drastic measures that often cover up their own feelings of helplessness and sadism (Fine, 1979). Wilhelm Reich's (1949) "orgone box" and having his patients attend therapy sessions in the nude probably gratified the therapist's voyeuristic wishes and other sexual fantasies.

The constant silence of a therapist may mask wishes to reject and defeat the client, and constant talking by therapists may be an attempt to alleviate their own anxiety. Techniques like mirroring, in which the therapist apes and mimics the client, can mask sadistic and retaliative wishes. Constant supportive remarks can sometimes be viewed as a way of acting out the desire to ingratiate oneself with the client.

Very often when therapists themselves are currently in treatment, they act out feelings with their clients that they have toward their own therapist, feelings that have not been resolved in their own treatment. One issue that often bothers therapists is feeling like a "second-class citizen" with their clients, because they are in treatment, too. Rather than examine their fears and wishes to be submissive, they act out their resentments with their clients.

Janet Rothschild, a social worker in private practice, was also in psychoanalytic training and therefore saw her own therapist several times a week. She was treating Ms. I., a graduate student in her late twenties. Ms. I. sought treatment because she found herself in constant power struggles with family, friends, teachers, and colleagues. As she started to face in treatment some of the issues that sparked her proclivity to act out her interpersonal struggles, Ms. I. developed a rather strong negative transference toward Janet Rothschild.

For the first few weeks, while the client's negative transference was being examined by client and therapist, Janet Rothschild compassionately helped Ms. I. to put into words her hatred of her therapist. She also enabled the client to discuss how the therapist reminded her of her "ungiving mother" and "cold father." However, as the negative transference was mutually examined further, Janet Rothschild found herself coming late to the sessions with Ms. I. At first she was only five minutes late and the latenesses were infrequent. Eventually, however, Janet found herself coming late for almost every session, and sometimes she was 15 to 20 minutes late.

Ms. I. now had "good reason" to resent her therapist. She described the latter as "irresponsible, hostile, and rejecting." Initially Janet Rothschild was quite defensive and tried to cope with her client's angry accusations by making interpretations about Ms. I.'s dynamics, particularly how her "past was being used to distort the present." Yet, Janet Rothschild soon began to feel contrite, depressed, and helpless and found it increasingly more difficult to relate to her client.

As Janet Rothschild examined her acting out in her own personal treatment, she learned that through her behavior she unconsciously provoked Ms. I. to voice the hostility and contempt that Janet Rothschild was feeling toward her own therapist, a hostile contempt that Janet Rothschild did not feel safe enough to express toward him directly. Also, by coming late to the sessions, Janet Rothschild was able to show her client the derisive attitude that she thought her own therapist had toward her. Said Janet Rothschild later to her therapist, "I made Ms. I. feel like the miserable child I feel with you, you big boss!"

CONSCIOUS OPPOSITION AND OPPOSITION OCCURRING WITH THE BEST OF INTENTIONS

Several writers have categorized resistances into subgroups: those which appear as deliberate and conscious as contrasted to those which appear ego-syntonic and completely unconscious. Thus, Menninger (1973) refers to those clients who "consciously oppose" and "pretend" to be skeptical of the therapy and independent of the therapist and contrasts them with those clients who cling to the notion that it is their temperamental makeup that, for instance, leads them to dawdle or delay, that is, they resist "with the best of intentions." One of the limitations of this type of dichotomy is that it overlooks the fact that unconscious processes are always at work to form any expression of resistive behavior. Though a therapist or client can consciously and deliberately resist talking, relating, or arriving at sessions on time, these particular resistive behaviors are always fueled by unconscious id wishes and/or unconscious superego mandates and/or unconscious ego defenses. The reason it is important to emphasize that the unconscious is always operative in all resistive and counterresistive behavior is that it helps the concepts of resistance and counterresistance to lose some of their pejorative connotations. As we have stated several times in this chapter, resistance and counterresistance are always operative in every therapeutic session—from the initial consultation to termination—and need to be assessed in as nonjudgmental a manner as is possible.

Most clients and therapists frequently rationalize their resistive behaviors by commenting on their "best of intentions." It is rare for either to refer to their resistive behaviors as accompanied by "the worst of intentions." When a practitioner dawdles or delays, acts out or is too inhibited, is too early or too late for sessions, or interprets with seductiveness or belligerence all of his or her own psychodynamics, we repeat, are at work in the counterresistive behavior.

Similar to Menninger's formulation is Stone's (1973) categorization of resistances into two types: (1) "tactical resistances" which deal with "manifest process phenomena of ego resistances" [that is, overt signs of resistance—lateness, absence, and refusal to pay fees]; and (2) "strategic resistances . . . those largely subsumed in the 'silent' group [for example, delays or failure of expectable symptomatic change, omission of decisive conflict material . . . inability to accept termination]. They relate to the depths of the patient's psychopathology and personality structure and to his total reactions to the [therapeutic] situation, process, and the person of the [therapist]" (p. 46).

Again, we have to point out that when a therapist (or client) overtly resists the therapeutic encounter by lateness, absence, or reluctance to deal with fees, these issues also "relate to the depths [of the therapist's] psychopathology and personality structure" (Stone, 1973, p. 46).

Whether counterresistances (or resistances) are ego-alien—that is, appear foreign, extraneous, and strange to the therapist's reasonable ego (such as when the practitioner, for no apparent reason, feels that the client hates him and is about to leave treatment) or ego-syntonic—that is, experienced as familiar, rational, purposeful, well-established, habitual patterns of behavior (such as excessive compliance, extreme punctuality, marked orderliness) (Greenson, 1967)—both forms also relate to the clinician's "psychopathology and personality structure" (Stone, 1973).

What we have said about the categories of Menninger (1973), Stone (1973), and Greenson (1967) may be said of Reuben Fine's (1982) categories as well. Fine divides resistances into those in which the client refuses to comply with basic requests and those of a more subtle nature. Clients and therapists can both rebel against fulfilling certain basic requirements around appointment times, fees, and so on, and they can also somaticize, be without feeling, or act out. Whether they resist subtly or do not fulfill certain requirements, their resistive behavior must be understood by studying their full "psychopathology and personality structure" (Stone, 1973).

Robert Langs (1981) categorized client resistances in a way that may be utilized to better understand certain features of a therapist's counterresistances. According to Langs, a resistance "may, by design, protect the patient—and often the therapist—from (1) threatening perceptions of the therapist; (2) threatening fantasies about the therapist; or (3) threatening perceptions and fantasies related to persons outside of the therapeutic relationship, but which usually have a significant bearing on the therapeutic interaction" (1981, p. 536).

Although not acknowledged frequently enough, therapists can have threatening perceptions of the client. The latter can emerge in the therapist's mind as a cruel mother, abusive father, seductive sibling, or lost girlfriend (Strean, 1988). Threatened by his or her perceptions of the client, the practitioner can act out, be punitive, withdraw, or resist the appropriate therapeutic role-set in one way or another. Similarly, the clinician can have erotic or murderous fantasies toward the client that create anxiety in him or her; therefore, he or she can resist trying to understand and empathically treat the client. Finally, the therapists can be having difficulties in their current interpersonal relationships that can have an impact on their therapeutic work. We will elaborate on this issue in a later section of this chapter.

According to Langs (1976), the most effective resistance a client can use is one that is offered or sanctioned by the therapist. As Langs has stated on numerous occasions, "Patients are exquisitely, though unconsciously, sensitive to such offers, and will characteristically exploit their presence" (1981, p. 537). His major thesis is that a study of unconscious communication between therapist and client always demonstrates the presence of some element of counterresistance in every intervention by the therapist (Langs & Stone, 1980; Langs, 1981). Therefore, Langs concludes that the therapist "is always contributing in some meaningful way to the presence of resistances in [the client], and it is incumbent upon the therapist to ascertain his own contribution to each resistance before dealing with those sources which arise primarily from within [the client]" (1981, p. 540).

RESISTANCE TO COUNTERRESISTANCE

Just as many clients resist facing the fact that they have transference reactions to their therapists, have responses in the treatment that can be described as id, ego, or superego resistances, and can derive epinosic gains from the therapy, clinicians can resist facing these same issues in themselves and can also deny their existence. Gill (1982) suggests that many clients would like to believe that their irritation, infatuation, or idealization of the therapist are natural responses to the situation; likewise, many clinicians would like to view their own irritation, infatuation, or idealization of their clients as natural responses, devoid of countertransference fantasies, defenses, and superego injunctions. Thus, just as every response of a client to the therapist is composed of a rich and complex set of variables, the therapist reacts similarly to the client.

Therapists can tell themselves that they are probably resisting facing their countertransference reactions and other counterresistive behavior when several clients during a short period of time describe them similarly. If a therapist is told several times by several clients during the course of a week that he or she is behaving coldly, seductively, aggressively, or dogmatically, there would seem to be sufficient consensual validation to motivate the therapist to start examining what is going on in his or her own life or psyche.

One of the early pioneers of psychotherapy, Sandor Ferenczi (1950), took the position that many therapeutic impasses occur because the client is aware of the therapist's unrecognized hostility or sexual fantasies toward the client. Ferenczi warned therapists against being too rigid with their clients, which may make the clinician appear as much too distant. This attitude on the part of the practitioner squelches the development of a spontaneous transference in the client. Ferenczi viewed this rigid demeanor of the therapist as a resistance against facing his or her countertransference reactions because it suggested that the therapist was frightened "to let himself go during the treatment as [psychotherapy] requires of him" (Ferenczi, 1950, p. 188). Ferenczi contended that the therapist should try to maintain a happy medium between responding too readily to the client's emotions and being overcautious and rigid in his or her own emotional responses.

COUNTERRESISTANCE AND THE THERAPIST'S DAILY LIFE

Regardless of their theoretical predilections and regardless of which therapeutic modalities they prefer, virtually all practitioners concur with the notion that what is transpiring in the client's daily life at a particular time will very much influence his or her productions in the treatment encounter. A client's illness, pregnancy, loss of a loved one, abandonment by a spouse, lover, or child, or being fired from a job will certainly influence the client's transference reactions toward the therapist and affect the evolution of other resistances, as well.

Whether the life event is a potentially unhappy one—such as the death of some one near and dear—or a possible joyous one—like a job promotion—all clients are affected and react in their own idiosyncratic manner. The sensitive therapist recognizes that not all individuals respond the same way to the same event (Hollis, 1964; Strean, 1978). Unemployment can be devastating to one client, while it can be a relief to another. Pregnancy can activate joy in one prospective mother, despair in another, and ambivalence in still another. Frequently, a situational event induces a variety of emotions in most individuals, but the complex picture varies from one person to another.

Although the daily events in the client's life, particularly the inevitable crises, have been studied comprehensively by practitioners (Parad, 1965), the same cannot be said about a comprehensive study of how the daily life of therapists, particularly the crises they endure, affect their counterresistances in the treatment situation. However, in recent years a move in this direction has been initiated. The pregnancy of the therapist and its contribution to resistances and counterresistances have been discussed by, among others, Goldberger (1991), Applebaum (1988), and Lax (1969). Illness in the therapist and the therapist's emotional reaction to it have been examined by Lasky (1990), Abend (1982), Dewald (1982), and others. The effects of aging on the practice of psychotherapy has been studied by Eissler (1975).

These articles on illness, pregnancy, aging, and a few other events in therapists' lives and how they affect counterresistive behavior have made for stimulating contributions; however, many dimensions of the clinician's life and its impact on therapeutic behavior have not been forthcoming as yet. What about a therapist's separation, divorce, marriage, or remarriage and the impact on his or her counterresistances? What happens to the clinician when he or she is particularly elated by a particular event—a daughter's or son's engagement, an award, the acceptance of an article in a prestigious journal? If the therapist has had an argument with his or her spouse, how does that affect the state of his or her counterresistance? Many therapists are in treatment themselves. How does a particular session or sessions with his or her own therapist influence the practitioner? These and many more dimensions of the practitioner's life and how they affect the evolution of countertransference and other counterresistances need much more attention. Usually, if an event is taking place in the clinician's life, it has an impact on how he or she behaves with many clients.

THE THERAPIST DIVORCES

Ann Silver had been a successful psychotherapist in private practice for over two decades. During her twenty-first year of practice, she and her husband divorced. Though Ann went through various emotional reactions during her divorce—elation, depression, relief, and despair—she thought she was well aware of her feelings and how and why they appeared in her work with clients. Nonetheless, she found, to her dismay, that a year after her divorce several of her clients separated and divorced from their mates and a few more were facing serious marital conflict.

As Ann Silver studied her behavior with her clients, she discovered that her divorce made her feel, among other emotions, guilty and lonely. Slowly, she was able to realize that she had unconsciously used her clients to be "partners in crime." Their separations and divorces helped her feel less lonely and less guilty.

Phenomena similar to the case of Ann Silver and her clients transpire frequently. They need to be studied much more intensively along with other counterresistive behaviors. These behaviors affect treatment in a basic way, particularly in the initial phase of treatment, which we will discuss in the next chapter.

2

Counterresistances in the Initial Sessions

It is virtually axiomatic among psychotherapists of all persuasions that for the prospective client entering treatment is a most difficult decision that requires considerable courage. To reveal to a stranger one's forbidden fantasies, shameful memories, hostile actions, embarrassing inhibitions, and irrational notions is a very anxiety-provoking experience, which activates a vast array of resistances in almost every prospective recipient of therapeutic help. Those entering a treatment relationship worry a great deal about how they will be judged and often wonder if they will be demeaned, ridiculed, criticized, or rejected for what they will reveal to the practitioner.

Although the literature is replete with case illustrations, research findings, and much theorizing on the rich diversity of resistances that prospective clients present in the initial stages of treatment, there has been limited consideration of how and why practitioners covertly and overtly resist the initial therapeutic encounter. Just as clients feel uncomfortable about telling their distressing story to a stranger, many therapists feel uncomfortable in listening to a stranger tell his or her distressing story. And similar to clients who avoid or oppose the therapist, practitioners have their own ways of avoiding or opposing their prospective clients.

It is much more acceptable for recipients of treatment to acknowledge that they would rather be elsewhere instead of participating in an initial consultation interview than it is for therapists to admit the same sentiment. Clinicians are loathe to confess that they would rather be at home, in a museum, or outdoors than at work in their offices. Most practitioners possess consciences and ego ideals that condemn shirking their work responsibilities; usually the voices of the superego affirm the notion that listening, empathizing, and understanding prospective clients are eminently desirable activities that should never be avoided.

Yet clinicians, if they acknowledge their humanness, will admit that they are

43

frequently quite anxious about meeting a stranger—even though they need money to survive and though they love people and deeply want to help them. They also are concerned about how they will be judged. They also fear that their therapeutic role-partners will criticize, deride, or devalue them. To ward off these possibilities and other upsetting ones, therapists can be cold and aloof in the initial telephone conversation with the applicant, can appear too late or too early for the initial interview, or they can even forget about the intake appointment. Clinicians, in coping with their own anxieties as they evolve in the initial interviews, can become over-talkative, ingratiating, hostile, seductive, or show a combination of these and other forms of resistance.

In order to enable an applicant for psychotherapy to accept the role of client, helpers must be able to say to themselves—and to really believe it—*"This person in front of me in many ways is like me. I, too, have had and probably still have many neurotic conflicts, immaturities, difficulties in interpersonal relationships, pathological character traits. I, too, have felt and still feel embarrassed about exposing myself to a stranger."*

Although clinicians can eloquently and brilliantly describe how psychotherapy should be arranged for most men, women, and children in every society—and often go so far as to point out that only the strong can ask for help, as indicated in Chapter 1—many practitioners find it quite difficult to accept the role of client for themselves and concomitantly maintain a positive self-image. Starting with the early followers of Freud, such as Otto Rank who bragged that he did not need therapy for himself (Jones, 1953; Novey, 1983), and continuing to this day, many practitioners need to maintain an air of omnipotence and deny that, like all human beings, their conflicts and imperfections necessitate therapeutic assistance if they are going to function at their optimum so as to love maturely and to work productively.

Practitioners who have a genuine desire to help applicants for psychotherapy become actively participating clients have to feel reasonably comfortable with their own sexual fantasies—heterosexual and homosexual; their own aggression—assertive wishes and murderous impulses; their own defenses—adaptive and pathological; their own superego admonitions—punitive commands and ethical imperatives. To feel comfortable with the aforementioned is an ideal that practitioners can only approximate. Consequently, resistances to the range of feelings that therapists experience in initial interviews are inevitable. Variations in sexual practices are diverse among clients, and practitioners can have inhibitions to listen to their clients and to understand such sexual practices as sadomasochism, bisexuality, and transvestism. They can feel uncomfortable with applicants' presentations of physical battles, addictions, antisocial behavior, and antisocial fantasies. In sum, therapists' superego injunctions can activate many counterresistances to listen and to relate to all kinds of client behaviors and wishes.

Not only may practitioners resist relating to unfamiliar sexual and aggressive practices of applicants for psychotherapy, but also they may resist "accepting the client as he is" (Hamilton, 1951). The therapist may want to get a full history of the client's life, while the the client may want to stay exclusively in the present and discuss the here and now. The therapist may want to discuss the details of the client's sexual life, while the client may want to discuss everything else but that. The therapist may have many questions to ask the client, while the client may be more interested in asking the therapist questions about the clinical process and/or the therapist's personal life. The therapist may want to arrange a fee and a time for a weekly appointment, while the client may wish to discuss why he or she does not need therapy in the first place. These conflicting expectations between practitioner and client often stir up anxiety and conflict in both individuals. However, it is largely the practitioner's responsibility to become aware of the anxieties and conflicts of the applicant as well as those of his or her own, ascertain the nature and meaning of the initial resistances and counterresistances, and try to resolve both. This is a formidable task, so much so that it may help explain why only approximately one-third of applicants for psychotherapy remain in treatment beyond the first couple of interviews (Strean, 1985/1990).

As you can see, the resolution of the practitioner's counterresistances in the initial phase of treatment is extremely crucial to the eventual success of the therapy. Therefore, we will devote this chapter to a review and discussion of the many counterresistances that emerge from the first telephone call of the applicant through the next several interviews.

THE FIRST TELEPHONE CALL

When an applicant for psychotherapy makes a telephone call to a private practitioner, to a mental health clinic, or to a social agency, the applicant rarely does this impulsively. He or she has spent hours, days, weeks, months, or often years going back and forth considering the idea of treatment. As we have noted, it is often difficult and frequently painful to say to a stranger, "I cannot cope with my marriage, my job, with my children, with my parents." It is quite upsetting to tell a person with whom we are not familiar, "I am depressed, hostile, feel like a failure, and am suicidal on occasion." Although there is more acceptance of different lifestyles in the 1990s, it is still difficult to get on the phone and tell the unknown listener, "I am having difficulty accepting my homosexuality, bisexuality, extramarital affair, celibacy, or promiscuity."

Because the initial telephone contact is such an anxiety-provoking event for applicants for psychotherapy, they erect many overt or covert resistances that block their proceeding with their request for treatment. Some applicants quietly hope that the therapist or agency will be too busy to help them. Others will make requests of the prospective helper, anticipating that these requests will not be gratified. Many uninitiated clients will try to convince themselves that the therapist is professionally unqualified. Often the office of the practitioner will be considered too inconvenient for the prospective client to reach and/or the time and day of the initial consultation will be completely impractical. Occasionally, the applicant will consciously or unconsciously provoke an argument with the professional and conclude that therapy and therapists must be shunned forever.

The major job of the practitioner who receives a telephone request from an applicant for psychotherapy is to help the applicant feel accepted with his or her doubts, hesitancy, skepticism, and anxiety about psychotherapy. The practitioner should also try to assist applicants to feel comfortable enough with all of their resistances so that they will want to make an appointment for an initial consultation and discuss their problems further. This is a complex task for the clinician because the resistances of clients inevitably activate many counterresistances in the therapist.

"Selling" Psychotherapy and Promoting Themselves

Perhaps the most popular expression of a therapist's counterresistance on the telephone is the attempt to convince a reluctant client to come in for an appointment. When a reluctant client is pressured, he or she then resists treatment strenuously.

> Arnold Temple was an intake worker in a child guidance clinic. One early Monday morning, Mrs. H., a mother of a five-year-old child, called him and said, "My child needs help. He refuses to go to school. Can you help him?" Arnold Temple responded affirmatively and said, "Sure. First we'll see you, get a picture of the problem, hear about your family and your history, then see the child in play therapy, and then see you and your husband in counselling." Mrs. H. said, "That's a tall order! Do we have to do all that? I just want him to get to school!" The intake worker then asserted, "I know you want him to get to school and that's why we have a diagnostic evaluation process and treatment plan to insure it." Mrs. H. commented that she did not think so much "probing" was necessary and suggested that she "would try another facility."
>
> Arnold Temple tried to persuade Mrs. H. to come to his clinic—it was "the best equipped facility to help." The more he insisted on helping Mrs. H., the more she resisted making an appointment. After telling Arnold Temple that she would call back the next day to work out an appointment for a consultation, she called a private therapist and arranged for therapy for her son and counselling for her husband and herself.

Very often when therapists are invested in doing their job well, they forget about their prospective clients' fear of help and avoid conveying to them that psychotherapy can activate discomfort and distress. When therapists are so narcissistically involved that they "must make a sale" and convince prospective clients that they *must* have treatment, the latter become alienated, feeling that they are not being supported but exploited instead.

Although practitioners usually want to convert an applicant for psychotherapy into a client, they have to try to monitor their id wishes to promote themselves and to feel less intimidated by superego commands to work hard. These understandable counterresistances are probably close to universal among practitioners, but they have to be well understood and well mastered.

The mature and competent therapist can feel free to verbalize to a prospective client that the latter may wish to postpone moving ahead in the therapeutic process. He or she does not necessarily have to feel like a failure if the applicant does, indeed, refuse further involvement in treatment.

In the example above, if Arnold Temple were not so interested in "selling" his program, he might have empathized with Mrs. H. when she told him over the phone that she could not get her son to go to school. He could have told her that a child not going to school can be quite burdensome for a mother, and that he would like to try to help her with her problem. Instead of describing the diagnostic process in detail to Mrs. H., which was experienced by her as a series of demands, Arnold Temple might have inquired about the nature of the youngster's school phobia and how long it had existed.

When practitioners are as invested in promoting themselves as Arnold Temple was, they can temporarily forget what they know. Most practitioners in child guidance clinics realize that a school phobic youngster like Mrs. H.'s son is usually unconsciously "helped" to stay at home by the parent. Consequently, Mrs. H., like virtually all clients, was not that eager to overcome her conflicts so readily. Therefore, she probably would have been helped much more if she were told that *maybe* she would like one appointment to discuss her son's problem *a little* further. Perhaps this would have given her the impression that she was being understood and supported instead of being pressured.

OVERLOOKING THE CLIENT'S APPREHENSIONS ABOUT TREATMENT

The reason why it is so important for practitioners to monitor their wishes to be pressuring salesmen is because of what practitioners have noted for decades, namely, prospective clients in many ways are reluctant to receive help and often hope it won't be forthcoming.

Sally Ungar, a school social worker, was asked by school personnel to see Jack G., a 12-year-old youngster who seemed very depressed and inattentive in class. Because he seemed to be suffering very much, it was firmly recommended that Sally Ungar begin seeing him immediately.

After Jack G. and Sally Ungar were introduced to each other by Jack's teacher and an appointment was made, Jack G. "forgot" to come to see Sally Ungar on three separate occasions. When Sally Ungar decided to make a visit to Jack's class and suggested to Jack that maybe he didn't feel like coming to see her, Jack told her he "definitely wanted" to see Sally, but he "really forgot." Sally Ungar then told Jack that she would "pick him up" and bring him to her office so they could talk; Jack agreed to this plan.

When Jack G. was brought to the social worker's office, he was practically mute during all of his interviews. Although Sally Ungar tried to verbalize all of what she thought Jack was experiencing, such as his "not wanting to talk," "fear of a stranger," and "not liking school," she was not able to face the fact that her client was feeling forced to be the recipient of therapeutic help and hated the idea. Had Sally Ungar showed Jack G. that although he was suffering a great deal, he *really did not want to see her and did not have to do so*, she might have emerged as more of an ally to him. If she had given him permission not to be a client, the prospect of being one might not have seemed so forbidding to him. And, if she did not chase after him and force him to come to her office for interviews, he may have emerged as less apathetic in her office.

A competent and mature therapist has to be able to cope with rejection. Many times clients such as Mrs. H. and Jack G. are viewed countertransferentially as rejecting parents, rejecting siblings, or rejecting significant others. Rather than face themselves with how they feel about being rejected and later possibly explore with their clients who are rejecting what they don't like about them, practitioners can resist coping with rejection by trying to convince clients to accept them. Without realizing it, practitioners can emerge as rejected children with their clients and cope with feelings of vulnerability by coming close to begging for love.

What Are Your Qualifications?

In any new situation, all human beings tend to feel somewhat vulnerable and inadequate. Because of this truism, many therapists are inclined to feel quite tense when an applicant for psychotherapy asks about the practitioner's professional qualifications. Usually when applicants ask of the therapist over the phone, "What are your qualifications?" they have doubts about the professional's capacity to help. If the professional realizes this, then he or she also realizes that a presentation of professional credentials will not satisfy a dubious consumer. Rather, some acknowledgment of the consumer's doubts should be shown. However, if practitioners have questions about their own professional competence, and have to defend against accepting their imperfections, they might feel obliged to present their achievements and accomplishments to the prospective client. Usually this has negative results.

John Van Wort, a psychologist in private practice, was called by Mr. F., a man in his mid-thirties who wanted help for sexual difficulties. On the phone,

Mr. F. asked John Van Wort, "Have you taken courses and do you have a certificate in sexual counseling?" "Sure," replied John Van Wort. "Where did you get it?" queried Mr. F. John Van Wort told his prospective client that he took courses at a Masters and Johnson facility, had courses on sexology in his doctoral studies, and had further clinical training and clinical experience beyond the completion of his doctoral studies.

After assembling a great deal of data on John Van Wort's background, Mr. F. then told John Van Wort that he wanted to compare the latter's credentials with those of other professionals. Obviously irritated, John Van Wort told Mr. F. he was "a therapy shopper," which prompted Mr. F. to comment, "I did not call you to be put down."

If practitioners realize that questions about their qualifications are really statements that imply that the practitioner's competence is in doubt, they can say over the phone to the applicant, "Perhaps you are not sure whether I'm competent enough to help you." Although the applicant may not acknowledge the truth of this statement, he or she may feel sufficiently understood and supported to consider coming in for an interview to discuss the problematic situation further.

Clients Who Think That They Themselves Are Underqualified

Just as there are prospective clients who feel that the prospective therapist may be underqualified, there are some applicants for psychotherapy who do not feel that they are well-equipped to be clients. They question their own capacity to be sufficiently interesting, stimulating, and challenging to the therapist. They are unsure whether they will be accepted by the therapist and tend to perceive their application for treatment as if they are applying for membership in a country club, fraternity, or sorority, and they are very worried about the possibility of being "blackballed."

There is a tendency on the part of most practitioners, particularly on the phone, to reassure self-effacing applicants that in spite of their protests, they are acceptable and desirable candidates for psychotherapy. When given reassurance, these clients tend to reason the way Groucho Marx did when he contended, "I wouldn't join any country club that would accept me as a member."

Laura Wolfe, a psychiatrist in private practice, was called by Ms. E., a single woman in her early twenties who wanted help for her heroin addiction. Over the phone, Ms. E. was quite critical of herself for being "on a fix" and warned the psychiatrist that she "would not be an easy patient." On hearing Ms. E.'s constant self-accusations, Laura Wolfe told Ms. E. that she would be glad to work with her and that "people with addictions" can be helped, and she had assisted many of them.

The more reassurance Ms. E. was given, the more resistant she became to making an appointment. She continued to point out that she was not an easy person to get to know, that she found it difficult to talk about herself, and that she was sure that Dr. Wolfe had patients who gave her more pleasure than Ms. E. would offer. When Laura Wolfe again reassured Ms. E. that the latter was "eminently treatable," and that she should make an appointment, Ms. E. acquiesced. However, she never did appear for the appointment. Despite repeated phone calls in which Laura Wolfe reassured Ms. E. that she was "treatable," Ms. E.'s protests grew more vehement and she told Laura Wolfe to "stop calling."

The telephone contacts between Ms. E. and Laura Wolfe demonstrate that self-effacing individuals are rarely reassured when told that they are acceptable, regardless of how firm the reassurer is. What most practitioners do learn about self-hating clients is that they harbor a great deal of rage toward others about which they feel very guilty. Their self-castigations are in essence self-inflicted punishments for their hateful wishes. Consequently, when they are told they are desirable and can be helped, they are very suspicious of the one who tries to console them. They do not want to be absolved of their hatred so quickly because within their hearts they are dimly aware of their murderous impulses (Strean & Freeman, 1991), which they believe are evil and unforgivable.

Had Laura Wolfe suggested to Ms. E. over the phone that she realized that Ms. E. did not have much faith in herself and was all set to be rejected, Ms. E. would probably have felt better understood and may have trusted Laura Wolfe a little more. With a feeling of being understood, Ms. E. might have been a little more willing to come in for one appointment, rather than for treatment over a period of time.

Therapists who constantly reassure masochistic clients like Ms. E. are usually overidentifying with them. Like their clients, these therapists have not been able to master their own sadistic fantasies, berating themselves instead. Practitioners who constantly reassure self-hating clients of their worth are trying to prevent themselves and prevent their clients, albeit unconsciously, from facing their respective sadism. Reassuring therapists are those who have not faced their own guilt about their own sadistic fantasies. By reassuring their clients that they are "okay individuals," they are trying to reassure themselves that they are "okay" too.

Reassurance is a popular form of counterresistance. However, it is rarely helpful to any client. At best it is like giving a weak aspirin to a person suffering from a powerful migraine headache. It provides little consolation for the client and only temporary diminution of anxiety for the therapist. When therapists find themselves reassuring a client, they should begin asking themselves, "What feelings, thoughts, or memories am I trying to keep away from myself?" They usually get their clue by examining how and why they are trying to protect the client. Laura Wolfe eventually realized that she was protecting herself from facing two issues: her own addiction to smoking and her own oral sadistic fantasies, which were somewhat gratified by the smoking.

Telephone applicants who can stir up all kinds of counterresistances in therapists are the men and women who make many demands. These are the applicants who want to know over the phone how long the treatment will last, want a description of the clinical process in advance, must have the time and dates for the next several appointments, need to have a thorough familiarity with the qualifications of the practitioner, and much more.

Very often these clients have tremendous doubts about becoming clients. However, rather than face their own ambivalence about going into treatment, they raise questions about the therapist and the therapeutic process.

What is sometimes difficult for practitioners to accept is that trying to gratify the demands of ambivalent clients usually does not diminish their ambivalence or the anxiety that creates it. Rather, giving answers to questions applicants pose on the phone often compounds their ambivalence. Their doubts about the therapist and the therapy are not actually being addressed when they are given the clinician's curriculum vitae, or the fee structure of the agency, or a description of a hypothetical clinical process.

When some therapists offer answers to prospective clients' questions over the phone, this usually indicates they are fearful of the applicant's possible hostility when he or she is frustrated by the therapist. Some applicants do become quite angry when they are told, "I'm sure that question (e.g., the therapist's theoretical orientation, his or her preferred therapeutic modality, or usual fee) is important to you and I'd like to answer it now, but I think it would be better to discuss it further face-to-face." It is always important for a practitioner to become aware of why he or she is frightened of the client's hostility at a particular time.

Most often therapists are frightened of a client's hostility, real or anticipated, when they feel that they deserve it. And, therapists believe that they deserve to be castigated when they are so identified with the client that they are quite convinced that the client's request is legitimate. Some practitioners feel so positive that a prospective client has a right to know, for example, the practitioner's professional qualifications, that they furnish the requested information without realizing its therapeutic implications.

Some clients want to know about prospective clinicians' qualifications when they think the clinician may be unqualified. Consequently, if a client believes that the practitioner is unqualified (and this is based, almost always, on myriad unconscious wishes, defenses, superego injunctions, childhood history, etc.), telling the doubtful client that the practitioner has a Ph.D. from Harvard and is a member of the American Psychiatric Association may only cause the client to doubt the merits of Harvard's curricula and the appropriateness of A.P.A.'s membership requirements. In this case, the therapist fails to be in touch with what the applicant is feeling. Although there are exceptions to the rule, usually when practitioners furnish their curriculum vitae to an applicant they are not too comfortable with nor confident of their therapeutic talents and skills. Often their own doubts about their qualifications need to be explored further with a colleague, supervisor, or personal therapist.

When practitioners answer applicants' questions over the phone without knowing the issues that propel the questions, they can appear like parents who feed their child food when the child is in distress for a reason other than hunger. A child who is anxious, fearful, or ambivalent needs a parent to understand and verbalize these feelings—not give gum drops or ice cream.

> Tom Xavier, a social worker, was on intake at a mental health clinic associated with a metropolitan university. A graduate student in psychology, Ms. D. called and asked over the phone, "Do you do didactic analysis for prospective therapists?" Tom Xavier replied, "Yes." Ms. D. then queried, "Do you know what I mean by didactic analysis?" "I believe I do," responded the intake worker. "Well, then, what is it? I'm not sure I know," admitted Ms. D. "It's therapy for those individuals who want to do therapy," answered Tom Xavier. "Do you do it?" Ms. D. asked. "Oh, sure," said Tom.
>
> "Well, what are your qualifications?" Ms. D. wanted to know. Tom told Ms. D. that he received his M.S.W. from a midwestern university and had training at several institutes. "Oh," said Ms. D., "I'm reading a book on the therapeutic process and the author advises psychotherapists not to answer questions so fast. How come you do?" Tom Xavier laughed over the phone and then said, "Why don't you come in and talk it over?" Ms. D. then responded, "That's what you should have said at the beginning! I'll try somebody else."

In this day and age telephone applicants are quite sophisticated about the nuances of psychotherapeutic practice. Many of them have read books and articles on the subject and want to test the practitioner's abilities almost immediately. It is quite easy for therapists to resist the idea that they are being tested, particularly by an applicant for treatment who seems in distress and calls for information over the telephone.

Many practitioners like to give information and exhibit their knowledge like Tom Xavier in the above case. Practitioners always have to monitor their desires to show how much they know, be able to benignly frustrate queries of applicants, and try to abort the applicant's hostility, if necessary.

In the above case, when Ms. D. asked if Tom Xavier offered "didactic analysis," he could have responded with, "Is that what you are interested in?" and see what Ms. D. had to say when he explored her requests further. This would have required Tom Xavier to frustrate his own wishes to gratify Ms. D. and monitor his desires to enhance his own professional self-image.

Although a positive initial phone contact between applicant and practitioner can pave the way for the client to feel relatively comfortable at his or her initial consultation—and, therefore, is a crucial dimension of the therapeutic process—it has not received the attention it deserves in the professional literature. Yet, the resistances of the applicant and the counterresistances of the practitioner on the phone are one of the major determinants in the success or failure of the initial phase of treatment and deserve much more consideration.

THE CLIENT'S PRESENTING PROBLEM AND COUNTERRESISTANCE

Whether clients present their problems over the phone and/or in the consultation room, practitioners have reactions to the problems themselves and the way they are presented. Although all therapists ideally should be able to say, "I could be this applicant," it is often difficult to empathize with those who hate what we love, and champion what we decry. If we love children, it may be difficult to empathize with a rageful parent who shows no guilt as he or she describes physically abusing a youngster. If we are against racism, sexism, or civil injustice, and a prospective client makes racist, sexist, or homophobic remarks, it may be difficult to sensitize ourselves to the vulnerabilities and anxieties of the prospective client. Most practitioners abhor a negative bias toward any human being, but they can become quite prejudiced toward a prejudiced client.

> Ms. Young was an intake worker at a family agency and received a telephone call from Ms. C., who requested help for a housing problem. Ms. C. had been living in a low-cost, city-sponsored apartment complex for senior citizens and wanted the agency's assistance in moving to an apartment complex in another neighborhood.
>
> In exploring Ms. C.'s wish to change her residence, Ms. Young learned that Ms. C. was not favorably disposed toward Blacks, and since there were many Afro-Americans in her apartment building, she wanted to move. Without being aware of the anger in her voice, Ms. Young asked, "What do you have against them?" Her question exacerbated Ms. C.'s antipathy and she began to hurl slanderous racial remarks over the phone, calling Ms. Young "a nigger lover," and she slammed down the phone.
>
> If Ms. Young had received a call from a prospective client who expressed the desire to move away from his or her spouse, she probably would not have asked the applicant what he or she had against the mate. Rather, Ms. Young probably would have suggested that the applicant come down to her office to discuss the situation in more detail, face to face. However, she dealt with an angry, prejudiced woman like Ms. C. in a different way. Rather than monitor her anger and eventually try to understand it so that she could empathize

with the client, Ms. Young acted out her hostility toward the client by asking a question in an abrasive manner.

THE CLINICIAN MAKES PUNITIVE REMARKS

Often when we are quick to ask a question in response to a remark of a hostile client, we are unwittingly involving ourselves in a power struggle rather than attempting to understand our client's anxieties and defenses. Attitudes and behaviors of applicants and clients can be abhorrent to us, but they do demand our understanding. Often when we "protest too much" about clients' attitudes, we are protesting against our identification with them.

> Max Zaro, a psychologist in a child guidance clinic, received a call from Mr. B. who identified himself as the father of eight-year-old Joe. Mr. B. told Max that his son was "playing hookey" from school. "I've been beating him up a lot, punishing him as much as I can, but the kid still plays hookey," lamented Mr. B.
>
> Max found himself feeling very angry toward Mr. B. because of his very punitive attitude toward Joe. Mr. B. was so verbose over the phone that Max could silently assess his own punitive response toward Mr. B., which was fortunate for both Max and for Mr. B. At first he realized that he was identifying very strongly with Joe and was absorbing in fantasy the aggression that was being directed toward Joe. However, when Max Zaro asked himself a further question, "Why am I making myself such a beaten-up kid?," his associations led him to the realization that he always wanted to "play hookey" from school as a youngster, but never had the courage to do so. It dawned on Max, too, that as an adult, he often felt like taking time off, but never could allow himself to do so. Consequently, because Max Zaro felt quite critical toward the rebellious youngster in himself and thought that youngster should be punished, Max was unconsciously agreeing with Mr. B. but could not accept his own hypercritical attitude.

Practitioners rarely view a presenting problem neutrally, although most of them would like to be as nonjudgmental as they can in their overt behavior as they listen to the client present the problem. To appear therapeutically neutral and assess a client's problem objectively, therapists should try their best to know how and why they overidentify and underidentify with clients' problems, when and why they feel hostile, and when and why they feel too compassionate.

THE THERAPEUTIC SETTING AND COUNTERRESISTANCE

Most therapists are keenly aware that the unique setting where the treatment is conducted almost always affects the evolution of the therapist's counterresistances. For example, if an agency consists of experts in marriage counselling or child therapy, the case dispositions made and the plans favored for clients will be heavily influenced by the priorities of the agency (Siporin, 1975).

Social agencies can become preoccupied with their distinctiveness, and some of the unique needs of the clients may be overlooked as a result. A professional subculture emerges that has its own value system and accepted ways of operating (Compton & Galaway, 1975).

Within the professional subculture, a hierarchal system forms and therapists are usually required to review their work with a supervisor who upholds the setting's values and priorities. Therefore, if a psychotherapy applicant requests over the phone to be seen in a one-to-one interview, the therapist may be inclined to instruct the prospective client to bring in her spouse and children for a family interview, if that is the preferred therapeutic modality of the agency and one which the supervisor probably upholds. Similarly, if a mental health center places a high priority on short-term treatment, the therapist may steer a client in this direction without carefully assessing if the client's conflicts call for a different form of treatment.

Very often a practitioner strongly submits to a supervisor's predilections and the agency's value system (Rosenthal, 1958). Thus, he or she appears much like a compliant child with an overbearing parent.

Sheila Yeager, a social worker in a mental health clinic, was asked by the chief psychiatrist "to get a history on Peter A.," a six-year-old child who was being considered for treatment at the clinic. Sheila Yeager complied with the psychiatrist's orders, called Mrs. A., Peter's mother, and asked her to come to the clinic for an interview so that the clinic could get a history on Peter. Mrs. A. agreed and made an appointment.

When Mrs. A. arrived for her appointment, she was not particularly interested in presenting a history, but seemed to have a strong wish to discuss her trials and tribulations in her relationship with Peter. She told Sheila Yeager that she didn't know what to do about Peter's temper tantrums, phobias, compulsions, headaches, and tics. Instead of relating to Mrs. A.'s desperation and pervasive anxiety, Sheila asked Mrs. A. for material relating to the history of Peter's symptoms. When Mrs. A. responded with terse replies and/or evasive answers and then returned to a discussion of her own anguish, Sheila Yeager persisted in trying to get a history on Peter. Finally, Mrs. A. felt so frustrated and misunderstood that she asked of Sheila, "Are you an obsessive-compulsive who believes more in rituals than in people?" Sheila was left speechless as

Mrs. A. went on to tell her that she was going to take Peter to another facility "where I can get help for both of us."

All too often the therapist views the rules and regulations of the clinic or agency setting and the requests of a supervisor or administrator as commands from an exacting superego with which he or she must comply. As a result, histories are demanded of the applicant when the latter would prefer to discuss his or her conflicts. Often application forms take precedence over emotional and interpersonal issues that appear more pressing to the prospective client, and fee arrangements can dominate the interview when the client has other interests.

FIGHTING THE TREATMENT CENTER'S RULES AND REGULATIONS

Although some practitioners can comply too readily with the dictates of the setting's policies and practices, others, by contrast, can rebel against them too strenuously. From time to time practitioners turn colleagues into sibling rivals and supervisors and administrators into punitive parents with whom they want to compete. Often the competition becomes more salient than the client's conflicts.

Jerry Xenia worked as a resident psychiatrist in the outpatient clinic of a mental hospital. All of his clinical experience prior to working in the outpatient clinic was in a medical setting where the M.D. was the boss. Consequently, it was somewhat difficult for him to be supervised on some of his cases by a social worker and almost equally difficult to attend a weekly seminar led by a psychologist.

Jerry Xenia was assigned to treat the mother of a youngster, Sam B., who was in treatment with this psychologist. While making his first appointment with Mrs. B. over the phone, he found himself telling her how "very provocative" Sam was and "how very sorry" he felt because she "had to deal with such a difficult and troublesome child."

As Jerry Xenia reviewed some of his responses to Mrs. B., he slowly realized that he was really voicing his hostility toward Sam's therapist, the colleague with whom he felt very competitive. Jerry also became aware that he was trying to get Mrs. B. to join with him in a battle against Sam and his therapist and gain a supporter in his own fight.

Another issue related to the therapeutic setting and counterresistance, although not sufficiently recognized and discussed, is that practitioners in private practice also participate in a professional subculture. They, too, have supervisors and seminar leaders and have transference reactions toward them. Often practitioners in private practice are candidates in training at psychoanalytic and other types of educational institutes where certain theoretical biases exist and where particular therapeutic modalities and treatment techniques are championed. Therefore, clients with certain diagnostic labels such as "narcissistic character disorder" or "borderline personality" may either become abhorred or adored, and, knowing this, the candidate can unconsciously, and sometimes quite consciously, choose certain clients to diagnose and treat in a very prescribed manner. In effect, the values of the therapist's professional subculture become more pertinent than the needs of the client.

THE PRACTITIONER'S THERAPIST AND COUNTERRESISTANCE

Perhaps one of the major influences in the private practitioner's practice is his or her own therapist or analyst. The way the latter is perceived is frequently emulated by the practitioner, even if the client he or she is working with is diagnostically very different from himself or herself.

Amy Wolfson, a social worker in private practice and psychoanalytic training, was in an intensive personal analysis. During the fourth year of her analysis, she became aware of some severe sexual inhibitions of her own and as she discussed some of her resistances to sex as well as some of her sexual fantasies, she began to feel more liberated, both in her personal life and in her professional life. In her preoccupation with her own sexuality, she found herself constantly investigating her clients' sexual fantasies and sexual behavior.

When Mr. C., a young man in his early twenties, called Amy for a consultation, Amy decided to conduct a brief interview over the phone. After learning that Mr. C. was depressed and lonely, she asked him if he had a girlfriend. To his response that he did not, Amy Wolfson then queried, "Then how often do you have sex?" Mr. C. told Amy that he preferred to discuss this issue with her in her office. Despite the fact that Amy agreed with this proposal, Mr. C. did not show up for a consultation and refused to have one when she called him several times.

There are several lessons to be learned from Amy Wolfson's contact with Mr. C. First, most prospective clients do not want to discuss their problems over the phone and resist very strongly any attempts to investigate their lives before they meet the therapist. Even when applicants try to discuss their issues over the phone, most of them respond positively to the practitioner's suggestion that perhaps it might be more helpful to discuss the issue or issues in the consultation room. Second, it behooves practitioners to review quite frequently what is going on in their own personal and professional lives and determine what their predominant concerns are at a given time so that these concerns are not prematurely and insensitively foisted on the client. Finally, most applicants for psychotherapy need some time to get to know and be known by the therapist before they can respond to questions about their sexual behavior and sexual fantasies.

THE CLINICIAN'S ATTIRE AND OFFICE DECOR

It is a truism that people reveal a great deal about themselves by their selection of clothes, furniture, cars, and other personal possessions. A depressed person is often dressed in a disheveled manner as opposed to a self-confident person who usually appears well-groomed. Similarly, the furniture in a house, as well as its physical condition and neatness, suggests some things about the owner's self-esteem and self-image.

The choice of particular clothes and other accoutrements can also be used for defensive purposes. Men or women who have doubts about their sexual identity often dress in an ostentatious manner to mask their defective body images and to cover up their self-doubts.

Although clients will selectively perceive and distort how the practictioner's consultation room appears and how he or she dresses, practitioners do reveal a great deal about how they feel about their work, their clients, and themselves by their office and waiting room decor and the way they are groomed. If a waiting room has broken chairs, stained rugs, and torn magazines that are also outdated, a message is transmitted to clients which may make many of them feel repelled and/or unwelcome. Further, if the male therapist needs a shave, or the female therapist has smudged makeup, clients can feel alienated.

Just as the therapist's comments are designed to help the client grow and develop, his or her office decor and attire should be designed to do the same. If decor and attire, either for their lack of care or their excessive embellishment, attract undue attention or are experienced by clients as inappropriate, therapists should ask themselves why they may want to present themselves in such a way that can interfere with the treatment process. For example, if therapists hear that their office looks very luxurious, they should ask and try to answer some of these questions: "What am I trying to cover up in myself by calling attention to my ritzy office layout and lavish clothes?" "Why don't I want my office and my physical appearance sufficiently neutral?" "Am I unconsciously trying to deflect certain transference fantasies and intensify certain resistances by calling my clients' attention to issues they really should not have imposed on them?"

Although practitioners are usually quite sensitive and alert to what clients are expressing by the way they are groomed, and despite the fact that practitioners make many diagnostic inferences about what their clients' possessions convey, the issues of the professional's attire and office decor have received limited attention in the therapy literature. Some research may reveal certain unconscious counterresistances and other dynamic issues at work that have not been sufficiently considered.

THE REFERRAL SOURCE

Clinicians are usually quite alert to the fact that how prospective clients feel toward the individual who referred them for therapy will very much influence their attitude toward the therapy and the therapist. If a well-liked and trusted physician makes the recommendation for treatment, there is a good possibility that the applicant will be ready to form a positive relationship with the practitioner. On the other hand, if a disliked and dogmatic court official makes psychotherapy part of a sentencing procedure, the client will probably be ready to view the therapy as a form of imprisonment and the therapist as a type of warden.

Therapists, as we have reiterated, are psychologically similar to their clients. Consequently, how they greet and relate to the prospective client over the phone and in the initial interviews will be a function, at least to some extent, of how the therapist feels toward the referral source. If a highly esteemed and well-liked supervisor or colleague makes the referral, the therapist is usually in a receptive mood when he or she meets and greets the prospective client. However, if the referral comes from a colleague who is "too busy to take on new patients" and "doesn't accept low fees," the therapist's feelings toward the condescending and insensitive referral source may very well become displaced onto the client and color the therapist's work with the client.

Frequently, referrals come from supervisors, teachers, and other senior colleagues whom the clinician wants to impress. As a result, hoping that the prospective clients will tell the supervisor or teacher how well they were treated, the clinician may become overactive in the telephone interview with the applicant and try to appear very knowledgeable in the initial interviews. Inasmuch as practitioners respond to pressure in different ways, some of them, with their keen desire to impress their senior colleagues, can become tongue-tied and say next to nothing in the initial contacts with a client.

Many referrals come from clients who are in treatment with the practitioner. These clients refer friends and family members to therapy for a variety of motives (Strean & Blatt, 1976). Some may be expressing gratitude, admiration, and respect, while others may wish to deride, demean, and disrespect their helpers. Many times the client in treatment who is making the referral is expressing a mixture of loving and hateful feelings. If the therapist has not investigated with the client the latter's motives in making the referral, he or she may be in for some surprises and not always pleasant ones.

Tim Viola, a therapist in private practice, was treating Mr. D. The client, a man in his mid-twenties, had come for treatment because he was experiencing sexual difficulties with women, often becoming impotent for several months at a time with a number of different women.

After being in therapy for a year, during which he became much more relaxed and potent, Mr. D. decided to refer to his therapist the young woman he was currently dating. Tim assumed that Mr. D. was expressing his gratitude to him through the referral and thought that perhaps Mr. D. was hopeful that his girlfriend would become a better mate as a consequence of Tim's therapy with her.

When Tim Viola met Ellen, Mr. D.'s girlfriend, he found her to be very attractive but very unfriendly. Inasmuch as Mr. D. had described Ellen as warm and engaging, and Tim thought he could trust Mr. D.'s judgment, he was very baffled by Ellen's attitude toward him. When Tim eventually asked Ellen how she felt about being in therapy, Ellen had many negative attitudes toward it and in many ways resisted the idea of being a client. Her sole reason for seeing Tim Viola, she pointed out, was to please Mr. D. who seemed to feel very strongly about her being in treatment and with Tim.

Fortunately, Tim Viola and Mr. D. had a good working relationship and could discuss some of Mr. D.'s fantasies about Ellen being in treatment with Tim. Slowly, a latent competitive transference that Mr. D. had been harboring toward Tim emerged. Said Mr. D. in one session, "Yeah, I wanted to show Ellen off to you. It makes me feel like a big shot as I picture you admiring me for being able to have a woman like Ellen admire me." Later, Tim was told by his client, "It's kind of fun to know that as a therapist you can't even put your arm around her, but I can have sex with her all of the time." Finally, a strong oedipal transference was expressed loudly and clearly when Mr. D. acknowledged, "I think the greatest piece of fun in all of this is that Ellen really doesn't want you as a therapist, but she does want me as a boyfriend. I think that her excluding you turns me on!"

As we reflect on Mr. D.'s referral of Ellen to Tim Viola, several points emerge. One, a referral can be made by a client to promote a latent negative transference which, if left unexplored, can retard the treatment of a client who is really acting out the negative transference by making a referral. Second, many individuals are quite aware that they do not want to come for therapy but nevertheless appear for an interview. If the practitioner resists facing the idea that someone is in his office who doesn't want to be there, as was true of Ellen, the therapist runs the risk of not only alienating the individual referred, but the client doing the referring can become alienated when the gift he or she wants to give turns out to be anything but a gift. In the case above Tim could have lost both Ellen and Mr. D. as clients by not exploring Mr. D.'s wish to refer Ellen.

Fortunately, Tim was able to discuss with Ellen her tendency to comply with demands, even when she knows she does not want to acquiesce to them. As a result of this discussion, Ellen eventually became motivated for therapy. Also, it was helpful to Mr. D. and his work with Tim that the two of them, Mr. D. and Tim, were eventually able to face and resolve their mutual resistance. In effect, they colluded in *not* exploring Mr. D.'s referral of Ellen—an example of the client's resistance and the therapist's counterresistance supporting and reinforcing each other.

REJECTING REFERRALS

Some therapists believe that client referrals are always a subtle form of acting out and therefore refuse to accept referrals from clients. We believe that just as accepting referrals can be an acting out of resistance and counterresistance, refusing them can be an expression of counterresistances of the practitioner, as well. Some therapists may be too inhibited to face what receiving a referral from a client means to them—being seduced, controlled, or manipulated. By refusing to accept a referral, they may be refusing to accept some of their own human desires, such as the wish for passivity, dependency, sexuality, or intimacy.

Martha Ungar, a private practitioner, routinely rejected referrals from clients she was seeing in therapy. She contended that to accept referrals was an acting out of transference and countertransference that, instead of being gratified, should be investigated in treatment. When a client of hers, Ms. E., wanted to refer a woman friend for treatment and Martha refused to accept the referral, Ms. E. went into a deep depression and eventually had to be hospitalized. As a result, Martha Ungar was forced to analyze more carefully her resistances to accepting referrals from clients.

As she reflected on her counterresistance problems related to accepting referrals from clients, Martha began to realize that she had unconsciously experienced the individual referred as an intruder who was disrupting a treasured symbiosis with the client she had in treatment. Further self-scrutiny helped Martha realize that she experienced men who were being referred as her younger brother, "the guy who in many ways took my mother away from me." Women being referred by her clients were often turned into her mother toward whom Martha Ungar felt much animosity and envy and was "the lady who wouldn't let me have my father to myself."

When Martha Ungar courageously faced her counterresistances as they emerged in the referral process, she was able with more objectivity and equanimity to study her clients' wishes to refer friends and family members. Eventually, she could help her clients face the fantasies, transference issues, and subtle resistances that were motivating their desire to refer clients. It later dawned on her that by refusing Ms. E.'s referral, she was also refusing to face Ms. E.'s homosexual transference fantasies and her countertransference fantasies.

Accepting or rejecting referrals from clients, colleagues, friends, or family members should be based as much as possible on the needs of the client being referred.

If it is a client in treatment doing the referring, the state of the client's current transference, current resistances, and current situation should be given top priority. Therapists, like clients, have a vast array of feelings toward those who refer clients. In order to use ourselves in as productive and helpful a manner as possible, we should try to review comprehensively how we feel toward and experience transferentially the referral party.

THE FIRST INTERVIEW

What Is a Psychotherapeutic Interview?

A psychotherapeutic interview is a purposive conversation, involving verbal and nonverbal communication between individuals, during which ideas and feelings are exchanged. In any interview, the participants reciprocally influence each other (Kadushin, 1972). In the psychotherapy interview, however, the therapist is considered the director of the process. The therapist helps clients formulate their reasons for seeking help, helps them consider what they would like to alter in their lives, and focuses the interviews so as to help them talk about and reflect on their current and past stresses and presses.

Because the central purpose of the psychotherapy interview is designed to serve the interests and needs of the client, interviewers conduct themselves in a manner that encourages interviewees to reveal a great deal about themselves while the practitioner reveals very little (Garrett, 1951). This affords clients the opportunity to feel, perhaps for the first time in their lives, that another person is devoting exclusive attention to them—to their wants, needs, conflicts and external pressures.

A good interviewer in the psychotherapeutic process is always a good listener. This simple statement, however, is too often overlooked in practice. It usually takes many years of experience for clinicians to truly master the notion that when clients are given the opportunity to have an empathetic listener attend to their thoughts, feelings, ideas, and memories, tensions are reduced and energy previously utilized to repress and suppress disturbing feelings and thoughts becomes available for more productive functioning.

Most individuals who become clients do so because there is no one in their immediate environment to listen to them. Furthermore, most listeners who are not trained in the art and science of listening, when hearing someone else describe a conflict, voice indecision, or discuss feelings of loneliness, helplessness, hopelessness, anger, loss, and grief, often feel obliged to give quick advice, offer notions and experiences from their own pasts, or in some other way try to offer immediate and usually impulsive first aid. They fail to realize that one of the most effective means of helping an individual feel less anxiety and stress and more self-confidence is to permit interviewees plenty of latitude to voice what is really on their minds (Barbara, 1958).

Practitioners in general underestimate the enormous value of nonadvising, noncritical, nonintrusive, nonjudgmental, quiet listening. They are not always sensitive to the wonderful things that can happen when clients are given the opportunity of being with a professional who does not ask anything for himself or herself but focuses interest solely on them. But several wonderful things inevitably do happen when clients are the recipients of patient, warm, quiet listening. They begin to feel they are people of value, and this feeling of self-worth often frees and strengthens them to use their coping mechanisms more effectively. As they begin to trust the empathetic interviewer, their significant others begin to appear more trustworthy. As they feel that being listened to enhances self-esteem and induces warmth, they unconsciously identify with their helper as they interact with others. In doing so, significant others begin to value and to trust them more and, hence, a positive spiralling goes into effect in which clients begin to esteem themselves and others more, and others respond similarly to them.

Psychologist Carl Rogers described effective, nonjudgmental listening as offering the client "unconditional positive regard" (Rogers, 1951). As we suggested, clients sense that when they are regarded positively by the interviewer, which is usually transmitted by nonintrusive listening, they begin to regard themselves more positively. However, interviewees who harbor much self-hatred often react with suspicion to compliments and other supportive remarks of the interviewer. They may feel that they are being patronized and demeaned when the interviewer uses these seemingly well-intentioned procedures (Benjamin, 1974). They then create distance between themselves and the interviewer.

Good listening, of course, means following what is implied as well as what is being said. It requires being expectantly attentive and receptive, with a relaxed alertness in which the interviewer extends himself or herself fully to appreciate what the interviewee is saying (Kadushin, 1972). Most interviewees sense when the interviewer is psychologically somewhere else; silent listening without being attentive to the clients' spoken and unspoken messages rarely achieves very much of a therapeutic alliance.

As we noted in the Preface and in Chapter 1, just as clients in the initial sessions resist telling the therapist salient themes of their past and present life, clinicians can resist listening, either by silently wandering away from the client's productions, as noted above, or by talking too much. Just as there are clients who feel forced to attend a consultation, and dread it, there are practitioners who feel the same way. The client's resistances in the initial interviews are ubiquitous, as are the therapist's counterresistances. In the remaining part of this chapter we will attempt to identify common counterresistances in the initial sessions, try to assess their meaning, and offer some ways to resolve them.

Resistances to Listening

Just as there are probably an infinite number of reasons why clients resist discussing their problems and inhibit themselves from exposing their feelings, fantasies, thoughts, and memories in the initial interviews, there are probably an infinite number of reasons why therapists resist listening to their clients' productions. In this section we will deal with some of the dynamics that contribute to a therapist's failure to listen.

Perhaps one of the major factors contributing to a therapist's failure to listen attentively are his or her feelings toward the client, that is, his or her countertransference reactions. As we have already indicated, transference and countertransference are universal phenomena; consequently, every time a clinician meets a new client, the client stirs up feelings toward and memories of important figures of the therapist's past. The new client can be viewed as mother, father, sister, or brother by the therapist. Or, the client can become a previous girlfriend or boyfriend, a former or current boss, a son or daughter, grandmother or grandfather, cousin or colleague, or a composite of many of these figures. Similar to clients who turn the therapist into an idealized parent or lover, therapists can do the same with their new clients. Occasionally, therapists fall in love with their new client in the first few minutes of the first interview, or they can find themselves feeling acute resentment toward the new client in the first few minutes of the first interview.

Of course, when clinicians have strong feelings toward the new client, they find it difficult to listen. For example, if the therapist experiences the client as a former boyfriend about whom she has many warm memories, she may be more interested in recalling her fond memories than in listening to how her new client cannot get along with his tyrannical boss. Or, the same therapist may find it difficult to listen to her new client because she is trying hard to curb erotic fantasies toward her client who has become a boyfriend for her and therefore she feels as if she is on a date rather than conducting an interview.

As suggested, a new client can also stir up unpleasant memories and negative feelings in the practitioner. Affects toward an envied sibling or a disliked parent or an abusive parental figure may be provoked. Again, it should be pointed out that it is difficult to listen attentively to a client's productions when the therapist has to cope with memories of old power struggles and fracases, while the client may be seriously depressed because his favorite uncle has just died.

As a client's transference reactions to the therapist influence what he or she selects to present to the practitioner, a therapist's countertransference reactions toward the client in many ways determine what material he or she selects to listen to carefully. If the client induces positive feelings in the therapist, there will be a tendency to listen to those productions that present the client as a decent, lovable character. Furthermore, if the client is very positively cathected, the practitioner may not only select certain dimensions of the client's personality and life circumstances with which to empathize and identify, but also the therapist may color his or her perceptions of the client's productions and alter their meaning so that the client is maintained as the transference figure that the practitioner wants the client to be. Similarly, if the new client is negatively cathected, in all probability the practitioner will selectively perceive and retain those observations and impressions that conform to his or her negative countertransference reaction.

THE CLIENT'S STORY KINDLES MEMORIES AND FANTASIES IN THE THERAPIST

Because transference reactions of client toward therapist or those of therapist toward client are usually intense and complex and have been reinforced on many occasions over a long period of time, they are not easily modified or worked through quickly. Just as a client's transference reactions to the therapist usually take much time to resolve, the same can be said of the therapist's countertransference reactions toward the client.

Bob Thompson, a therapist in private practice, was conducting an initial consultation with Ms. F., a 30-year-old married woman who was having marital conflicts and was seriously thinking of leaving her husband. As Bob listened to Ms. F.'s presentation of her marital conflicts, he found his mind wandering. An experienced therapist, Bob hypothesized that if he was wandering away from his new client, her presence and story were stirring up feelings toward somebody important in Bob's past or present.

Bob followed his mental roamings to see where they would lead. He soon found himself thinking of his teenage years, particularly of young women he admired from a distance but with whom he did not feel free to initiate much contact. As Bob became aware of the fact that he had become preoccupied with young women of his past with whom he could not relate intimately, he realized that he was reviewing Ms. F. in the same way.

Although it took Bob several weeks to feel comfortable with Ms. F., he was able to begin resolving his resistance to listening—that is, his initial counterresistance in his therapy with Ms. F.—once he acknowledged to himself that he was defending against sexual fantasies toward his client. Bob's next step in overcoming his sexual inhibitions with Ms. F., which was the main factor in his mental wandering, was honestly and directly to face his forbidden sexual fantasies toward her. As he allowed himself to fantasize embracing Ms. F., and having sex play with her, he began to realize that he was trying to have a teenage romance with her—something he deprived himself of frequently during his adolescence.

One of the best ways to resolve a counterresistance is first to acknowledge its existence. Just as clients need to be confronted first with their resistances, and helped to acknowledge that their resistances do exist, practitioners first need to confront themselves with the fact that they are resisting, for example, not listening attentively. Once therapists confront their resistances, their next task is to clarify for themselves what wishes, feelings, fantasies, and memories they are trying to repress and suppress. In the above case illustration, after Bob confronted the fact that he was not listening carefully to Ms. F., he then faced the fact that he was avoiding her in the same way he avoided his girlfriends of the past. Finally, Bob could interpret to himself that he was using his counterresistance to avoid facing specific adolescent sexual fantasies that were emerging in his work with Ms. F., chiefly pregenital wishes usually gratified in sexual foreplay. Like all resistances and counterresistances, Bob had to permit himself sufficient time to work through his inhibitions toward Ms. F. by reviewing the above issues several times. These steps of confrontation, clarification, interpretation, and working through (Greenson, 1967) are the procedures utilized in helping clients resolve their resistances and are certainly applicable to the resolution of counterresistances.

REVERSING ROLES WITH THE CLIENT

Therapists often find that when their reluctance to listen emanates from negative feelings toward the client, the resistances are more difficult to resolve. As we suggested in Chapter 1, practitioners' superego injunctions often forbid them to harbor hostile feelings and fantasies toward clients. Consequently, they feel guilty and ashamed when they become aware of their resentment toward their clients. Furthermore, because negative feelings usually evolve from a sense of threat, it is often difficult for practitioners to admit that they, who are charged with helping threatened clients to feel more comfortable with them and others, have reversed roles (A. Freud, 1946) with their therapeutic partners.

Mona Stanton, a psychiatrist in private practice, was having an initial interview with Ms. G., who sought help because she was unable to advance in her position as a professor of psychology at a large metropolitan university. As Ms. G. presented her problems, honestly admitting her competition with colleagues and superiors, Dr. Stanton found herself feeling agitated, restless, and not able to concentrate on the content of Ms. G.'s material. As Mona found herself interrupting her client at one moment and then not listening at another, she became increasingly depressed in the interview. As she started to reflect on her strong discomfort, Mona did not acknowledge that her own dynamics were at work. Rather, she felt that her discomfort in the interview was "an induced countertransference reaction" (Spotnitz, 1976), that is, she was experiencing feelings that the client wanted her to feel.

Mona reasoned that the boredom, restlessness, and irritation that she was experiencing in the session were probably the same boredom, restlessness, and irritation that Ms. G.'s colleagues and students most likely experienced in their contacts with her. Consequently, Mona asked Ms. G. toward the middle of their first interview, "Do you find that your students and colleagues move away from you when to talk to them, and that they seem bored, restless, and irritated?" Ms. G. denied this possibility immediately, but went on to ask Dr. Stanton why she asked her this question. Mona asked then, "Why do you think?" and then Ms. G. became silent for several minutes.

When Mona asked her client why she was quiet, Ms. G. responded with tears and lamented, "I feel very hurt by you. But you are the expert, so maybe I do bore and irritate others without knowing what I'm doing."

Mona Stanton then began to feel very sorry for her client and told her she would like to help her understand how she "subtly provokes others without realizing it." Therapist and client agreed to make another appointment for the following week. During the intervening time between appointments, Mona found herself thinking of her client several times. Although she could acknowledge to herself that she was quite "harsh" with Ms. G., she also found herself saying, "But Ms. G. has it coming to her. She's a bitch and needs to face it!" Yet, Mona made up her mind to try to be "a little softer" with Ms. G. in the second interview because she had "given her a rather strong dose of medicine."

Despite Mona's intentions to be "a little softer" in the second interview, client and therapist participated in a similar form of interaction. Ms. G. again described her struggles with her colleagues and Mona again found herself sometimes interrupting her client and other times not concentrating. Mona then thought to herself, "I didn't affect her in the first interview. The damn woman is doing the same thing today." But again, Mona Stanton did not take much responsibility for her own helplessness, irritation, and agitation. Instead she asked her client, "Do you find that when people show you how you can be irritating, you ignore them?" And, true to her own characteristic script, Ms. G. responded, "I'm not aware of other people pointing out things to me. But if you say that I ignore people, I guess that's what I must do," and she wept again and quite profusely.

Mona Stanton eventually realized that she and her client were participating in continual sadomasochistic orgies in these early sessions. So she discussed these sessions with her supervisor and later in her own personal therapy. Over time, Mona was able to realize that Ms. G. reminded her of her younger sister toward whom she felt quite rivalrous and secretly envied. Her sister, like Ms. G., was also an educator and also intellectually gifted but emotionally quite insensitive and unaware of her own foibles. As Mona became more conscious of her "sibling rivalry" with her client, she could slowly begin to listen to her more and compete with her less.

There are clients who frequently rationalize their transference reactions toward their therapists and contend that they are "induced," but some therapists tend to do the same—perhaps to even a greater degree. Regardless of a client's unconscious intent and provocation, each practitioner responds to each client on the basis of his or her own personal history, dynamics, and psychic structure. In the above example, there was no doubt that Ms. G. was a competitive woman who provoked many people. However, it was important for Mona Stanton to realize that she was responding to Ms. G.'s provocation and competitive attitude with her own provocative remarks and competition. Ms. G.'s hostile, competitive attitude was not understood well by her therapist because the therapist used the client's belligerence to turn her into her envied sister.

Another major reason for clinicians being unable to listen to the client's story is that the story can be upsetting to them. Clients enter treatment because they feel depressed, dejected, and demoralized. Often their feelings of helplessness and hopelessness overwhelm them. They cite instances of being abused in the past as well as in the present. Sometimes they describe violence enacted toward themselves by others and/or toward others by themselves. Some clients are suicidal. Many feel very lonely. Most have a poor self-image and low self-esteem. Unfullfilling marriages are ubiquitous; dysfunctional parent-child and family relationships are frequent; and serious physical and mental illness are more than occasionally described. Guilt is practically universal.

It is never easy, and perhaps it is impossible, to relax completely when one meets somebody for the first time and hears the stranger talk in pain about sexual or emotional abuse, family wars, and other personal and interpersonal conflicts. Clinicians, although they do not permit themselves to do so frequently enough, are entitled to have their own feelings, thoughts, and fantasies as they listen to their clients present severe problems, which often appear horrendous. They are entitled to feel revulsion, anger, sorrow, and pain. They have a right to experience excitement and lust, and feel it with heartbeats and other physical sensations that often accompany these emotions.

When practitioners do not listen to their clients' presentations, they are usually not able to listen to their own emotional reactions. If they have to repress, suppress, or deny what they are feeling in the interviews, they are going to arrange *not* to listen to what stirs up affects in themselves that they cannot contain.

Competent, effective, empathetic clinicians are those who can allow themselves to experience a wide range of emotions. If they can tolerate their own murderous and erotic wishes, they can be more tolerant of hatred and lust in their clients. When they can accept the infant in themselves, who is characterized by dependency, greed, passivity, and impulsiveness, they will be able to accept these human characteristics in their clients.

When Fred Ryan, a psychologist in a community mental health center, met his client, Mr. H., for the first time, he took an instant dislike to him. Mr. H. had been referred to the mental health center by the courts because he had been "guilty of domestic violence." In the intake interview, Mr. H. bragged to Fred Ryan that when he did not like what his wife said or did, he "slapped her face, socked her in the nose, and made her bleed."

As most caring professionals would probably feel, Fred Ryan felt protective of Mr. H.'s wife. His wish to protect and defend her made him feel like "getting even" with Mr. H. and "beating him up." Fred could not listen to Mr. H. during most of their first interview because he was busy fantasying himself in a physical duel with him.

After his first interview with Mr. H., Fred Ryan found himself mentally boxing and wrestling with Mr. H. for several days. As he reflected on his own wish to fight, he first became aware of how identified he was with the victim, Mrs. H., and that by fighting with Mr. H. in fantasy, he was acting out his revenge toward all of the bullies he had confronted during the course of his life, particularly during his childhood. Although recognizing and accepting his own identification with Mrs. H. was helpful to Fred, in that he could now see that much of his rage toward his client emanated from a desire to ward off feelings of weakness and vulnerability in himself, this was not the complete answer. What was painful and difficult for Fred to face was "the Mr. H. in himself.," the part of himself that had wishes to beat up his own wife. Fred's extremely punitive attitude toward Mr. H.'s physical violence was his way of warding off a confrontation with his own violent impulses.

When we feel very condemning and punitive toward a piece of a client's behavior, or very critical of a client's particular attitude, we are usually being too hard on ourselves for feeling capable of the same behavior or having the same attitude. As Fred Ryan slowly became aware of the Mr. H. in himself, as well as the Mrs. H. in himself, he could begin to listen more attentively and with more compassion to his very disturbed and conflicted client.

Counterresistances with Clients Who Withhold Material

From time to time, every clinician resists listening to the client during the first interview and in later sessions as well. Nonetheless, there are many instances, particularly in initial interviews, when the clinician is very ready to listen but the client is most reluctant to talk.

As suggested in Chapter 1, there are many reasons why clients do not want to talk to a therapist. They worry that they will be derided, demeaned, or debased for their sexual and aggressive wishes and deeds. They fear that issues in their past and present about which they feel guilty and ashamed will be revealed in the therapy and they think they will be judged very negatively by the therapist, often fantasying some form of censure. Entering psychotherapy is often experienced by the client as being relegated to a status of "second-class citizen," an ignoble, submissive position in which one has given up control. One way of restoring control is by with-holding information from the practitioner (Noble & Hamilton, 1983). If the client feels weakened by saying, "Yes, I will go for a consultation with a therapist," he or she feels that some strength can be gained by proclaiming, "No, I won't talk."

When a man, woman, or child is pressured to see a therapist by an external authority, such as a court or school, it is not too difficult to understand why the client wants to withhold data—he or she does not want to be in the therapist's office in the first place! However, sometimes it is difficult to fathom why a client who feels enormous pain seeks out a practitioner, is ready to pay a lot of money in the hope that his or her suffering will abate, enters the consultation room, and then is most unwilling to talk about anything but superficialities. The client may even say in the interview, "I know I can't be helped very much if I don't speak to you, but I just can't." By saying little, the client not only feels some pseudostrength and pseudoindependence, but also feels that he or she is diminishing the power and authority of the therapist.

Even though most practitioners agree that pressuring a reluctant client to talk only compounds the client's resistances, many of them cannot resist nagging their untalkative clients about the value of discussing their problems with the therapist. One of the main reasons that practitioners try to persuade reluctant clients to talk is to relieve themselves of frustration and irritation. Men and women become therapists, in part, in order to gratify wishes to know and to see. When their clients stop them from knowing and seeing, usually they do not like it. Also, those who become therapists want to help their clients do something to change their dysfunctional and unfulfilling lives. If their clients do not give them the data they need to do their therapeutic jobs, they can feel very disappointed, even dejected. Finally, most therapists welcome the respect and esteem they are usually given by their clients when they are made confidantes by them. Consequently, it is often demoralizing for practitioners to be told overtly or covertly that they are not going to be in the position of a confidante.

When information is withheld by the client, if clinicians do not handle their frustration and irritation by pressuring the client, they may instead cope with their tensions by using "negative suggestion" or what has been termed "joining the resistance" (Spotnitz, 1976). "Joining the resistance" of the client who is reluctant to talk involves telling the client, "It is not necessary for you to talk" or, "You should try not to talk" or even, "Therapy works best when the client talks very little." Clients usually sense the manipulation and sadism involved in such "therapeutic" procedures. Unless they are very masochistic and submissive, and are prone to idealize the therapist regardless of what the latter says or does, the majority of clients eventually reject this form of "help."

Most people who come into treatment have secrets (Fine, 1982; Greenson, 1967; Strean, 1985/1990) and usually it takes much time for the therapist to understand their etiology and even longer for clients to discuss them in therapy. The sensitive therapist is neither lax about attending to the client's secrets nor pressuring the client to reveal them. What is important for both therapist and client to realize is that when a client has difficulty exposing material, he or she feels in danger and it is the danger that should be the focus of discussion.

THE THERAPIST BECOMES IMPATIENT

When psychotherapists find that they are not empathizing and discussing with their clients the dangers the clients are experiencing when they say very little in the initial interviews (or in later ones, too), but are either lax or pressuring, saying nothing or saying too much about the client's reluctance to talk, they should try to investigate what their inactivity, overactivity, or inappropriate activity is all about. Some of the more common practitioner reactions to a client's unwillingness to present pertinent material in the initial interviews are feeling impatience, for example, "Damn it, why don't you give me what you are supposed to give me, you withholding so and so!"; feeling teased, for example, "Come on now, come out with it; stop dangling a carrot in front of me!"; and feeling threatened and weakened, for example, "I'm not the jerk you are trying to turn me into. Cut it out." Although the aforementioned remarks are usually said silently to themselves, practitioners' verbal and nonverbal communication reveal the reactions, albeit subtly, to clients.

George Quinn was an intake worker in a family agency, and was interviewing Mr. I., a man in his forties, referred to the agency by the court for exhibiting himself sexually to children. George Quinn, rather early in the intake interview, recognized in many ways that Mr. I. did not want to be at the agency. He also encouraged Mr. I. to voice his resentment toward the judge who ordered him to come to the agency. However, George had trouble getting Mr. I. to discuss the sexual problems that prompted the exhibitionism.

George told Mr. I. that he understood how difficult it was to talk about his exhibitionism and to share his difficulties with a stranger. Despite George's understanding attitude, Mr. I. repeatedly told George that the charges levelled against him by the court were false and "even if they were true, I wouldn't want to talk to anybody about them." On George's asking Mr. I. why he wouldn't talk to anybody about his problems, Mr. I. tersely responded, "It's nobody's business."

The more reluctant Mr. I. appeared to reveal information about himself, the more irritated and pressuring George Quinn became. When the power struggle between client and worker heightened, George threatened to send Mr. I. back for resentencing for failure to cooperate with the agency. Feeling intimidated and overpowered, Mr. I. finally relented and said, "Okay, what do you want to know?" Slowly realizing that he had been bullying his client, George Quinn tried to resume his therapeutic posture by saying, "I've been giving you a hard time, haven't I, Mr. I.?" Although Mr. I tried to be more cooperative, he gave a very controlled and unrevealing report of his exhibitionistic activities. He returned for a few interviews, but treatment never did get off the ground.

It was only after treatment discontinued that George Quinn could get in touch with the issues that activated his counterresistances toward Mr. I. George eventually realized that he unconsciously experienced his client's with-holding information as if he, George, was being controlled and bullied. George ascribed strength and power to Mr. I. as if his stubbornness was weakening George. In response to feeling demeaned and controlled, George became controlling and demeaning with his client.

When we sensitize ourselves to George Quinn's sense of threat and his need to overpower Mr. I., we realize why therapists in general, and psychoanalysts in particular, have tended to view resistances as "forces to overcome." Unconsciously, resistances have been experienced by practitioners at times as enemies ("forces") that have to be vanquished ("overcome"). Hence, the client can be perceived as an opponent, not as someone with whom one has "a therapeutic alliance" (Greenson, 1967).

When George Quinn shared his counterresistance difficulties in a supervisory seminar, he became aware of the fact that he had experienced Mr. I. in part as his own father who would stop talking to him as part of punishment. George felt weakened and rejected by his father when he stopped talking to him. As George later reflected, "I was feeling like a weak, castrated boy next to Mr. I. and I made him my strong, authoritarian father who wanted me wiped out. Just because Mr. I. wanted to wipe me out, I did not have to oblige him. As a kid with my father, I didn't have much choice. With Mr. I., I did."

When clinicians speak of "induced countertransference reactions," they are really describing something akin to what happened to George Quinn in his initial interview with Mr. I. The client probably did want to make George feel impotent and vulnerable. But George did not have to comply with Mr. I.'s unconscious agenda. Perhaps we can use the term "induced countertransference" when the therapist unconsciously complies with the client's overt and covert demands and wishes for the practitioner to behave in a certain way.

Very often a client's withholding of material is experienced by the therapist as if something is being sexually withheld, and again sometimes this is precisely the client's intent.

Natalie Pearson, a sex therapist in private practice, was conducting an initial consultation with Mr. J., a married man is his mid-thirties who was referred to her by his family physician because of frequent impotency. When Mr. J. was greeted by Natalie Pearson in the waiting room, he commented on the good choice of magazines she had selected for her clients to peruse. He was also quite complimentary regarding Natalie's "fine appearing" office. When Natalie nodded, showing her appreciation of Mr. J.'s "kind" observations, Mr. J. went on to tell Natalie Pearson that he could understand why she became a sex therapist because she was indeed "a sexy woman." A little embarrassed by Mr. J.'s provocativeness, Natalie remained quiet. After a short silence, Mr. J. asked, "Don't you have anything to say about your sexiness?," to which Natalie asked, "Perhaps it's a bit difficult for you to talk about your sexiness?" Mr. J. smiled and said, "I asked you first!"

The "one-upmanship" interaction like the above continued during much of the remainder of the interview, with Mr. J. wanting the therapist to reveal more of herself while he withheld as much as possible, and Natalie wanting Mr. J. to reveal more of himself while she revealed very little about herself.

When the initial consultation between client and therapist was reviewed a couple of days later in supervision, Natalie was able to recognize that she and Mr. J. were involved in a mutual teasing contest as if each was trying to get the other one to get undressed first. Natalie associated to the many times she felt teased by young boys when she was a little girl, such as when they wanted to "play doctor" with her and she was conflicted about it. Natalie further realized that now that she was a doctor in reality—and in addition a sex, perhaps sexy, doctor—and she found herself feeling in the same position as the young boys were with her. As "doctors" they commanded her to take off her clothes, which either she did most reluctantly or not at all.

As Natalie thought more about her interview with Mr. J., she also realized that she felt somewhat uncomfortable and a little guilty in her role as "a sex doctor" having to tell people, as she experienced it in her fantasy, to take off their clothes. She had a tendency to think of herself as if she were a provocative, aggressive, young boy while enacting the role of sex therapist. Consequently, she could not relate to Mr. J.'s provocativeness in the interview and tell him it appeared as if they were playing the game, "I'll show you mine if you show me yours." In effect, her fear of her own fantasied aggression inhibited Natalie from "calling the shots" in the therapeutic situation.

In her second interview with Mr. J., Natalie Pearson felt more confident and clearer about how she could deal with her client's reluctance to reveal information. When Mr. J. made some more references to "the sex doctor's" attractiveness, Natalie suggested that he seemed to be interested in flirting with her. To this Mr. J. flushed and said, "Yeah, I like to flirt, but I can't get it up! When the woman wants me sexually, I don't know what happens, but I shrivel up."

Although Mr. J. made further attempts to flirt with Natalie Pearson, she realized that his flirting was clearly a form of teasing. And, like most teasing, Mr. J. was demonstrating how very frightened he was of his own sexuality as well as of hers.

When clients wish to tease the therapist by withholding data, it is helpful for the practitioner to keep in mind that the client is feeling like a frightened child who is trying to reduce his or her own sense of threat by putting the interviewer on the spot. Perhaps of more importance, practitioners should be familiar with their usual responses to teasing, be able to recall times in their lives when they have been teased, and/or did some teasing themselves. They should try to be in touch with how they experienced themselves and the significant other when this took place. If therapists find themselves feeling unduly irritated, retaliative, or inhibited in the face of the client's teasing, they can probably assume that they are too invested in being teased and teasing than invested in helping the client get in touch with why he or she is engaged in provoking the interviewer.

As implied earlier in this chapter, one of the main reasons that practitioners find it difficult to feel comfortable as they deal with clients who tend to withhold material is that they feel their position of "boss" is being undermined. Although the therapist is the director of the treatment process, and should be able to accept the fact of therapeutic life with equanimity, mature practitioners should also be able to sustain their state of comfort as directors of the therapy even when their clients want to remove them from this role.

Tolerating the Client's Competition

To be able to feel secure with clients who wish to defeat us almost as soon as they meet us, we have to be able to tolerate their competition with us and face some of our own competition with them. If we become intimidated by our clients' immediate wish to denounce us, and return their competition with some of our own (Schafer, 1983), we cease being the director of the treatment process. Clients then succeed in manipulating the drama that they unconsciously have intended to produce—to get us to "give up" so that they do not have to enter treatment.

Jean Olson, a psychologist in a child guidance clinic, was conducting an intake interview with Ms. K., mother of nine-year-old Elizabeth. The child had a severe school phobia, making it impossible for her to go to school. The guidance department of Elizabeth's school called Ms. K. and said that a consultation at the local child guidance clinic was recommended.

In the first few minutes of the intake interview when Jean asked Ms. K. how long it had been that Elizabeth was frightened to go to school, Ms. K. replied, "First of all, I don't think knowing how long this has been going on will cure it!" Although it was quite clear to Jean Olson that Ms. K. had a strong, unconscious investment in keeping her daughter at home under her own surveillance and not a teacher's, Jean, nonetheless, felt quite threatened by Ms. K.'s very aggressive attitude toward her. Rather than trying to investigate what was making Ms. K. angry, she asked another question about Elizabeth's activities at home. This question activated even more ire in Ms.

K., and this time she said, "I don't think you are very well qualified to do this job. Here the kid is upset about going to school and you are trying to find out what she does at home. Are you nuts?"

As Jean listened to Ms. K.'s accusations and criticisms, she told herself that she was dealing with a very paranoid mother who was extremely worried about having her strong symbiotic relationship with her daughter exposed. Despite her clarity regarding Ms. K.'s dynamics, all Jean was aware of was that under the impact of Ms. K.'s bombastic attacks, she found herself retreating.

The more Ms. K. attacked, the more Jean retreated. Either Jean found herself saying nothing or she asked questions that Ms. K. deemed to be inappropriate. The interview ended prematurely on Ms. K.'s initiative. Ms. K. said that she felt exasperated and vowed that she would "never see a shrink again."

There are some clients, like Ms. K. in the above vignette, who seem so threatened by the possible exposure of their deep secrets that they appear very determined to defeat the therapist and the therapy regardless of the practitioner's activity or inactivity. Very often, these clients induce the therapist to conclude that to work with them is a complete waste of time and effort. Although there are clients who feel compelled to defeat their therapy and therapist and do not view their victory as self-destructive, some of them can be helped to remain in therapy if the practitioner copes with the counterresistances that emerge.

When clients want to defeat us, we can go on the war path and use "interpretations" to put them in their place. Usually, when this happens, clients leave treatment and, feeling rebuffed, they correctly conclude that they are dealing with an angry therapist. Another way of coping with a belligerent client like Ms. K. is to react the way Jean Olson did—retreat and submit. However, then the client usually feels contemptuous of us and leaves prematurely, worried that he or she can destroy us.

What sometimes can be helpful to clients like Ms. K. is to level with them and point out how eager they are to fight with the therapist and are bent on destroying the possibility of treatment. Although these clients may use such statements as fuel for more fighting, some may feel a little understood and begin to examine themselves. This seemed to occur with Natalie Pearson and Mr. J. in an earlier vignette.

When Jean Olson reviewed her interview with Ms. K., she realized that she felt so angry in the face of her client's belligerence that she became speechless, lest she "destroy" her. Often when practitioners find themselves speechless in their initial consultations, they are fighting the expression of forbidden impulses—often aggressive feelings, but sometimes other feelings such as sexual desires.

Jean Olson was so upset with her own anger that she could not even think of confronting Ms. K.'s anger with her own. In addition, Jean felt so identified with

Elizabeth and Ms. K.'s mistreatment of her that she transferred onto Ms. K. qualities of her own mother, who Jean felt was at times very restrictive and punitive.

Frequently, when we feel demeaned by a client, we are making the client a parental figure of our past and assigning ourselves the role of a helpless child. We do this when we resist assuming the role of "boss" or director—obviously an adult role. If we believe that being an adult boss will make us appear too big and belligerent, we can regress, feel like a child, and turn the client into a big and belligerent parental figure. If we do turn clients into powerful parental figures and resist modifying our countertransference positions, we are usually on the brink of giving up.

Coping with Clients' Wishes for Advice and Other "Therapeutic" Interventions

Although most clinicians do appreciate the importance and value of listening to their clients' presentation of problems without interruption, many of them feel "on the spot" when, toward the end of the first interview, the client asks, "So, now that I've spoken for over 40 minutes and you've been quiet, what do you think?" Or, the client might say, "Since you are the expert and I'll be spending good money, could you give me some advice on this?" And if the client is particularly bold, he or she might say, "Is this the way it's always going to be? I do all of the talking and you say nothing?"

It usually takes many years of experience for therapists to feel comfortable enough *not* to gratify a client's requests and instead explore what the client is feeling and thinking or make some other intervention. Practitioners often feel, particularly in the initial interview, that if they do not give clients what they request or demand, their clients will become angry and not return for further therapy. Therapists can place themselves in the psychological position of parents who are overidentified with their needy children. To say "no" to their hungry children makes them feel cruel, because in their overidentification, they are quite convinced that their children are being severely hurt by their frustrating behavior. Clinicians eventually realize that the most helpful therapeutic procedure, particularly in the initial interviews, is to investigate what is behind the request.

What usually leads to solid emotional growth in therapy is frustration accompanied by sensitive understanding. Although therapists may intellectually accept the concept that successful weaning, successful toilet training, and other maturing experiences involve the imposition of limits, many clinicians find it difficult to transpose this virtual axiom to the treatment situation. Why is this so?

Many, if not most, men and women who become psychotherapists have strong omnipotent fantasies. The wish to be a god who reigns over a therapeutic universe, taking care of his or her dependent children, is a very common fantasy among those who wish to help people in trouble. Complementing this, people in trouble often want the therapist to serve as an omnipotent parent (Freud, 1937). As a consequence, we frequently find a phenomenon taking place, particularly in the initial interview, of unconscious collusion between client and therapist in which the client wants to be the recipient of consistent feeding, soothing, loving, and nurturing by an all-giving combination of omnipotent mother and father, and the therapist is only too pleased to oblige.

Overgratifying the Client

If client and therapist unconsciously create a blissful symbiotic relationship, the client, supported by a doting parental figure, remains a psychological infant. In addition, if clients are indulged indiscriminately, they eventually become very depressed and irate, because no therapist, no matter how hard he or she tries, can consistently satisfy the demanding client. Sooner or later the client's fantasy of therapist as omnipotent parent becomes punctured. Therapists do have lives of their own with their own mates, children, friends, extended family, and colleagues and cannot be "on call" for the client all of the time. They also have to sleep and take care of other human needs. Therefore, if they cannot resolve their wishes to be omnipotent therapeutic gods, they will eventually disappoint many clients who will feel very let down and misunderstood. If the client expects a Santa Claus to be present at every interview, and the therapist has this expectation as well, the practitioner will eventually run out of gifts and the client will understandably see himself or herself as a victim of broken promises.

Bernard Nelson, a therapist in private practice, was seeing Ms. L., a single woman in her early thirties, for an initial consultation. Ms. L. was interested in receiving therapeutic help because she found herself "continually in frustrating relationships with men," and was choosing men who did not "satisfy" her. She also mentioned in her consultation with Bernard Nelson that her experiences in therapy had been unsatisfying. Said Ms. L., "I kept wanting feedback from the two guys I saw in therapy but they did not come through for me."

In describing her history, Ms. L. referred to both of her parents as "ungiving and unfulfilling." Therefore, she told Bernard, "I need someone who I feel is there for me. My parents weren't there, my therapists weren't there, and the guys I've dated haven't been there for me either."

Although it was clear to Bernard Nelson that Ms. L. was trying to gratify fantasies in all of her relationships that she could not get gratified, he found himself in the first interview competing with her previous therapists, past boyfriends, and with her parents. Toward the end of the interview, Bernard told Ms. L. that she had led a life of frustration and did not derive much pleasure from her relationships. He would try to help her "have a different experience" with him.

Feeling supported and reassured by Bernard Nelson, Ms. L. asked several questions about therapy and therapeutic procedures. Instead of exploring with his client the feelings that prompted her questions, Bernard answered her queries. He talked about "corrective emotional experiences," "transference," and "resistance," but particularly of the importance of "a good relationship between client and therapist."

Although Bernard's statements and definitions were clear and correct, he did not seem to appreciate how much he was "feeding" a client who was insatiable. At the end of the first interview, Ms. L. profusely thanked Bernard for his kindness. Then Ms. L. made several phone calls to Bernard before her second session. These were questions about insurance, fees, and frequency of sessions. Instead of suggesting to his client that she talk about these issues at her next appointment, Bernard again answered Ms. L.'s questions directly.

One question answered by Bernard led Ms. L. to ask another. By the third interview, Bernard felt deluged with more and more questions and more and more demands. He began to realize that he was behaving more like an acquiescent parent than an understanding therapist. As a result, toward the middle of the third interview, Bernard decided to investigate what was going on with Ms. L. that prompted her "many questions." Ms. L. responded very angrily to Bernard's query, saying, "You seemed like such an understanding gentleman but now I see you are like all the rest! From a nice guy you've become a cold shrink."

Although Bernard Nelson tried to empathize with Ms. L.'s anger, showed her that he understood how and why she felt let down by him, it seemed to be too late for Ms. L. She left treatment after the fifth interview even though Bernard extended the time for 15 minutes beyond the usual session.

When clients are realistically gratified by the therapist, they have every right to expect an "encore." When they do not receive an "encore," they also have every right to view the therapist as an inconsistent person; hence their anger seems quite legitimate and they have to distrust the therapist.

Very often when the above scenario transpires, the therapist's wish to be the all-giving Santa Claus interferes with the therapy. The client is not receiving more self-understanding, but more indulgence. What usually occurs, though, is that those therapists who want to surpass all of the caregivers in the client's past and present find they eventually get exasperated by all of the demands placed on them and begin to show irritation. The client senses the irritation, feels misunderstood, and leaves treatment.

To keep a client in treatment, therapists from the very beginning of their contact should try to monitor their rescue fantasies. Bernard Nelson's strong wish to rescue Ms. L. from all those individuals, particularly men, who had not gratified her the way she wanted them to satisfy her, paralleled her wish to be rescued. This collusion between the therapist and client—their mutual wish to rescue and be rescued—was doomed to defeat. Insatiable desires can never be fulfilled. Instead, they should be understood. When therapists find themselves repeatedly answering questions of clients, they should be alerted to the possibility that they are in a neurotic competitive struggle in order to emerge as the best gratifier in the client's life. Once a therapist is embarked on such a journey, the client is being helped to regress in a way that will never lead to maturational growth. Clients need their questions and requests explored with the therapist rather than gratified. When the client's motives for questioning or demanding become clearer to him or her, she or he usually feels stronger and more competent.

Ground Rules and Counterresistances

Regardless of the therapeutic setting and the modality used, all clinicians and their clients have to agree to certain ground rules. The appointment times for sessions, the amount of the fee, when the fee is paid, and confidentiality are among many of the ground rules that pervade all therapies.

How and why clients cope with ground rules the way they do have received a great deal of attention in the therapeutic literature (Fine, 1982; Langs, 1973; Strean, 1985/1990). Many clients do handle ground rules in a cooperative manner, arriving punctually for every appointment, paying their fees faithfully at the last session of each month, saying everything that comes to mind regardless of the shame and guilt that accompanies their revelations and confessions, and avoiding discussion of the content of their sessions with anyone other than the practitioner.

The cooperative behavior, like any form of overt behavior, has a unique meaning for each individual who enacts it. For one client, the cooperative behavior can be an attempt to manipulate the professional to love the client. For another client, the cooperation may be a massive defense against the expression of defiance. Or, the cooperative behavior can be a function of a strict, punitive superego, whereby the client is strongly complying to the dictates of powerful inner voices. Any one of these possibilities, alone or in combination with others, may explain the cooperative behavior of the moment. And, these explanations do not exhaust the list; there are others, including the possibility that the client's cooperative behavior is essentially conflict-free (Hartmann, 1958).

Clients, of course, can handle the ground rules in a defiant manner, missing sessions, arriving late for them, not paying fees, and talking over sessions with friends and family. Again, the rebellious behavior can have many different meanings and/or combination of meanings. The defiance can be a wish to defeat the therapy and the therapist, a powerful defense against a passive wish to comply, or a fear of loving the practitioner.

Although clients use and abuse of ground rules as a means of expressing their resistance to therapy have been richly explored, how clinicians utilize ground rules as an expression of their counterresistance has received limited consideration.

In this section we focus primarily on how practitioners express their resistance to the therapy in their handling of ground rules in the first session and in the one or two sessions that follow.

Although there are individual differences among clinicians regarding their feelings about ground rules, two major perspectives regarding the establishment of ground rules in the initial sessions can be gleaned from the literature. One view takes the position that the therapist should establish the ground rules in the first session: the therapist talks about payment for all sessions regardless of whether the client shows up for them, vacation times, and the "fundamental rule" of saying everything that comes to mind, and so on (Langs, 1973).

The other perspective is one in which the discussion of the ground rules evolves from the ongoing interaction between therapist and client in the initial sessions (Strean, 1985/1990). For example, if a client has some doubts about the competence of the therapist, it may be more helpful to the furthering of the therapist-client relationship if a discussion of ground rules is postponed for a while. On the other hand, if a client is in a severe crisis, has a strong wish to talk, and is eager for therapeutic contact, it may be reassuring to the client to establish a routine in the first session for the next two weeks of therapy. Several appointments a week may be agreed upon with the further agreement between client and therapist to reevaluate the frequency of sessions at the end of the two weeks.

An important, but often forgotten aspect of the therapist establishing ground rules in the first sessions is that the therapist's doing so has transference meaning to the client. Inasmuch as most clients have a strong tendency to project their punitive superegos onto the therapist, the therapist's proclamation of rules and regulations in the first session can make the practitioner emerge as a tough taskmaster to be feared. On the other hand, if a therapist does not have anything to say about ground rules to a prospective client who is fearful of an impending rejection by the therapist, the client may conclude that there will be no further contact. One such client did not return for more sessions when the therapist ended the initial session after 50 minutes with, "We have to stop now." This self-doubting and self-loathing client who heard "We have to stop now" concluded that treatment contacts for him were finished.

EXCESSIVE PREOCCUPATION WITH GROUND RULES

Therapists can find themselves taking different positions on ground rules with different prospective clients. With some, they can be firm and exacting; with others, they can be lax and permissive; and with still other clients, they can time their discussion of specific ground rules according to the needs of the client and according to the nature of the ongoing interview. Regardless of practitioners' approaches to ground rules in the initial sessions, the position they take can offer important clues about how they are experiencing their clients.

Larry Morse, an intake worker in a short-term mental health clinic, was conducting a first session with Ms. M., a senior citizen in her late seventies, who was referred for help because of alcoholism, depression, phobias, and suicidal tendencies. After Ms. M. described her debilitating symptoms, Larry Morse told her he "needed to get some history" from her. Ms. M. faithfully complied. On concluding her presentation of a very traumatic history, Ms. M. said, "I've had it kind of rough and I need lots of help!" Larry responded to this cry for help by telling Ms. M. that the "clinic rules" allowed for "a maximum of 12 sessions at a rate of once a week, 45 minutes each." Ms. M. looked a bit bewildered but agreed to the ground rules. Then Larry told Ms. M. that the fee for the service would be based on her income. After informing Larry that her sole income was from her social security check each month which amounted to $340, Ms. M. was told that her weekly fee would be $11 a session. Larry then asked for $11 for the intake session, told Ms. M. he would make an assignment of a therapist during the week, and the therapist would call her within the week.

When the assigned therapist called Ms. M. to make an appointment, Ms. M. told him that she had "found another facility that can really help me." She informed the therapist that she could be seen for more than 12 sessions, would also be in a group, and would have "a kind man to help me."

When Larry Morse reviewed his session with Ms. M. in supervision, he recognized his undue preoccupation with the ground rules and realized that his mechanical approach in the interview warded off many feelings he had toward Ms. M. The client's pervasive and deep pathology made Larry feel both overwhelmed and helpless. Further reflection also helped Larry realize that the client reminded him of his deceased grandmother who had a prolonged and painful illness before she died. Larry felt many of the same feelings that he experienced with his grandmother—helplessness, hopelessness, and being overwhelmed. Furthermore, Larry also recalled that with his grandmother he had tried to cope with his many anxieties by doing many mechanical chores for her.

Usually when we find ourselves unduly preoccupied with ground rules, we are unconsciously trying to move away from the client because the feelings we have appear "too hot to handle."

Larry Morse was unable to realize during the course of his interview with Ms. M. that he was making his client his dying grandmother. Had he been in touch with his countertransference reactions, he may not have resisted empathizing with Ms. M. as much as he did. And if he had been able to listen to his client a little more, he would have been less compulsive in dealing with the ground rules.

As suggested earlier, practitioners occasionally find themselves being lax about ground rules. They may let several sessions go by without discussing a fee policy, ignore the client's lateness or absence from initial sessions, or not relate to the client's having discussed his or her impressions of the therapist with significant others.

Very often when practitioners ignore issues like the aforementioned, one of several possibilities is at work. The clinician may be intimidated by the prospective client and too frightened to face the client's hostility. Sometimes the client's defiant attitude stirs up defiant fantasies in the therapist, and by ignoring the rebellious behavior of the client, he or she derives some vicarious gratification.

OVERLOOKING GROUND RULES

From time to time, a practitioner meets a client for the first time who activates such warm, friendly feelings that the interviewee appears to be more like a friend or relative than a client. In response, the practitioner fails to remember anything about ground rules because the issue at hand seems to be the furtherance of a friendship and not an attempt to establish a therapeutic relationship.

> Brian Lawrence, a psychologist in private practice, was conducting a consultation with Mr. N., a man in his mid-twenties. Mr. N. consulted Brian Lawrence because he found himself obsessed with the possibility of having AIDS, even though he tested negative. A homosexual man, Mr. N. had been very cautious and discriminating in his sexual contacts, so that, everything considered, it appeared that the client's preoccupation with AIDS was unrealistic and neurotic.
>
> In his interview with the client, Brian felt a profound warmth toward and concern for Mr. N. His empathy helped Mr. N. talk about his past and present with freedom. At the end of the first interview, which was extended about 20 minutes, client and therapist agreed to meet again in a few days.
>
> At the second interview, the same warm rapport between Brian and Mr. N. continued. Mr. N.'s obsessive ruminations about AIDS had diminished and the client continued to discuss his present and past life, but did so as if he were involved in a friendly chat with Brian. Again, the session was extended about 20 minutes and, as had occurred in the first interview, neither client nor therapist brought up the fee.
>
> Brian, an experienced professional, realized after the second session that he was "overinvolved" with his client and was treating him more like a fragile son than as a mature man. As he let his mind wander, Brian had two very helpful associations. The first one was to a physically handicapped friend from elementary school who depended a great deal on Brian for emotional and physical support. His second association was to a time, again in elementary school, when Brian yearned for a big brother or for an older male friend who would nurture and support him.
>
> On examining his associations, Brian was able to see that he was turning Mr. N. into a child who needed a great deal. A combination of his physically

handicapped friend from childhood and his "lonely boy self," the client appeared as a fragile boy who could not be asked for anything much. Not bringing up the fee, extending the sessions, and permitting "chatty" talks rather than exploratory interviews were all manifestations of Brian's resistance to helping Mr. N. become a client in therapy.

How we relate to ground rules with each prospective client during the initial sessions can tell us a great deal about our initial reactions toward the client. We have to be vigilant about our use and abuse of ground rules. Too early and too much concern or a lax attitude are helpful clues to us that we may be ignoring certain counterresistances.

FEES

A dimension of the therapeutic process that can activate intense affects in both the client and practitioner is the paying and receiving of fees. As Eissler (1974), in one of the few comprehensive papers on the subject, said, "We are not always able to keep our attitudes to money free of what may be called irrational infusion" (p. 96).

Clients vary considerably in their attitude toward paying a fee and many seeming paradoxes appear in practice. Very wealthy clients have sometimes insisted that they should pay the therapist next to nothing, and impoverished clients have been known to be very firm in their contention that they should pay high fees. Similarly, very experienced and competent clinicians have charged low fees, while some who have had limited experience and demonstrate limited competence charge very high fees.

In American culture, and in other societies as well, there is a tendency to judge one's worth as a person and as a professional by how much money he or she earns. Consequently, the therapist charging a high fee may connote to some clients and practitioners that the therapist's skills should be valued. As early as 1913, Freud warned against a low fee, contending that this would not enhance the value of the treatment in the patient's eyes. The implication of Freud's stance is that paying the therapist a low fee may maintain a patient's low self-esteem. He averred that "free treatment enormously increases some of a neurotic's resistances" (1913, p. 132). Yet, Eissler argued that although there are patients who are ready to make sacrifices involving basic needs in order to secure treatment, he advised the practitioner to "not consider treatment under such circumstances, since they provide masochistic gratifications of such magnitude that a successful treatment could hardly be expected" (1974, p. 75).

If the 1990s can be characterized as a time when a sexual revolution has taken place in that most prospective clients are freer than ever before to discuss their sexual behavior and attitudes in the first session with an interviewer who is a virtual stranger, the 1990s may also be regarded as a time when financial secretiveness is *au courant*. Many prospective clients can be very open about their sexual lives but quite closed about their income, financial assets, and expenses. Similarly, therapists can be much freer to discuss their sexual countertransferences and their resistances to facing sexual fantasies toward their clients than they are in revealing their fee policy, fee ranges, and procedures regarding payment for missed sessions.

A frequent occurrence in initial interviews is prospective clients asking therapists what their usual fee is and then immediately asking for a fee reduction. Therapists often feel uncomfortable when asked to reduce a fee and feel obliged to either say "yes" or "no" rather than explore the prospective client's income, expenses, and so on to ascertain whether a reduction in usual fee policy is warranted. Many practitioners, if asked by clients to modify an interpretation, would feel quite secure in exploring the client's feelings in the here and now; however, the same practitioners may very well resist asking the client about his or her current financial assets and liabilities when asked to modify a fee policy. Why is this so?

Many practitioners can distort the meaning of an inquiry into a client's financial picture. They feel that they are becoming voyeurs and are asking the new client to get undressed prematurely and to display his or her physical assets and liabilities. Projecting their own discomfort onto the client as they picture themselves in the same situation, they resist asking appropriate and pertinent questions about the client's finances.

> After Jennifer Knight, a therapist in private practice, completed most of the initial interview with Mr. O., who consulted her because of his mixed feelings regarding an extramarital affair in which he was involved, the client asked her what her fee was. "My usual fee is $85 per session." Mr. O. then asked with a smile, "How about letting me pay an unusual fee?" Not exploring the meaning of Mr. O.'s wanting something "unusual" from her, Jennifer assumed that the client wanted to pay a lower fee, and without clarifying this, lowered the fee to $75 per session.
>
> In his second session with Jennifer Knight, Mr. O. told her that after thinking about his interview with her, he realized that she reminded him of the woman with whom he was having an affair. When Jennifer asked, "In what respect?" Mr. O. was quick to respond, "You seem very flexible. When I wanted to do something 'unusual' with you, you were ready."
>
> Jennifer became alerted to her client's seeming wish to sexually manipulate her and to "reduce" her by getting his fee reduced without any real exploration of his finances. As she reflected on her resistance to explore Mr. O.'s request to have an "unusual fee," Jennifer realized that she fantasied herself being manipulated in having some "unusual" sex with him. Because she was unable to confront her own sexual fantasy (and possibly the fantasy that Mr. O. was trying to induce), Jennifer quickly discussed a specific financial arrangement with Mr. O. instead of facing her fantasy of a mutual sexual arrangement.

The interaction between Jennifer Knight and Mr. O. suggests that discomfort regarding finances and fee payment between the therapist and client may cover up certain sexual anxieties. Although men and women, children and teenagers may be able to talk about certain aspects of sexuality with more freedom, and even participate in sex with less anxiety, the inability for many clients and clinicians to have frank discussions about financial transactions between them may cover up a reluctance to face certain mutual sexual fantasies.

Certain therapists are so reluctant to tell clients what their usual fee per session is that, when asked, they often respond, "How much can you afford?" If the client says "$50 per week" and the therapist wants $100 per session, he or she may retort, "Then I'll see you every other week for $100, which means you will pay me $50 per week." This approach to fees not only suggests a resistance of the therapist to state openly what amount of money is desired, but it also suggests that the therapist making $100 per session is more important to him or her than are frequency of sessions and other therapeutic needs of the client.

Some clients are so masochistic that they can easily submit to all kinds of untherapeutic financial practices. Some charismatic therapists can get away with the procedure of charging a client $300 or more for a session and see the client once a month.

Just as there are masochistic clients, there are, of course, masochistic practitioners. These practitioners, though well-trained, empathetic, and disciplined in many respects, tend to project their own dependency needs onto the client. As a result, their fees are too low. Their clients may not feel comfortable in addressing the issue with them and a resistance–counterresistance collusion can go undetected for a long time.

Therapists have a difficult task in therapeutically addressing their fee policies. They have to learn what the going rate is in their communities, determine what they deserve as they compare their training and experience with their colleagues, evaluate carefully their clients' financial needs so that they can lower their fees if they wish to work with particular low-paying clients, and assess carefully what money and disclosure of finances means dynamically to their clients and to themselves. As they do this, they can more objectively and empathetically help clients deal with financial issues as they emerge in and out of treatment.

Dynamic Assessment and Counterresistance

Assessing the client's dynamics is an ongoing process. From the moment the applicant makes contact with the therapist over the telephone until the last words are said in the last session, the practitioner is constantly trying to assess the meaning of the client's feelings, thoughts, fantasies, and behavior. As clinicians participate in this ever-present activity, they base many of their diagnostic inferences on their own reactions. If, for example, the therapist finds himself or herself obsessed with sexual fantasies during the course of several interviews, there is a good possibility that the client has some sexual fantasies toward the therapist. Although practitioners should always be striving to separate their own idiosyncratic reactions from the clients' individualized transference reactions and resistive behavior, this is an ideal that is never fully and permanently achieved. Recognizing that counterresistances are always present is a belief well worth achieving, and trying to understand and master our counterresistances is a worthwhile and constant undertaking.

One way of achieving a better understanding of our counterresistances is to observe the form our dynamic assessments take. As we suggested in Chapter 1, diagnostic labels and dynamic assessments can be used pejoratively. Our pessimistic prognosis of a client can be expressed by labelling the client "borderline" or "narcissistic character disorder." Our hostility can be shown when we refer to the client as being a "psychopath" or "sociopath." Similarly, when we say "ego functions are very weak, superego is very fragmented, and the client is impulsive," we may be feeling somewhat hopeless about the client.

Yet, when we refer to "highly developed ego functions, sound ego ideals, and adaptive mechanisms that work well," we are implying that we like the client and are pleased to work with this person.

Since there is a tendency in all of us to see much pathology in those clients we dislike and much health in clients we like, sometimes our feelings can color our observations so that we do not see maladaptive mechanisms in clients we like nor adaptive strengths in clients we dislike.

It is always a helpful exercise for us to review our diagnostic and dynamic appraisals to determine how we are feeling toward our clients. If we are feeling very positive, very negative, or very ambivalent, these are signs that counterresistances are active and we may as yet not be aware of them. Particularly when we find ourselves saying to ourselves or to our colleagues that we think a client whom we assessed as "a high-functioning neurotic is really a low-functioning ambulatory schizophrenic," we have probably modified many of our attitudes toward the client and his or her treatment.

Sometimes practitioners are so wedded to a particular therapeutic modality that they impose it on the client without fully assessing the client. For example, if the practitioner is a classical psychoanalyst, he or she may be too quick to recommend five days a week analysis to an uncertain, doubting client who does not have much of an observing ego. Similarly, a specialist in short-term behavior modification may overlook the fact that the client can profit a great deal from long-term psychodynamic therapy.

Diagnostic Labels as an Expression of a Negative Countertransference

Usually when we are very ready to see a client in long-term intensive treatment, we feel quite positive toward the client. However, the client may not yet be ready for the experience. Often when it is suggested that a client be seen in short-term treatment and/or is referred elsewhere, the feeling toward the client is quite negative.

> Barry Jackson, a social worker in a family agency, after having seen Ms. P. for three intake interviews, wrote the following dynamic appraisal: "Her ego functions are fragile, particularly her object relations. The narcissism of Ms. P. is ever-present and she forms a very dependent, oral transference. Her pathology is extreme, although her motivation for therapy is high. Ms. P. should be seen in weekly treatment for about three months. Short-term therapy is obviously the treatment of choice."
>
> On being asked in a training seminar why he selected short-term therapy as the treatment of choice, particularly since the client had high motivation, after much discussion and reflection, Barry was able to say, "Who the hell would like to be with that bitch for so long?" Recognizing his intense negative countertransference was helpful to Barry. Once he could discharge his anger, Barry could then get in touch with Ms. P.'s extreme feeling of vulnerability and with that in mind, change the treatment plan.

Occasionally we can prolong and intensify a treatment plan when we feel warmly toward and attracted to the client, even though the client may wish to have less. Consequently, it is extremely helpful to ask ourselves what we feel toward and about the client as we plan the frequency and intensity of any individual's treatment plan.

The first few sessions of treatment are probably the most important part of any therapy. If clients are listened to empathically and little is imposed on them, if they are helped to talk freely while the therapist tries to talk little, a therapeutic alliance forms. This alliance can and usually does spark what has been termed "the therapeutic honeymoon" (Fine, 1982), which we will discuss largely from the therapist's perspective in Chapter 3.

3

The Therapy Honeymoon and the Therapist's Counterresistances

An insufficiently appreciated and discussed phase of psychotherapy is what has been referred to as "the therapy honeymoon" (Fine, 1982). In reality, this honeymoon should be viewed as a dramatic expression of a mutually positive transference and countertransference relationship between client and therapist. Until now, however, the honeymoon has been examined almost exclusively from the client's perspective. Hence, the originator of the term, Reuben Fine has referred to "the honeymoon" as:

> a period of blissful expansion for the patient. Everything seems to be going well. He or she has one new insight after another, feels better on the job, and functions better at home. (p. 77)

From the client's point of view, there are many reasons for entering into a honeymoon period with the therapist. Possibly for the first time in his or her life, the client has a unique relationship with another human being who gives the client exclusive attention and asks for none, listens quietly in a nonjudgmental manner, and demonstrates an unconditional positive regard toward virtually everything the client says or does (Rogers, 1951). By having the opportunity to experience consistently uncensored catharses, continual lack of superego criticism, and uninterrupted warm attention, the client's self-esteem rises, the need for self-punishment diminishes, and energy previously tied up in maintaining maladaptive defenses is now available for more productive living and more mature loving.

In thinking about the client undergoing a therapy honeymoon, we are reminded of one version of the Greek myth involving Pandora's box. When Pandora let the evils out of the box, she kept one tiny creature from escaping. That entity was hope, and as the myth goes, it gave people a ray of light to combat the suffering unleashed by the newly escaped demons. Usually when clients begin treatment, they are in a state of agony and despair. As the therapist listens and does not judge or punish while the client "lets the evils out," agony yields to equanimity and despair surrenders to hope.

As suggested, the therapy honeymoon is not completely understood if one focuses solely on the client. All honeymoons are dyadic encounters in which two human beings deeply affect each other. Just as "it takes two to tango," it takes two to have a honeymoon—no man or woman is an island! Furthermore, the result of this interactional process does not depend merely on the two personalities of therapist and client, but also on how these two personalities influence each other (Wolman, 1972).

One might wonder why the therapist's role, activity, and countertransference reactions during the honeymoon phase have been essentially shrouded in secrecy. As we have implied in previous chapters, the therapist's counterresistances have been insufficiently considered in all phases of the therapeutic process. However, the practitioner's role in the honeymoon has been extremely inconspicuous in the literature and, we believe, for special reasons. "Honeymoon" usually implies that two lovers are blissfully enjoying each other on an ecstatic vacation. Sex is considered to be their most prominent activity, while work and serious contemplation are shunned. In many ways, the pleasure principle reigns supreme.

It may be hypothesized that therapists have a great deal of difficulty acknowledging that they are active participants on a honeymoon, because it is difficult for many to accept the fact that they are psychologically similar to vacationing lovers enjoying a blissful encounter—and concomitantly getting paid for it! This picture runs counter to the idealized image that many therapists like to have of themselves. The model therapist likes to see himself or herself as hardworking, not vacationing; as a student of interpersonal affairs, not participating in love affairs; and as an object who is cathected, not a subject in love! Hence, the originator of the term "analytic honeymoon" overlooks much of what he knows about love and its vicissitudes when he describes in one sentence the therapist's feelings on a therapy honeymoon: "For the therapist [the honeymoon] is particularly gratifying; he feels like a fond parent watching a child grow up" (Fine, 1982, p. 77).

It is much more acceptable for therapists to experience themselves with their clients as "fond parents" rather than as "excited lovers" or "romantic partners." Similar to the tabooed libidinal feelings many parents experience with their children, which they try to turn into fond feelings, many therapists try their best to convert erotic wishes into fond feelings.

Because therapists have been quite reluctant to face their own proclivities to "fall in love" with their clients, this form of counterresistance may be one of the main reasons that many therapies terminate during the first few months of treatment. As the therapist resists feeling excited with his therapeutic partner and instead shows discomfort, distance, and deadpan expressions, the client can feel devalued and misunderstood and leaves treatment in anger and with great disappointment.

In studying in more depth the therapist as a honeymooner, we may find that our exploration also helps us to understand better the popularity of short-term therapy. When proponents of brief treatment (Sifneos, 1987; Wolberg, 1968) assert that some very major changes occur in clients during the first several weeks or months of treatment, they are correct! As Fine (1982) suggests: "[The honeymoon] is a period of blissful expansion for the patient" (p. 77). However, when therapists observe that their clients have improved a great deal after a couple of months of treatment, it does not necessarily imply the gains will be sustained, nor that treatment can be terminated. What it does mean is that the client is feeling enthusiastic and positive because he or she is in love. Usually the therapist feels enthusiastic and positive when with the blissful client, but the therapist can also be in love—although he or she rarely acknowledges it.

When therapists cannot accept their own passion or their clients' passion for what it is, namely a temporary state of affairs, they may respond in a variety of untherapeutic ways. Many therapists, afraid of their own libidinal feelings, as well as those of their clients, do not see their clients' progress as temporary. In the service of defending against their own discomfort, therapists can declare treatment as successfully completed.

If therapists are honest with themselves and are truly empathizing with their clients, when they are with them it will be inevitable for them to feel within themselves the intense excitement, keen enthusiasm, and boundless energy of a honeymooner. When clients tell their therapists they have never felt better in their lives, that they feel full of love, are creative and productive, that everybody is praising them, and that this is all due to the therapist's skilled help, how should practitioners react? If they allow themselves to be human beings—to feel loved, appreciated, and admired—usually they will respond with warmth, gratitude, and pleasure. Similar to their therapeutic counterparts in the initial phase of treatment, when clinicians are unconditionally regarded in a positive manner, considered unique, and never criticized, their self-esteem will rise, too, and they will value themselves more.

There is a tendency for most human beings to love and appreciate those who love and appreciate them. Therapists are no different from clients in this regard. When the client considers the therapist's words as "pearls of wisdom," when the therapist's empathy is considered powerfully poignant, and when the client ascribes many visible changes in his or her life to the therapist, the latter is bound to experience loving feelings toward the client. The therapist's optimism about helping the client is buttressed by the client's optimism and lessened despair. Therefore, the enthusiasm of each therapeutic partner becomes reinforced by the other so that the two individuals form a mutually gratifying symbiosis. This is essentially no different from the behavior of any two individuals in their early stages of being in love.

Dynamically, what happens to both client and therapist in the therapeutic honeymoon is that they *both* feel well mothered. When two individuals enjoy being the recipients of maternal love from each other, they idealize each other and project their own ego ideals onto the love object. This results in a simultaneous increase in the self-esteem of both partners (Chasseguet-Smirgel, 1985; Freud, 1914b).

Kernberg (1991) pointed out that in falling in love, there is usually "a sense of transgression, of overcoming the prohibitions implied in all sexual encounters" (p. 346). This characteristic of erotic desire helps us understand the therapist's resistance to acknowledging his or her honeymoon fantasies. Just as Gill (1982) comprehensively demonstrated that many clients resist becoming aware of their transference fantasies because of the dangers they believe will confront them, therapists do the same. If therapists fear that they will transgress or feel too guilty for having honeymoon fantasies, they will resist facing them. In defending against their countertransference fantasies they will subtly or overtly oppose the emergence of the therapy honeymoon.

Experienced practitioners easily comprehend the common occurrence of a client's inability to recognize certain feelings toward the therapist. Instead, the client dwells at length in sessions on such feelings as he or she experiences them toward a surrogate, someone with whom he or she has a current relationship (Jaffe, 1991). The same phenomenon, although rarely discussed, happens to therapists as well. Many therapists who cannot bear to confront their honeymoon fantasies obsess instead about sexual fantasies toward a colleague, friend, or relative, not consciously realizing that these fantasies are sparked by an interaction with a particular client. Although clinicians will sometimes acknowledge that they have displaced aggression onto a spouse that originated with a client, there are few reports in the literature of clinicians discussing how they were sexually stimulated by a client and then displaced their erotic feelings onto a mate. The best example of this is of Breuer (Breuer & Freud, 1895) who could not cope with Anna O.'s honeymoon fantasies toward him nor his own toward her. In desperation, he ended the therapeutic honeymoon between them, stopped the treatment, and went off with his wife to have a baby. It should be mentioned that Breuer himself did not report on his counterresistance with Anna O.; it was inferred by others.

No practitioner should be criticized for wanting to have a second, third, or fourth honeymoon with a spouse, nor should he or she be censured for wanting to have a baby with a mate; if a desire becomes desperate and compulsive, like Breuer's rejecting behavior toward Anna O., the motives underlying the desperate compulsiveness should be investigated.

Recognizing that every therapist is a unique individual who has his or her own idiosyncratic responses and fantasies toward each individual client, there are two major forms of counterresistance that are prevalent during the honeymoon phase of treatment: (1) those activities of the therapist, either by omission or commission, that prevent or retard the development of a honeymoon phase of treatment; and (2) those activities of the therapist that exploit the honeymoon phase and interfere with the client's therapeutic growth. We will discuss these two forms of counterresistance in detail in this chapter.

PREVENTING THE DEVELOPMENT OF THE
THERAPY HONEYMOON

Although there are many clients who try to prevent themselves and their therapists from becoming therapy honeymooners, practitioners are equally adept, if not more so, in resisting the process. In this section we will discuss the variety of ways the therapist can block the development of the therapy honeymnoon.

The Therapist Is Overtalkative

Although we alluded to the very common counterresistance of the therapist being overtalkative, it is a particularly frequent recourse that therapists utilize in opposing the development of a therapy honeymoon.

As we also suggested, it is a virtual axiom of dynamic psychotherapy, if not of all psychotherapy, that the more the client can talk about what hurts, angers, upsets him or her, or induces guilt, and the more the practitioner can quietly and benignly listen, not only will the client's self-esteem rise and his or her anger, hurt, and guilt abate, but the client will feel warmer toward the therapist for what he or she has provided. Particularly in the early phase of psychotherapy, if the therapist listens and the client talks, a positive transference evolves in most cases.

Although therapists can talk a great deal to dispel their own anxieties about anything that disturbs them, what we want to take note of here is how the therapist's talking too much can unconsciously serve as an antidote to the development of a therapy honeymoon.

Herman Inniss, a psychologist in a mental health center, was seeing Ms. Q., an elementary school teacher in her early thirties. Ms. Q. had sought treatment because she found her relationship with youngsters to be overwhelming. The students' belligerent behavior made her feel quite helpless; consequently, it was difficult for her to limit them. As a result, the children were continually unruly and Ms. Q. became more depressed and agitated, eventually losing most of her self-confidence as a teacher.

During the first five sessions of weekly treatment with Herman Inniss, Ms. Q. poured out her heart and talked of how much anger she felt toward her unruly students. Because she talked nonstop, it was quite easy for Herman Inniss to listen quietly. As Ms. Q. ventilated her anger, her depression and agitation diminished and in the fifth session she told her therapist how much he had helped her. Ms. Q. mentioned to Herman that when she observed how he could tolerate her anger and did not seem overwhelmed by it, she identified with his demeanor and started to behave similarly with her students.

Feeling and functioning better in her work, Ms. Q., a single woman, began to talk about her loneliness inasmuch as she had "no man in my life." As she talked about her eagerness to form "an intimate relationship with a man," Ms. Q. came to the interviews in brighter and more appealing clothes. Although Herman took note of his client's increasing attention to her appearance, he did not consciously appreciate its transference implications.

As Ms. Q. talked about how difficult it was to meet men in the large city in which she lived, Herman Inniss began to "universalize" her plight. He told Ms. Q. that statistically there were more women than men in her city, that many men were threatened by an intellectually sophisticated woman like Ms. Q. who had a master's degree, and like many women in her "category," she had it very rough.

In sharp contrast to his quiet demeanor when Ms. Q. was talking about her difficulties in teaching, Herman was extremely active when his client came to the interviews attractively dressed, looking for a man. Not able to cope with the fact that Ms. Q. was feeling warmth and gratitude toward him, and therefore was eager to make Herman her man, he subtly rejected her. His comments about men not being that accessible in a large city, particularly for a bright woman like Ms. Q., were unconscious attempts on Herman's part to make himself inaccessible. In effect, he was trying to talk Ms. Q. out of being interested in him as a man.

For the seventh interview, Ms. Q. was dressed in rather drab clothes, and she told Herman that she was functioning much better on the job, realized that she had "to accept reality" and learn that men were just not that available for her. She also told her therapist that he had done a very effective job and that she was now ready to try it on her own. Herman concurred with her sentiments.

The experience of Herman Inniss with Ms. Q. is an excellent example of how a case that was considered statistically successful short-term treatment was really an example of a therapist's discomfort in facing his client's and his own honeymoon fantasies. If Herman, instead of "universalizing" the client's plight, had empathized with Ms. Q.'s loneliness and explored further with her the kind of male companion she was looking for, Ms. Q. would probably have begun to describe someone like Herman Inniss. Had Herman accepted her interest in him, his client would have felt more valued as a woman and may have carried this increased self-confidence and improved self-image into her interpersonal relationships with men. Perhaps she would have had some erotic fantasies toward Herman that could have been aired, understood, and mastered.

When he reviewed his work with Ms. Q. in supervision, Herman Inniss realized that he was afraid to appear "too seductive with Ms. Q. only to disappoint her later." This is often the sentiment of clinicians when they resist the formation of a therapy honeymoon. In effect, they are unable to master and to monitor their own fantasies to seduce the client and therefore they distort the meaning of an exploration of a client's honeymoon fantasies. As Herman later acknowledged, "I guess if I let her talk about wanting a man and that led to her wanting me, I'd feel like a seductive lover who was turning her on. Then, when I didn't come through, I'd feel sadistic."

One of the most difficult parts of doing psychotherapy, as well as in receiving it, is recognizing its "as if" quality. Herman and Ms. Q. both had to acknowledge to themselves their real feelings of warmth and pleasure with each other, face their honeymoon fantasies, but not go on a real honeymoon with each other! When a honeymoon phase occurs in a treatment situation, the therapist has to be able to allow it to evolve.

Therapist and client during a therapy honeymoon are to some extent like a parent and child during an oedipal love affair. Not only does the child want the parent of the opposite sex as a mate, but the parent, if he or she is honest, enjoys the adulation. However, the mature parent, while enjoying many of the concomitants of a love affair, helps the child to master his or her wishes, not through seduction but through frank discussion.

Just as parents who can tolerate their own libidinal feelings toward their children and those of their children toward them can talk frankly about love affairs with their offspring, and not fear regressing or acting out, maturer clinicians can do likewise with their clients. Usually those therapists who subtly or overtly push their clients away, as Herman Inniss did, are frightened of their own strong love feelings and tend to view their clients and themselves as provocative seducers if they discuss honeymoon fantasies.

THE PRACTITIONER IS RELUCTANT TO ACCEPT THE CLIENT'S TRANSFERENCE POSITION

The therapy honeymoon, of course, takes place regardless of the sexes of the practitioner and client. If a client is listened to empathically in a quiet nonjudgmental manner, he or she tends to fall in love with the therapist, regardless of whether the therapist is male or female. What is not always easy for the therapist is to be experienced transferentially as a woman when the therapist is a man, to be perceived as a man when the therapist is a woman (Kulish, 1984, 1989; Mayer & deMarneffe, 1991).

Harvey Hollis, a therapist in private practice, had seen Mr. R., a man in his late thirties, for about 10 sessions. Mr. R. sought treatment because he was very unsuccessful in his relationships with women. Sexually, he was frequently impotent; interpersonally, he was very self-effacing, inarticulate, and ingratiating, but particularly so with the women he dated.

During the 10 sessions with Harvey Hollis, Mr. R. was very open about his deep yearning to talk with someone like Harvey because Mr. R.'s father died when he was 12. "As a result," said Mr. R., "I've been hungry for a warm father-figure like you."

Mr. R. filled the therapy hours with frank discussions about his discomfort with women, particularly focusing on his sexual anxiety. Observing that his therapist empathically listened, taking in all that Mr. R. was saying but without much comment, Mr. R. felt "reassured, supported, and loved." Inasmuch as the client was responding positively to the treatment and also because he seemed to have a lot on his mind that he wanted to talk about, Harvey suggested that Mr. R. consider coming for two treatment sessions each week. Without much consideration, Mr. R. jumped for joy at the opportunity and immediately decided that two sessions per week "was an excellent idea."

After accepting the idea of two sessions per week, Mr. R. described in his next session how, after the last session, he had raced down the street, euphoric and smiling at everyone. "You have become the father I've always wanted, Harvey," said Mr. R. with much enthusiasm. He continued to freely associate to his past and present, brought in dreams, analyzed them well, and soon decided to come for therapy three times a week. He asked to use the couch, feeling it "makes the therapy go deeper," to which the therapist complied.

Mr. R. grew by leaps and bounds. He began to date women, felt more self-confident, and became more sexually potent. He received financial increases on his job because of his superior work as a salesman. Throughout the first few months of therapy, Harvey continued to listen empathically and made very few comments. Mr. R. somehow knew that his therapist's quiet acceptance was the appropriate treatment for him because he frequently would say, "You know what you are doing and it's working!"

In Mr. R.'s dreams, during his fourth month of treatment, he began to make Harvey more and more a woman. Although Harvey said to himself several times, "The patient is frightened of his homosexual transference, does not want to see me, a man, 'going deeper' into him, and therefore projects onto me the woman he's afraid to be," his correct appraisal of Mr. R.'s transference reactions and resistive maneuvers did not give him that much solace. Harvey began to find that his warm, empathic, nonintrusive stance was waning. Feeling uncomfortable being experienced as a woman by his client, Harvey began to assert himself more. At one point, despite his own understanding of Mr. R.'s fears of his homosexual transference, he made a poorly timed and overly critical interpretation. Stated Harvey, "You want to castrate me and destroy me as a man, the way you wanted to do with your father. That's why you make me into a woman."

Harvey Hollis's critical tone reflected his discomfort in being experienced transferentially as a maternal figure. To compensate for his own castration anxiety, he "stood up" in the interviews and in effect said to his client, "I'm an erect man, I'm not your mother!" The client felt misunderstood and mistreated and returned to his impotent and depressed state.

Because Harvey Hollis was in a personal analysis at the time he was treating Mr. R., he could more directly face the part of himself that wanted to be a woman with a man and eventually did not have to fight it as much. As he learned to tolerate the woman in himself with more equanimity, he did not have to resist Mr. R.'s efforts and other clients' efforts to make him a woman in the transference.

Whenever practitioners find themselves talking a great deal in sessions, most likely they are trying to talk themselves out of feelings they are experiencing in the sessions. Frequently the feelings they are resisting in themselves are loving, erotic ones, but this is not always the case. Quite often a client's resistance to experiencing a honeymoon transference manifests itself by criticizing the practitioner. Many practitioners, not realizing their clients are defending against a positive transference, take the criticisms too personally and ward off facing their clients' anger as well as their own by talking themselves and their clients out of what seems to be a formidable therapeutic impasse.

Ruth Gangel was a social worker in a family agency treating Ms. S., a woman in her mid-twenties. Ms. S., a lesbian, sought therapy because she had recently been jilted by her lover. The client was depressed, suffered from insomnia, could not eat, lost interest in people, and was not concentrating on her work as a graduate student in psychology. In addition, Ms. S. found herself drinking large quantities of alcohol and was starting to take drugs habitually.

As Ms. S. mourned the breakup of her love affair and shared her hurt, disappointment, and anger in therapy, she began to feel better. She experienced Ruth Gangel as "a very nonthreatening woman," who in her "very quiet way," showed that she "really cares." Discharging her intense feelings to someone who cared helped Ms. S. regain her appetite for food, lessen her depression, and reduce her dependency on alcohol and other drugs. She also began to return to her studies with more eagerness.

During the fourth month of her treatment, as Ms. S. was continuing to make much progress in virtually all areas of living, she began to consider forming another love relationship. Although she was being helped by her therapist to fantasy the type of lover she was seeking, Ms. S. became critical of Ruth Gangel. She told Ruth that she would not be able to help her with the issues before them because Ruth was not a lesbian and therefore could not understand Ms. S.'s "problems and values." Being asked what "problems and values" her therapist could not understand, Ms. S., rather than trying to answer the question posed to her, ridiculed Ruth Gangel's voice, manner, therapeutic perspective, and "lack of empathy."

What baffled Ruth Gangel at this time was her client's hostility. Ms. S. had been helped in many ways and instead of showing warmth and gratitude, was displaying coldness and derision. Ruth did not understand that it was because Ms. S. had been very much helped and did feel very grateful to her therapist that she had to oppose her. Many clients, after being helped in a major way, do oppose the therapist. Why is this so?

One of the main reasons that the loving feelings of clients can turn into hatred after being helped therapeutically is because clients frequently cannot tolerate the position of passive dependency. They become very apprehensive about unleashing their appetites for consistent nurturing and are very uncomfortable as they feel so small next to their "big" therapists.

It is particularly difficult for gay or lesbian clients to weather the honeymoon period with a therapist whom they believe to be heterosexual. Feeling warm and grateful, their wishes for sexual contact with the therapist pose a particular dilemma for them (Fine, 1982; Socarides, 1978). They are convinced that the heterosexual practitioner will reject their homosexual wishes; hence, anticipating rejection, they attack the therapist for not being very attractive and/or not being competent. This is, of course, what happened to Ms. S. She could not tolerate her warm feelings toward Ruth Gangel because she was convinced they would not be reciprocated. Having just experienced a rejection from her lover, she could not take on another one from her therapist.

Not understanding that her client was behaving much like a latency child who had to defend against her loving feelings by using the defense of reaction formation, Ruth Gangel did not relate empathetically to Ms. S.'s defensive hostility. Instead of giving her client the time and space to voice her resentment, Ruth became very defensive when attacked by her client. She informed Ms. S. that she accepted all of her clients as they are and did not judge them. Consequently, she could under-stand Ms. S.'s "lesbian lifestyle." Ms. S. responded by saying, "The lady doth protest too much, me thinks!" To this, Ruth told Ms. S. that she wasn't giving her a chance to prove herself, to which Ms. S. agreed and left treatment.

Although many clients are very frightened of their honeymoon fantasies and need to defend against them by becoming negativistic, particularly after they have been helped in a substantial way, the wise clinician understands the phenomenon and does not become defensive or attacking (Schafer, 1983). Rather, wise clinicians real-ize that they cannot expect clients to remain consistently in a positive transference with them.

Very often, though not always, when clients who are protecting themselves from feeling warmth by acting coldly and hostilely are listened to without censure, debate, and false reassurance, they begin to question themselves about their own provocativeness. If the therapist is not too angry or afraid of the client's anger, he or she might be able to say, "Let's see what it is about liking me that annoys you?" This question cannot be asked, of course, until clients begin to question on their own their wish to provoke and attack.

It should be stressed, however, that clients such as Ms. S. need a great deal of time to vent their resentment, to test the therapist's patience, and to question the therapist's motives. It should also be emphasized that the therapist's attempts to reassure the client about his or her doubts concerning the practitioner's values, motives, or credentials only serve to make the client more suspicious.

When a client needs to defend against warm feelings by going on the attack, the client puts the practitioner into a situation described by Kafka in *The Trial*. Whatever the therapist says and does in his defense is used against him. His faults go beyond individual responsibility. He is guilty at the outset, and his guilt only increases as he tries to defend himself. He is in the grip of an inescapable logic and permanent blackmail (Meghnagi, 1991).

If practitioners find themselves reassuring clients and/or arguing with them, as Ruth Gangel did, they should ask themselves what they need to be reassured about and what they, the therapists, are doubting about themselves. In Ruth Gangel's case, she could not accept the accusation of being homophobic nor could she tolerate being disliked by her client after being helpful to her. Later, Ruth was able to discuss in a training seminar some of her own prejudices toward and discomforts with lesbian women. She also was able to explore some of her motives in needing to receive appreciation from clients after she helped them. Thus, she learned to become less defensive and more therapeutic when her clients criticized her and/or rejected her.

The Therapist Is Experienced as a Critical Superego

Most clinicians accept the notion that to help a client mature, the therapist should be experienced as a benign superego. The vast majority of individuals who enter psychotherapy are guilt-ridden people who are very eager to punish themselves for innocent acts which to them are serious transgressions (Reik, 1941). Because of their severe superego restraints, clients in treatment, if they are to lead more fulfilling lives that bring them more pleasure, need to perceive the therapist as more forgiving and accepting than the voices of their own punitive consciences (Fine, 1982). So, particularly in the early phases of treatment, clients should be able to feel free to discuss anything on their minds and not to worry about being censured for what they feel, do, or don't do.

Although few clinicians would disagree with the premise that an accepting, non-judgmental, nonpunitive attitude on the part of therapists helps clients to form a therapeutic alliance (Greenson, 1967) and eventually enables them them to enter a therapeutic honeymoon, many clinicians unwittingly emerge as superego critics. Inasmuch as clients are very ready to project their superego admonitions onto the therapist, it is often difficult for practitioners to realize that something in their own attitude and/or behavior has created or reinforced the client's readiness to feel attacked or criticized.

One of the ways that many practitioners rather innocently make themselves superego figures early in treatment is by announcing the ground rules of the treatment. This is easily rationalized as something clients need to know in order to provide them with security and structure (Langs, 1981). However, telling clients when fees are due, that they should obey "the fundamental rule" and say everything that comes to mind in every session, that they are responsible to pay for their therapy appointments whether they attend them or not, that they should take their vacations when the therapist plans to vacation, and other do's and don't's does not always create a feeling of security. It can also create anxiety and fear in the client. What practitioners sometimes overlook is that every utterance of the therapist's has transference implications. When therapists announce ground rules, they appear to many of their clients as straight-laced, punitive teachers or as some kind of strict parental figures of their pasts. If the therapist appears to be a superego figure of the client's past, the client is not going to find it too easy to relate comfortably, always fearing that a rule may be forgotten and broken. The client may be resentful that the therapist appears not as a confidante, but as a taskmaster.

It is quite possible for therapists to await discussion with their clients of missed appointments until an appointment is missed. Some practitioners prefer to wait for the opportunity to tell a client after he or she has missed an appointment that the first missed appointment will not incur a fee; in the future, if appointments cannot be made up, there will be a fee. Most clients can accept a fee policy made this way with little resentment because the therapist appears to be a more benign superego.

ANNOUNCING THE GROUND RULES TOO EARLY

When therapists feel compelled to announce ground rules early in treatment, they should try to explore the meaning of their compulsive attitude and to understand the anxieties that propel this counterresistive behavior. If we accept the definition of counterresistive behavior as anything the therapist does that interferes with therapeutic movement, then an early announcement of ground rules by the therapist usually needs to be looked at in this way.

In her first interview with Mr. T., Helen Grant, a psychiatrist in private practice, told Mr. T., a 40-year-old man who had been sent for treatment by the courts because of his constant voyeurism, that there were "several rules and regulations" that he "had to follow." She informed Mr. T. that he had to pay for missed appointments, he should arrive at every session on time, and the more he talked about his feelings with her, the less trouble he would be in with the law. Mr. T. agreed with "the doctor's rules" and promised he would obey them.

Although Mr. T. had not been in any trouble with the law for two weeks prior to seeing Helen Grant, immediately after his first interview with her he went to a department store and was found watching the women get undressed in a fitting room.

After being arraigned again by law enforcement officials, Mr. T. had another interview with Helen Grant. Sensitive to the fact that there might have been a connection between Mr. T.'s first appointment with her and his immediate return to voyeurism, Helen asked Mr. T. how he felt about their first interview. Mr. T. was defensive and laudatory of the therapist at first, but Helen eventually was able to help him discuss his resentment about being forced to comply with her rules and regulations. A few months later in the treatment, client and therapist both discovered that Mr. T.'s symptom of voyeurism started in his youth as a rebellion against his own parents who never gave him "the answer to anything" and always told him "to mind his own business."

As Helen Grant reviewed her policy of announcing ground rules in the first or second interview with her clients, she became aware of the fact that the practice was designed to protect her against experiencing some of her own doubts and anxieties, rather than as a sound policy for her clients. The policy provided Helen Grant with a temporary feeling of "security and structure." Fearful of her clients' acting out, anxious that she would not be paid, unconsciously condemnatory of antisocial behavior rather than understanding it, Helen's prematurely announcing her ground rules was really designed to placate the voices of her own punitive superego. As she became more understanding and less punitive of her clients' "breaking the rules," Helen Grant was able to forego her premature announcement of ground rules, she was able to keep more clients in treatment, and she was able to achieve sustained therapeutic alliances with many of them.

Still later, Helen Grant recognized that one of the main reasons that she announced ground rules prematurely was one that was unconscious for some time—an unwillingness to participate in a therapeutic honeymoon with a client because of a fear of her own and her clients' erotic wishes.

REQUIRING THAT THE CLIENT GIVE UP SELF-DESTRUCTIVE BEHAVIOR

Closely related to prematurely announcing ground rules is another practice of some therapists that can also make them appear as critical superego figures. This is the practice of not permitting a prospective client to enter treatment unless the client gives up immediately some debilitating symptom such as gambling, alcoholism, drug addiction or a sexual perversion. Aside from overestimating the clinician's authority by assuming that because the therapist gives an order the client will comply, this attitude also overlooks the fact that giving up anything—a phobia, a compulsion, an obsession, an addiction, an inferiority complex—is never an easy task. On the contrary, it is most difficult to do! Just as most clinicians would not consider it prudent to order a client to give up a self-destructive attitude or relinquish a maladaptive character trait pronto, there seems to be no legitimate therapeutic reason to expect a client to comply with a therapist's edict to give up something immediately.

When the practitioner makes relinquishing anything a condition of entering therapy, the practitioner emerges as a very exacting superego figure. In addition to appearing very rigid, the practitioner's orders may be considered something akin to emotional blackmail, which many children experience with ambivalent parental figures. Here the parental figure takes the position that love will be withheld unless the child submits to a parental edict such as performing a chore, eating certain foods, or getting a certain grade in school. By insisting that the client behave in a certain way before treatment begins, the practitioner implies: "I am a very judgmental person who will offer you my love only if you agree to do what I say! If you do not do what I say, I'll abandon you."

Invariably when the therapist insists on certain types of rigorous conformity as a condition of ongoing treatment, transferentially he or she emerges as a hated superego figure of the client's past. Obviously if the client feels antagonistic toward the therapist, a therapeutic alliance will probably not be formed and the therapeutic honeymoon will be next to impossible.

When giving up a certain behavior is a condition of ongoing treatment, the therapist is in a difficult position when the client confesses after several interviews that he or she resumed "an old habit."

Ed Flynn was a social worker in a clinic specializing in the treatment of addictions. One of the clinic's strong positions and firmly stated at the intake interview was that clients would not be taken on for therapy unless they agreed at the intake interview to stop taking the alcohol or drugs they were using. Ed Flynn's client, Mr. J., a man in his early thirties, was informed of the clinic policy by Ed at the end of his first interview with him. Mr. J. seemed to welcome being told to cease and desist imbibing alcohol and said to Ed Flynn, "If somebody like you did not tell me to stop, I'm quite sure I couldn't do it by myself! Thank you very much."

The interviews between client and therapist seemed to go quite well for the first three months of treatment. During this time, Mr. J. informed Ed Flynn that although the withdrawal symptoms he was enduring were painful, it was "worth it." He also mentioned to Ed that his relationship with his wife and children had improved and he was able to concentrate with more ease on his job as an accountant.

During the fourth month of his twice-weekly appointments, Mr. J. began to arrive late. When Ed asked Mr. J. what was going on now that made him arrive late, since he seemed punctual for the first three months of treatment, Mr. J. replied with a certain desperation in his voice, "I think I have to quit our good work with each other." Genuinely surprised, Ed spontaneously asked, "How come?" Answering the question with some hesitation and with an expression of guilt on his face, Mr. J. confessed, "I went on a binge a couple of weeks ago, got really drunk, and I haven't been able to tell you about it because I knew that I took an oath with you never to drink again. I let you down and I guess I have to pay the penalty!"

Ed Flynn was speechless for a few moments and then commented, "You've been such a cooperative person; I think one binge can be forgiven." Mr. J., although pleased with his therapist's "understanding attitude," implied that Ed Flynn was appearing to be an inconsistent parental figure because he asked, "Don't you mean business?"

Although Mr. J. remained in treatment with Ed Flynn and made a lot of progress, the continuation of the treatment was very much influenced by Ed Flynn's coming to grips with his counterresistances. In discussions with his colleagues at the clinc, he realized first that if he threatened to stop the treatment if a client resumed his addictions and then did not keep his promise, he would not appear as a very dependable professional. As Ed and his colleagues further discussed in depth the clinic policy of "quitting" the addiction as a condition of treatment, they became aware of the fact that it reflected a very punitive attitude toward their clients. In effect, they were taking away from their clients one of the most needed ingredients in their clients' lives—psychotherapy. They realized further that their retaliative attitude toward addictions was "the function of a collective superego" which gave the staff the feeling of security as they dealt with their very troublesome and provocative clients (May, 1991; Smaldino, 1991).

One of the very positive consequences of Ed and his colleagues reevaluating the clinic's policy is they decided to share with each other their motives in getting into this profession. They learned that almost every one of them had either in the past or present an addicted relative who made life quite difficult for them. Getting into the type of clinic work they did not only reactivated certain rescue fantasies, but also it served to gratify retaliative fantasies toward their addicted family members. As Ed Flynn himself confessed, "By punishing Mr. J. and other clients like him, I got even with both my parents. I wanted to tell my parents thousands of times that if they didn't stop drinking, I'd stop living with them. I guess that's what I've been telling my clients—I'll stop 'living' with them if they don't cut out their drinking."

As we suggested in Chapter 1, very often certain counterresistive behaviors are bolstered by colleagues and supervisors. This certainly was true for Ed. Flynn. In his case, he courageously took up his counterresistance problems in staff meetings and, in addition to helping himself, he was able to assist several colleagues resolve some of their hostile attitudes toward addicted clients. As the staff members' retaliative fantasies toward their own family members were better mastered, they could form better working relationships with their clients.

DEMEANING THE CLIENT'S SIGNIFICANT OTHER

Sometimes practitioners can emerge as punitive superegos when they feel quite assured that they are appearing as just the opposite. This occurs in the early stages of treatment, although it can appear in later stages as well, when the client, feeling oppressed by a spouse, boss, or colleague, finds the therapist pointing out to the client how neurotic the significant other really is. The therapist, thinking that he or she is an ally providing strength to the client as the latter copes with a formidable enemy, is almost always overlooking a significant variable. That variable is that whenever a client feels chronically oppressed by somebody close, the client either unconsciously wants and/or unconsciously feels deserving of the oppression. In effect, part of the client for many possible reasons, such as unconscious guilt, sadomasochism, or wish for punishment, agrees with and can even idealize the oppressor (Reik, 1941). Consequently, if the therapist is critical of the client's spouse, for example, in many ways the client can experience the criticism for himself or herself, albeit unconsciously.

Ted Ernst, a therapist in private practice, was treating Ms. U., a woman in her late twenties who came to see him for help with her conflicted marriage. Her husband, Joe, frequently beat her physically and often she came to her appointments with bruises that Joe had inflicted.

Ted felt very protective of Ms. U. and very contemptuous of her husband. As he listened to Ms. U.'s reports on how she was being bullied, demeaned, and physically hurt, he had fantasies of beating up Joe and/or putting him behind bars.

Although he was very aware of his sadistic fantasies toward Joe, Ted, nonetheless, told Ms. U. that she found it difficult to accept the fact that she was married to an immature man who used fighting to cope with conflict, similar to what children do. On hearing Ted Ernst's remarks, Ms. U. seemed somewhat relieved. However, toward the end of the interview, which was still in the first month of treatment, she began to appear subdued.

When Ms. U. cancelled her next two appointments, Ted began to wonder if she was reacting to her last interview, in which Ted was critical of her husband. Consequently, before the following appointment, Ted called his client on the phone and told her he hoped she would be at the next interiew because he thought that perhaps their last one was upsetting and maybe they could discuss this. Although Ms. U. did not acknowledge the correctness of Ted's suggestions, she agreed to come in for the next interview.

Denying at first that she was affected by Ted's criticisms of Joe, Ms. U. eventually could say, "I think you want me to divorce him and if I do I don't know where I could turn. Also, I'm not sure you realize that he does not want to be mean to me—he just can't help it." On Ted's being able to recognize with Ms. U. that she was disappointed and angry at him for his remarks about Joe, Ms. U. then stated, "You see, Dr. Ernst, when people get married, they are one! It is okay for me to complain about Joe, but when you do, it's different. Then it becomes an attack on me. It's like members of minorities—Jews, Italians, Blacks—they can laugh at and criticize themselves, but if anybody else does, they take it personally."

Ted Ernst received some valuable information from his client. He realized once again that very frequently when a client refers to a significant other's remarks or actions, the significant other is really a stand-in for the client, representing part of him or her in the therapy sessions.

One might compare a client's constant reporting of being oppressed and mistreated as similar to reporting a dream. The client writes the complete script when he dreams, and when the client reports consistently being maltreated by someone like a spouse, boss, or child, it is always important for the practitioner to keep in mind that the client has written a good part of that script, too.

Overlooking a Client's Latent Negative Transference

Experienced therapists are always alert to the strong possibility that the client is being represented in the therapy when the latter reports that someone in the client's social orbit is being critical of the therapy and/or the therapist. It can almost always be inferred that when clients report on a friend, relative, or colleague's criticisms of the therapist or therapy, these clients in one way or another share the significant other's sentiment. They do not feel enough safety in the therapeutic situation, however, to be direct with the therapist. If the therapist does not relate to the criticisms of the therapy reported by the client, a therapy honeymoon will probably not evolve and the possibility of a working alliance will be greatly diminished.

Susan David, a psychologist in private practice had seen Ms. V. for about six sessions, helping her with some severe sexual inhibitions. A single woman in her twenties, Ms. V. had spent her time in treatment talking about her fears of men, as well as some of her resentments toward them. She realized in her contacts with Susan David that she had a fundamental distrust of men and felt very used by them, in and out of bed.

Although Ms. V. seemed to be feeling well understood and relaxed in her treatment sessions, at her seventh appointment she informed Susan of a discussion she had with one of her woman colleagues who worked with her as a co-editor on a magazine. Ms. V. told Susan that over lunch her colleague, on learning that Ms. V. was in therapy, became very critical of therapy and therapists. The colleague pointed out that therapists are obsessed with sex, quite emotionally disturbed themselves, and more concerned with making money than with helping their clients get better.

Not consciously aware that Ms. V. was in a disguised way attacking her, Susan was not able to ask her client how she felt about the criticisms but, instead, became quite defensive and said, "Yes, many people are threatened by therapy and therapists and have to criticize them to compensate for their own feelings of inadequacy!" Although Susan's manifest remarks probably contained some validity, they also reflected Susan's current emotional state. She felt threatened by the colleague's criticisms and rather than see what meaning they had for her client, demeaned the colleague "to compensate for her own feelings of inadequacy."

That Susan unconsciously recognized that she was being attacked by Ms. V. was probably true; otherwise, she would not have been very protective of therapy and therapists and quite aggressive toward her client's colleague.

Clients unconsciously recognize a therapist's defensiveness and Ms. V. seemed aware of Susan's. In her ninth session of twice-weekly psychotherapy, Ms. V. remarked, "I've noticed that when people are secure, they can take criticism instead of attacking other people." Although Ms. V. was referring to a defensive female supervisor on her current job, who reminded Ms. V. of a former school teacher "who thought she was teaching us but really wasn't," the client was unconsciously referring to her therapist.

Fortunately, Susan David was able to recognize that Ms. V. was referring to her when she talked about the supervisor and the teacher who were not doing their jobs properly. Consequently, she was able to get in touch with her client's latent negative transference and help Ms. V. discuss her own distrust of her therapy.

Very often when clients cannot feel free to express their doubts and resentments about their therapist, they do what Ms. V. did. They quote others and use them as representatives, invoking the words of a colleague or someone else close to the client. Or, as Ms. V. also did, they talk about other helpers in their past or present who have been or are insensitive, unkind, and unhelpful. Therapists, if they are not too anxious, defensive, angry, or suffering from some other vulnerability, should be able to help their clients eventually face their negative transference. When they cannot, they should look at their own counterresistances.

Susan David, in exploring her own counterresistances in her work with Ms. V. was able to recognize three issues that prevented her from initially dealing with her client's resentments. Susan realized in hindsight that she felt irritated with Ms. V. for not levelling with her. "It was as if she was getting away with knocking me, but not taking responsibility for her own hostility," reflected Susan in peer supervision. Also, Susan became aware of some envy she was feeling toward her client. Stated Susan, "My analyst never lets me get away with it. I have to face my own bitchiness all the time. She didn't look at hers and it made me very angry." Finally, Susan got in touch with how difficult it was for her to direct anger toward her own therapist. Frightened of her own anger toward her therapist, she overidentified with her client and unconsciously stopped her from doing what she, Susan, often stopped herself from doing in her own therapy.

Although seemingly paradoxical, another way of emerging as a critical superego figure is when the therapist praises the client. At first blush, it would appear that praising the client has a positive, reinforcing effect that can contribute toward a working alliance and a therapy honeymoon. However, when clients are lauded from time to time, they begin to feel they have to work laboriously in and out of treatment in order to continue to receive the supreme gratification in therapy—the practitioner's praise. However, if clients have to expend much effort to be lauded, they cannot be themselves and feel safe in the therapy. Rather, they feel pressured to be like compliant children and in response to the pressure eventually feel quite hostile toward the therapist and intimidated by him or her. Gradually, the therapist emerges as an austere, punitive, parental figure who has to be catered to in order that praise to the client will be dispensed. In response, the client feels more pressured and eventually becomes rebellious and may act out.

Misuse of Praise

Practitioners who utilize praise as a means of helping clients therapeutically, frequently are quite resistant to face their clients' wishes, fantasies, dreams, defenses, superego admonitions, and all that comprises their dynamic unconscious and unique metapsychology. Inevitably, those practitioners who resist relating to their clients' internal life are frightened to relate to their own internal life. They put the emphasis on the client's overt behavior as well as on their own overt behavior. Consequently, therapeutic movement is rare with these clients and dropping out of treatment is quite common.

> Patricia Connor was a psychiatric resident in a mental health clinic specializing in helping their clientele to move from unemployment to securing and maintaining jobs. She had been seeing Mr. W., a 32-year-old man, married with two children, for nine sessions, trying to help him overcome his reluctance to working on a sustained basis. During this time, Mr. W. brought out that he was going to have a job interview in a few days. Patricia praised him lavishly saying, "You are doing a wonderful thing. You have real courage!" Mr. W. enjoyed the praise, beamed, and thanked Patricia Connor for her help over the past two months.
>
> At the next session, Mr. W. did not mention the job interview. However, Patricia did, and wondered how it went. Mr. W. embarrassedly responded,

"I didn't get around to it." Patricia, obviously disappointed, spontaneously queried, "What happened?" Mr. W. stated he did not really know what happened, but maybe next week he would try again. To this, Patricia said, "Good!"

Mr. W. came late for his next two sessions and again did not make any reference to job interviews. Again, Patricia Connor asked him about the job interviews, and again Mr. W. had no answer. Inasmuch as Mr. W.'s resistances were not explored, he became more distant from Patricia and eventually left treatment.

Whenever therapists find themselves praising a client's behavior, they should ask themselves what investment they have in manipulating a client to achieve a specified action (Wolpe, 1958). Furthermore, even if they ardently wish to have the client behave in a certain way, and the client does not, they should ask themselves what is going on within themselves that forces them to bypass the exploration of the client's resistances and to focus exclusively on guiding and reinforcing certain actions of the client.

When Patricia Connor investigated the counterresistances in her therapeutic work with Mr. W., she learned a great deal about herself that helped her enormously with other clients. First, she realized how very work-oriented she herself had been all of her life and that to her the idea of flouting the work ethic was a virtual crime. For Patricia not to be gainfully employed was a horrible idea. It meant to her that she was a "good for nothing" and the ugly feeling that she could not tolerate in herself as she pictured herself not working was projected onto Mr. W. Not separating his values, superego admonitions, and anxieties from her own, Patricia assumed that Mr. W. was feeling as miserable and as corrupt as she would have felt if she were unemployed.

The ugly feeling attached to being unemployed that Patricia Connnor projected onto Mr. W. had to be wiped out. Consequently, she pressured him to get work, praised him as he moved in that direction, and withdrew praise when he did not. In response to her praise and reinforcement, Mr. W. felt rejected and admonished. Patricia learned that when she or any therapist does not permit a client to preserve his autonomy and self-determination, the client feels weakened and can flee the relationship.

What was perhaps the most beneficial lesson that Patricia derived from her work with Mr. W. was that when a client's resistances are bypassed, when his or her transference reactions are overlooked, and when the idea of trying to maintain a working alliance with the client is completely forgotten, usually something is very threatening to the therapist. What was most threatening to Patricia Connor was to face how ugly she would have appeared to herself, how devoid of self-esteem, and how self-loathing she would become if she were in her client's situation. Praising, reinforcing her client positively and negatively were all attempts on her part to avoid facing her client's inner life, which as is almost always true with any practitioner, was a strong attempt to avoid facing herself.

When practitioners cannot face themselves and thereby resist helping their clients to confront themselves, a working alliance does not develop. Usually this is what the practitioner is unconsciously seeking. As Patricia Connor learned, by rewarding and punishing her client, and bypassing an active exploration of his inner life, she was acting out her wish to reject him, and by so doing, would not have to face some of her own vulnerabilities.

If therapists want to avoid facing their own vulnerabilities that emerge with a particular client, they will unconsciously prevent the development of an intimate relationship. If they find themselves rewarding and punishing, it is usually a sign for them that they have an unconscious wish to prevent the development of a therapy honeymoon and the continuation of a solid working alliance.

GIVING ADVICE

Just as offering and withholding praise are means that practitioners utilize to prevent the establishment of an intimate relationship with their clients, the same may be said of offering advice to clients and answering their questions. If clinicians, particularly in the initial stage of psychotherapy, offer their clients advice and direction, they turn their clients into dependent, weak, passive children. Although this is partially gratifying to clients, with their autonomy squelched, creativity denied, and their introspective capacities blocked, they gradually lose respect for themselves. Disliking themselves, they do not feel like therapeutic partners in the treatment relationship, but like weakened objects. As a result, a therapy honeymoon becomes almost out of the question and a therapeutic alliance between the two adults is almost an impossibility.

Similar to rewarding and punishing, when therapists find themselves giving advice and/or answering questions, they have to ask themselves what is threatening them that prevents them from doing constructive psychotherapy. Sometimes practitioners cannot tolerate the content of their clients' concerns because it activates anxiety in themselves. To block the emergence of anxiety in themselves, they quickly give their clients advice, which is an attempt to get rid of their own anxiety quickly. As we pointed out in Chapters 1 and 2, advice is often given and questions answered because the practitioner cannot tolerate the client's expressions of hostility. Of course, if clients cannot express their anxieties, concerns, or hostilities, a close working relationship is prevented and, as we have suggested, this is often what the therapist unconsciously is trying to arrange.

When practitioners find themselves giving advice to clients and answering their questions, they might ask themselves, "Why do I have to appear so knowledgeable?" If they are honest with themselves, they will probably learn that their quest to appear omniscient and omnipotent is a defensive operation to mask their feelings of ignorance and impotence (Novick & Novick, 1991). Uncertain of their clients' dynamics, but frightened to feel baffled when with them; feeling vulnerable in the face of their clients' wishes, fantasies, defenses, and agonies, but unable to acknowledge this; insensitive to their clients' major resistances and prominent transference distortions, but unaware of their own emotional detachment, practitioners who freely give advice and frequently answer questions are keeping their clients in a childlike weakened position in order to protect themselves.

With their clients in the weakened emotional and interpersonal position that they have helped to create, therapists who dispense advice and answer questions derive a feeling of "pseudostrength" as they enact a role of "know-it-all." In so doing, they keep their clients from knowing too much about themselves and from knowing too much about their therapists—their therapist's biggest fear.

Just as there are therapists who propose short-term treatment to avoid the honeymoon, it may be hypothesized that some of the cases in private practice and in social agencies that go on for years, but with little therapeutic movement, are those conducted by practitioners who are not facing some important counterresistances. In giving advice and answering questions easily, they probably resist knowing much about their clients' fantasies. If they block the emergence of their clients' fantasies, they probably resist knowing too much about their clients' transference responses. And when therapists are uninterested in their clients' transference responses, they are probably frightened of an intense, intimate relationship with their clients, that is, a therapy honeymoon.

FEAR OF COMPASSION

As suggested several times in this chapter, counterresistances to the development of a therapy honeymoon are many and are unique to the individual practitioner. However, there may be one warning signal to all practitioners that alerts them to the possibility that they are resisting the development or continuation of the honeymoon. That is when the practitioner finds that he or she feels devoid of compassion in the therapy. When compassion is absent, passion is usually being opposed by the therapist, both the client's and his or her own. Arnold Bernstein (1972), in his paper "The Fear of Compassion," pointed out that a naive misreading of psychodynamic therapy tends to perpetuate the notion that to feel compassion toward a client is to act out countertransference problems. Yet, Bernstein attributes many treatment failures to the prohibition against compassionate behavior on the part of psychotherapists. We believe that many of the case illustrations in this section that demonstrated the therapist's fear of an intimate relationship and therefore blocked the emergence of a therapy honeymoon, derived from the practitioner's resistance to put himself or herself in the client's psychological shoes because the practitioner's anxiety was too great for him or her to bear. When the therapist's anxiety is too great, he or she resists identification with the client, empathy for the client, and help for the client. Then it may be inferred that the therapist's compassion is lacking.

We are inclined to concur with Bernstein whose contention is that if a psychotherapist is a healthy, mature, gentle human being,

> [his or her] human response to the expression of a need for help on the part
> of another human being is a feeling of compassion. Compassion is the socially
> complementary role response to a child or to a person in need of help or to
> any living creature in pain. (1972, p. 163)

EXPLOITING THE DEVELOPMENT OF THE
THERAPY HONEYMOON

Although many practitioners resist the idea of a honeymoon as a legitimate phase
of psychotherapy that helps the building of the working alliance and the subsequent
working through of the client's conflicts, there are also many practitioners who resist
continuing the work of psychotherapy. They instead exploit the client's honeymoon
state and prevent the client from experiencing further therapeutic growth.

By exploiting the client's emotional state of honeymooner, we are referring to those
activities of the clinician, by omission or commission, that are not designed to help
the client travel on the road that leads to self-discovery. Rather, they are designed
to help the clinician receive gratification of narcissistic wishes, fulfillment of sexual
desires, and reinforcement of maladaptive defenses.

Nearly 80 years ago in his paper, "Observations on Transference Love" (1915),
Sigmund Freud made many pertinent remarks that are applicable to the therapist's
sexual exploitation of the therapy honeymoon and bear brief review.

Freud cautioned the practitioner to *always* remember that the client's falling in
love is essentially induced by the therapeutic situation and is not to be ascribed
to the charms of the practitioner's personality. Freud further urged practitioners to
realize that they have no reason whatsoever to be proud of a sexual "conquest,"
inasmuch as the client is demeaning the therapy and the therapist if he or she wants
sex rather than treatment. Freud observed that if clients want to make love rather
than to examine their sexual fantasies, it is always an attempt on their part to move
away from therapeutic issues such as recalling a traumatic memory or confessing
a real or fantasied transgression.

Once the therapy becomes a sexual love affair, transferences and resistances cannot be further examined. Freud concluded that this type of love affair actually
"destroys the influence" of treatment and in the end becomes a "painful" experience
for therapist and client that usually ends in "remorse." Therefore, Freud asserted,
the more plainly therapists let it be seen that they are proof against every sexual
temptation, the sooner "will the advantage from the situation accrue" to the
treatment.

In his paper, Freud (1915) differentiates between the sexual love affair that the client wants and what happens when a man and woman are "really in love." "In real love" clients would "gladly choose the road to completion of the cure" in order to give themselves and the therapist value in their own eyes and in the eyes of the therapist. Freud thought that when clients "really love" they want to work together with the clinician to prepare themselves for "real life" where feelings of love "could find their proper outlet." By contrast, clients who pursue a sexual love affair show "a stubborn and rebellious spirit," have "thrown up all interest" in their treatment, and "clearly, too, all respect for [the therapist's] well-founded judgement." These clients, in effect, are "bringing out a resistance" under the guise of being in love.

With the possible exception of Freud's cautionary note to clinicians that the client's wish to pursue a sexual affair is a function of the treatment situation, and not because of the practitioner's charms, most of his observations on transference love refer to the client's contributions. However, what Freud has observed about the client is equally relevant to the therapist.

Sexual Exploitation

Just as the client's interest in pursuing a sexual love affair with the therapist should be viewed as an expression of resistance, that is, an attempt to avoid facing real life matters in the therapy, a therapist's wish to pursue a sexual affair with the client should be similarly regarded. When professionals want to turn their clients into sexual lovers, they are usually having difficulty coping with their own love lives. There are probably no therapists (or clients) who are having enjoyable sexual lives and are concomitantly responding to their therapy partners' sexual advances and/or making sexual advances toward them.

In addition to not being able to face their own personal and interpersonal conflicts, practitioners who act out their honeymoon fantasies with their clients are in most instances resisting the idea of doing therapy. Something in the day-to-day work with their clients angers and upsets them. Similar to their angry clients who are rebelling against self-examination and unconsciously wanting to demean the therapist and the therapeutic situation, therapists who have sex with their clients are fighting the therapy and unconsciously wanting to demean the client. These therapists are having trouble both in coping with life and in doing therapy.

> Ronald Baker was a 40-year-old married analyst treating Ms. Y. four times a week. Ms. Y., a woman in her late thirties, sought analysis because she was very depressed, phobic, suffered from many psychosomatic symptoms, and had little desire to do anything resembling work. Ms. Y. ascribed most of her difficulties to her "oppressive marriage." She found her husband to be "boring, sexually unappealing, and intellectually barren."
>
> Over a period of five months, Ms. Y. moved a great deal in her therapy. As she discharged anger in her sessions, her depression diminished and her

psychosomatic symptoms abated. Her self-esteem rose and she became more confident and much less phobic. Ms. Y. ascribed all of her growth to Ronald Baker's "magic touch." He was the man she "always desired" and she was positive if she could be married to a man like "Ron," " life would be ecstatic."

As Ronald was lauded in each session, as he was told how bright, competent, and sexually appealing he was, he began to feel very loving and sexual toward Ms. Y. In one session, during the sixth month of treatment, Ms. Y. had a dream in which Ronald comforted her, soothed her, embraced her, and then had sex with her. Ms. Y. associated to this dream by saying to Ronald, "You are the man of my dreams. Everything I did with you in the dream is what I desperately want. I'm positive if we become lovers, I will become a very happy woman."

Ronald became very moved by Ms. Y.'s adulation and began to feel that if she were in his life, he would become a very happy man. Slowly they moved from talking to embracing, and from embracing to actual sex. Two of the four sessions each week were entirely verbal and "exclusively psychoanalytic." The other two became sexual encounters followed by dinner together. Ms. Y. paid for all of the sessions but Ronald footed the bill for the dinners.

The combined sexual affair and psychoanalysis went on for about 18 months until Ms. Y. began to find the arrangement frustrating. As happens to many lovers, the time together was not enough for her. She wanted more time and commitment from Ronald. Since he was noncommittal and clearly very ambivalent about further involvement with Ms. Y., she became more rageful and less happy with him and with herself. Slowly she became depressed, and eventually all of her old symptoms returned. When Ronald refused to see more of her, she told her husband about the arrangement she had with Ronald. Mr. Y. insisted that Ms. Y. discontinue treatment with Ronald or he would leave her. After Ms. Y. left treatment, Mr. Y. successfully won a lawsuit against Ronald, which cost the therapist thousands of dollars as well as an enormous decline in his professional reputation.

When Ronald eventually looked at his own role in the relationship with Ms. Y., he learned a lot about why he exploited Ms. Y. and her honeymoon transference. First, he himself felt very unsatisfied in his own marriage. Like Ms. Y., he did not take very much responsibility for his own marital conflicts, projecting them onto his wife. Inasmuch as he was not in touch with the part of himself that unconsciously arranged for an unfulfilling marriage, he could not help Ms. Y. explore her own responsibilities and understand better her own role in her marital conflicts. By keeping himself blind to his client's contributions to her marital conflicts, he could protect himself more easily from facing his own contributions to his failing marriage.

What Ronald Baker had difficulty looking at is what most unhappily married individuals find upsetting to face—their own masochism (Reik, 1941). Masochistic spouses like to believe that they are being victimized by their sadistic mates, but do not like to believe that they have a role in provoking the abuse. Both Ronald Baker and Ms. Y. utilized this defensive posturing in their respective marriages. Consequently, because Ronald could not help himself overcome his wish to suffer in his own marriage, he was powerless in helping Ms. Y. come to grips with her own unconscious desire to suffer in her marriage.

For Ronald Baker to enjoy his wife, he learned, made him feel too guilty—too much like an oedipal winner. Therefore, he unconsciously arranged to have an unfulfilling marriage. This was similar to Ms. Y.'s conflict; she also felt too guilty to enjoy her marriage. In a psychodynamic sense, Ronald and Ms. Y. "were made for each other." Both of them were involved in sadomasochistic marriages; neither of them could accept his or her own responsibilities in his or her marital conflicts nor were they aware of the masochistic gratification that each was deriving from his or her respective marriages.

Although Ronald and Ms. Y. felt guilty for their oedipal wishes, neither of them realized that turning the therapy into a sexual love affair was his or her way of acting out these forbidden desires. In the end, they both suffered the "remorse" that Freud (1915) talked about in "Observations on Transference Love."

As Ronald Baker later realized, his sexual affair with his client was no different from his usual *modus vivendi*. Guilty and depressed because he had to punish himself for his forbidden wishes, he sought some relief from his misery through his sexual relationship with Ms. Y. However, the relief he sought was the gratification of the same forbidden sexual wishes that made him feel guilty and depressed. Therefore, he had to suffer for his acting out with Ms. Y. and had to punish himself severely for the misery he caused her.

Psychological Exploitation

OBJECT GRATIFICATION

As we have previously indicated, it is probably only a small percentage of therapists who act out their honeymoon fantasies and have sexual relations with their clients. There are, however, a larger group of practitioners who tend to make their clients into friends and colleagues and derive "support" for themselves as they tell themselves they are providing "support" for their clients. Although it is well documented how much the client "wants to obtain from the therapist some sort of object relationship which [will] provide the support and gratification he needs in dealing with the frustrations that come up in the treatment" (Stein, 1972, pp. 41–42), little attention has been given to the therapist's need for the same kind of support and gratification in the treatment situation.

As Tarachow (1963) pointed out and Gill (1954) and Stone (1961) corroborated, the temptation to reach out to the client for "object gratification" assails the practitioner very frequently. If the client loves and admires, the therapist wants to return the love and admiration. If the client is hostile, the therapist wants to fight. If clients mention that they have had a dramatic encounter with some individual the practitioner knows, he or she is tempted to inform clients of this interesting fact. Doing psychotherapy can be lonely and frustrating work that sometimes borders on the "impossible." Consequently, it is not a mystery why the therapist lets down barriers and interacts with the client as one may do with a friend or colleague or relative.

Despite the therapist being aware of the client's wish to obtain "object gratification," the therapist frequently rationalizes his or her own wish for the same kind of pleasure. Many practitioners who share personal facts and feelings with their clients, who gossip occasionally in the sessions, or who get into political discussions with their clients explain the behavior as providing "a corrective emotional experience" (Alexander & French, 1946), "support" (Stein, 1972) or "empathy" (Kohut, 1971, 1984). Rarely have authors discussed the aforementioned activities as emanating from their own needs and rarely have writers discussed how these activities have blocked the client's emotional growth. Although virtually every client sees the therapist as a real person (Stein, 1972; Viederman, 1991), notices some of his or her idiosyncratic reactions, is familiar with certain attitudes, and knows something about the lifestyle of the practitioner, we are referring here to consistent breaks from therapeutic anonymity that provide a regressive type of gratification both for the client and therapist, but little if no understanding or growth for the client.

What most clients are oblivious to in the therapeutic situation and which many practitioners tend to overlook is that for psychological growth to take place there needs to be consistent doses of frustration. All infants need to be weaned. All toddlers need to be toilet-trained and learn to accept "no" for an answer to many of their demands. All children need to learn how to curb their narcissism, share their parents with siblings, tame their oedipal fantasies, learn how to separate and individuate, and be able to cope with disappointments of all kinds. Psychosocial growth from the womb to the tomb requires the absorption of frustration. Certainly it must be part of every therapeutic relationship and coped with by both participants.

Therapists in using their clients for "object gratification" under the guise of giving corrective experiences and support are almost always rebelling against doing constructive therapeutic work. Inevitably, they cannot feel strong enough to cope with their clients' wishes, demands, or hostilities, and therefore they turn the therapy into a friendship or colleagial interchange or something nontherapeutic for the client.

Judith Applebaum was a therapist in private practice treating Ms. Z., a married woman in her mid-thirties, who had come to treatment because she was suffering from "an identity crisis." She was not sure whether she "should work or stay home," "have children or have the easy life," "get divorced [from her husband of two years] or make the best of it."

Over a period of five months, Ms. Z. made therapeutic progress, beginning to see that she could work and enjoy her marriage at the same time. Her self-esteem improved and she felt that her therapist was "an ideal role model."

During Ms. Z.'s sixth month of treatment, she noticed that her therapist was pregnant. When Judith was asked by Ms. Z., "What month are you in?," instead of trying to explore her client's fantasies and learn what she was feeling, Judith answered, "The beginning of the seventh." Ms. Z. congratulated Judith on her pregnancy and told her how pleased she was to know the details about it. "You are the role model, the good sister, the good mother, I've always wanted," said Ms. Z. enthusiastically.

Delighted with her client's very positive response to the revelations about her pregnancy, Judith began to share more information. Feeling strongly that Ms. Z. needed "permission" to have a child of her own, Judith decided that she would not only be "a benign superego" and give her client the needed permission, but Judith would "also be the role model with whom Ms. Z. could identify." Consequently, details of prenatal classes, changes of domestic routines, child care, and other personal matters were shared with Ms. Z. Judith relished giving her client the information she asked for as well as some unsolicited facts about her life, because the client "was eating it up" and "growing" from it.

Ms. Z. coped very well during the two-month absence after Judith's baby was born; however, a rather dramatic crisis ensued on Judith's return to work. Although Ms. Z. was able to accept the frequency of her treatment sessions being reduced from three to two times a week, upon her asking if she could see the baby in person, the crisis began. Judith said to her client, "Let's see what makes you want to see the baby," and Ms. Z. became indignant. Shouted Ms. Z., "For months you've treated me like a loved daughter, a devoted sister, and now you want to go back to that therapy junk! You've got your nerve!" When Judith said, "I've let you down," Ms. Z. said, "You're damn right. You can't be trusted."

Although Judith Applebaum and Ms. Z. sustained their relationship, it took months for the client to get back to therapeutic work. She needed a long time to vent her hatred toward Judith and even more time to show the similarity between the people in her life who betrayed her and Judith.

As Judith listened to Ms. Z. and reflected on herself, she realized how much she had exploited Ms. Z.'s honeymoon transference. She learned that by sharing the details of her pregnancy with her client, she was making her client the "good mother" and "good sister" who would support her. Judith also realized that she projected onto her client the part of herself that craved a woman to love her. She could not frustrate her client and help her discuss wishes and fantasies because she anticipated the intense anger from Ms. Z. that she, Judith, would have felt if frustrated under the same circumstances.

Pregnancy, like many other events in a therapist's life, is a time when the therapist does need support and understanding. It is very tempting to take the needed emotional supplies from someone who is very willing to give them. However, when the "someone" is a client who comes to the therapist's office and pays a fee to be helped therapeutically, it is abusing the client's treatment to use that client for support.

As Judith Applebaum subjected her activity and inactivity with Ms. Z. to further study, she learned that in many ways she was reliving something from her own past. As the oldest of five children, Judith had to endure her mother's pregnancies. This involved supporting and nurturing her mother and taking care of her younger siblings for many hours a day. Judith resented all of the nurturing she felt compelled to provide but never had a chance to discharge her animosity. Judith, in effect, put Ms. Z. in the same position she was in as a child. She identified with the aggressor (A. Freud, 1946) by becoming her mother and making Ms. Z. herself.

Similar to the child who has his or her tonsils extracted and then plays doctor by pretending to take out other children's tonsils, all human beings have a tendency to do to others actively something they experienced passively. Because therapists, perhaps more than many other people, have experienced a great deal of emotional pain, they can unconsciously exploit their powerful position as therapist and induce in their clients the pain they experienced in their past. These mechanisms of role reversal and identification with the aggressor seemed to be operating quite prominently in Judith Applebaum's interaction with Ms. Z.

Overidentification

Hervé Guibert (1991) in his insightful book, *To the Friend Who Did Not Save My Life,* presents a distraught account of how AIDS affects friendships. He strongly avers that no one who is healthy can truly accompany someone who is sick. Because illness is "a limbo of hope and uncertainty," limbo is a place where one lives alone.

What Guibert has described about victims of AIDS is a picture of how many of our clients experience themselves—lonely and unaccompanied by someone who really is concerned. Most therapists recognize this state of emotional isolation in their clients because they have been there themselves.

Although most clinicians are able to sense and relate to the mistrust and paranoia of their clients who feel very alone, when the practitioner is in strong identification with them, he or she can become too reassuring and gratifying. It is one thing to be able to empathize with a client who feels very isolated and deprived; however, to reassure and to gratify this client bypasses the work the client and clinician must do so that both of them understand how and why the client clings to the conviction of being emotionally impoverished and maltreated. If the therapist continues to reassure and gratify, the client will not come to grips with his or her mistrust and paranoia. On the contrary, the client will eventually make the therapist part of his or her world that can never be trusted.

When therapists do not explore, but reassure instead, when they do not try to promote insight but overgratify, they, the therapists, are really trying to reassure themselves about issues and conflicts that create anxiety within themselves.

Arthur Zimmer, a psychologist in an outpatient clinic of a general hospital, was treating Mr. A. for his abusive behavior toward his wife. Mr. A., a man in his early thirties, with very limited or no provocation, would physically hurt his wife, often resulting in her having black eyes and welts.

During Mr. A.'s first month of twice-a-week treatment, he did very well. His attacks on his wife abated, his frustration tolerance increased, and he became much more pleasant to be with, both at home and at work. At his eleventh session, while telling Arthur Zimmer about being "more relaxed" with his wife and referring to her several times as "a good woman," Mr. A. abruptly stopped talking and looked extremely anxious. When Arthur Zimmer noted the shift and commented on it, Mr. A. said, "I can't go on any further."

With some help from his therapist, Mr. A. was eventually able to reveal what was very upsetting to him. The client had been "suspicious" of his wife "for years," always wondering about her having an extramarital affair. Although Mr. A. could not provide any "real evidence," he had been obsessed with the idea for most of the eight years that he and Mrs. A. had been married.

Arthur Zimmer found himself feeling "enormous compassion" for his client and could feel within himself "the pain" his client "had to endure." In lieu of exploring with Mr. A. how, why, and when the obsession arose, Arthur told him "how horrible this situation" was. Rather than trying to expose the wishes, defenses, and superego injunctions that propelled the obsession, Arthur told Mr. A. that he was "worrying about it needlessly."

Arthur's attempt to reassure his client yielded poor therapeutic results. Mr. A. began to question how Arthur could be as certain as he was about Mrs. A.'s fidelity. On seeing that Arthur had no reassuring answer to this question, Mr. A. began to be quite suspicious of Arthur, wondering if he was "in cahoots" with Mrs. A. and was "being paid off for joining her."

Slowly Mr. A. turned Arthur into an enemy who was aiding and abetting his wife to cheat on him. In effect, Mr. A. made Arthur the same or similar person who was having an affair with his wife. From a position of being "relaxed" with his wife and "confident" with his therapist, Mr. A. regressed. His physical beatings of his wife resumed; he became acutely paranoid with her and with Arthur. His obsession became delusions and he had to be hospitalized after he was diagnosed as psychotic.

One of the important lessons that can be learned from Arthur Zimmer's work with Mr. A. is the futility and, at times, the danger of the practitioner reassuring the client. As we have noted, reassurance rarely helps clients get to the issues that make them doubtful and mistrustful; at best, it only covers up the client's doubts and mistrust for a brief period. More salient, perhaps, is the fact that if a husband or wife obsesses constantly about the mate having an affair, the husband or wife needs to believe this. Often the obsession we are discussing expresses homosexual anxiety and/or oedipal guilt. When the therapist tries to "take away" the obsession, the intense anxiety associated with forbidden oedipal and homosexual fantasies emerges.

What Arthur Zimmer overlooked in his work with Mr. A. was that the client's honeymoon fantasies were creating a homoerotic transference. As the client "relaxed" with Arthur, felt more "confidence" in him, he could not tolerate the emotional closeness and became more and more paranoid. Mr. A. seemed to experience Arthur Zimmer's strong compassion and very warm reassurance as sexual seductions, which made the client very uncomfortable. The more uncomfortable he became, the more Arthur reassured him. The more reassurance Mr. A. received, the more paranoid he became, until he had to be hospitalized.

A therapist always has to be vigilant during the honeymoon phase of a possible homosexual panic emerging in the client. Usually it takes the form of paranoid ideation. Clients are reassured, not when they are told to stop worrying, but, as we have demonstrated, when their doubts and distrust are given an airing. The airing of distrust and the anger associated with it make the therapist appear much less threatening.

As Arthur Zimmer reviewed his counterresistances with Mr. A., both in supervision and in his own personal therapy, he got in touch with many of his own conflicts that were operative with Mr. A. Married only a year, Arthur Zimmer had to fight the idea of his own wife being unfaithful to him. Thus he had to keep reassuring Mr. A. that his wife was faithful. Inasmuch as he was very identified with Mr. A.—overidentified—by reassuring Mr. A. that his wife was faithful, he was reassuring himself.

Arthur also realized that he defended against experiencing Mr. A.'s latent homosexual transference because he did not want to experience his own homosexual transference toward Mr. A. Of equal importance, at the same time he was fighting the acknowledgment of his own homosexual transference toward his own therapist, whom he was seeing several times a week in psychoanalysis.

As Arthur became more aware of the dynamics of his counterresistances with Mr. A., he became convinced of the fact that reassuring a client was frequently, if not always, a defensive maneuver by the therapist. He decided that whenever he found himself reassuring a client, he was going to try to find out what was occurring within himself that made him want the form of reassurance he was offering his client.

STRETCHING THE GROUND RULES OF TREATMENT

Earlier in this chapter, we pointed out how a rigid adherence by therapists to the ground rules could be viewed as an unconscious manipulation on their parts to prevent the emergence of a honeymoon transference and to prevent a later development of a working alliance. In this section we will discuss how stretching the ground rules can activate an initially strong honeymoon transference in clients only to have them feel teased, disappointed, and angry.

When they stretch the ground rules of therapy, many practitioners, under the guise of being benign superego figures who provide corrective emotional experiences, are frequently ingratiating themselves with their clients. If practitioners find themselves ignoring their clients' frequent cancellations, habitual latenesses, or constant vacations, on subjecting their oversights to examination, they usually discover that they feel intimidated by these clients. To investigate with their clients what the latter are feeling, fantasying, and fearing that moves them away from disciplined therapy, arouses in these practitioners the fear that they might antagonize their clients and provoke their departure from treatment. In lieu of risking this possibility, not only do they overlook occurrences like frequent cancellations of appointments or constant vacations of their clients, but often they do not charge a fee for these excursions and may even justify and support them; they do not realize that they are aiding and abetting their clients to act out their conflicts rather than to understand and to master them.

Initially most clients are pleased when their therapists stretch the ground rules. They tend to feel like a special child who is receiving special treatment. Also, the guilt that clients often experience when they depart from the therapy's routines can be diminished when the clinician "looks away." The client's departures from routines are frequently accompanied by hostile fantasies. If the clinician does not explore the meaning of the client's behavior, the client may feel relieved as if he or she "got away with something."

What is often overlooked by practitioners who stretch the ground rules is that their clients begin to wonder how seriously the therapist is taking the treatment. If my therapist "looks away," maybe my therapist doesn't think regularly scheduled appointments are that necessary? The client may then go on to consider the question, "Maybe I don't really need treatment that much anyway?" Then, the very thing the practitioner was trying to prevent occurs. The client leaves treatment reasonably convinced that the therapist did not think psychotherapy was that crucial to the client's life.

The "special" feeling that clients often experience when ground rules are violated leads to serious therapeutic impasses. On feeling special, clients have a tendency to want more evidence they are very much loved by the therapist. For example, the client who receives the therapist's encouragement to go on a vacation without paying for the missed sessions may follow this up with requests for a lower fee. The client who arrives late for appointments may decide to come even later and then may want the frequency of sessions to be reduced. Finally, if clients think they are special, they may begin to feel entitled to other favors like being loaned books by the therapist or using his or her kitchen or maybe even his or her office.

As we suggested a few times earlier in this text, sooner or later clients who are the recipients of the therapist's indulgences are going to have to be told, "No." Many clients can delay paying their bills to the therapist for a few months, or longer, but eventually the therapist is going to feel compelled to ask, "When are you going to pay me?" Yet, clients who have been consistently gratified by their therapists have every right in the world to feel angry when the goodies are taken away. When the fantasy of being gratified by an omnipotent parent—a wish every client harbors throughout most of the treatment (Freud, 1937)—gets squelched abruptly, on "the great parent's" returning to a more therapeutic role, the client feels robbed. Feeling robbed by the therapist, the client wants to rob the therapist. The best way a client can gratify the revengeful fantasy to rob the therapist is to quit treatment. This is frequently the final outcome when the ground rules of treatment are stretched. If the client doesn't quit treatment, he or she rarely grows from the experience.

One of the main reasons that clients who are accomplices in breaking ground rules of therapy either do not make much progress in treatment or quit treatment altogether is because their therapists have not encouraged them to examine their defiance, grandiosity, and whatever else propels their disruptive behavior. Their therapists have encouraged them, in effect, to act out rather than to try to understand themselves.

When therapists use the therapy honeymoon to provide an orgy of indulgences to their clients, at some point they are obliged to examine their antitherapeutic behavior. Those practitioners who do not want to enforce the ground rules of the therapy are those who usually derive vicarious gratification from their clients' non-adherence to the rules. They are similar to parents who aid and abet their children's antisocial behavior. As they observe their clients breaking rules, in many ways they experience themselves as breaking rules.

As suggested, if clinicians are frightened to be the target of their clients' hostility, usually they feel they deserve the hostility and also feel their clients are entitled to it. When therapists do not enforce ground rules, usually they do not want their clients to obey them and, like their clients, they have an abhorrence of rules. They do not want to analyze their own rebelliousness nor do they want their clients to analyze theirs. Unconsciously, they prefer to act out with their clients. If their clients quit treatment or do not grow therapeutically, these practitioners can derive unconscious satisfaction from their clients' final rebellious act—premature termination—

and also maintain their resistance to facing the rebelliousness in themselves and their client.

Beverly Yates was a social worker in a child guidance clinic working with Ms. B., a woman in her early thirties and the mother of eight-year-old Harold. Harold was referred to the clinic by school officials because of his very disruptive behavior in the classroom. He defied teachers, fought with peers, and seemed to have little motivation to learn. Ms. B. pointed out rather early in her treatment that Harold "was just as bad" at home. He defied both parents constantly and was very belligerent toward his younger sister.

During the six weekly sessions that Ms. B. had with Beverly Yates, the client spent most of the time talking about how difficult it was to limit Harold; no matter how hard she tried, it never worked. Beverly listened attentively, empathized with Ms. B., and told her how Harold was "one big handful."

Ms. B. arrived about 10 to 15 minutes late for her seventh, eighth, and ninth sessions, but Beverly did not comment on this. She felt that Ms. B. was under so much pressure that she did not want to put her under more.

At the end of the eleventh session, Ms. B. told Beverly that she wouldn't be in for her "conversation" with her the following week. An old friend from college would be in town and it was one of the few times that Ms. B. "would be able to just let down and gab." Beverly, again feeling concerned about the enormity of the pressure on her client, told her, "Have a good time, you need it!"

At the following session, Ms. B. arrived on time and told Beverly how much she enjoyed the meeting with her friend. She assumed that she would not have to pay the clinic for the missed session and told her therapist, "I not only had a good time, but I saved some money. I'm glad you are so understanding of how much I have to cope with, and I love you for how you try to reduce the pressure on me."

Ms. B.'s remarks encouraged Beverly to be "a kind mother figure who lets her daughter enjoy life." Ms. B. enjoyed Beverly's "kindnesses" and more and more came to the sessions looking and behaving like a teenager. She wore socks, sweaters with insignias, jeans, and used the language of a teeny-bopper. Concomitant with this regressive behavior, Ms. B. resumed coming to sessions late, missed appointments "to have fun," and accumulated a debt at the clinic.

On Beverly Yates's attempt to confront Ms. B. about the financial arrears, Ms. B. became very indignant. She bellowed at Beverly in a session during the fifth month of their work, "You are a real bitch. You told me to take life easy, that you want to reduce the pressures on me, and now you are on my back trying to get money out of me! What the hell is wrong with you?"

Beverly, shocked at Ms. B.'s vituperative behavior, became extremely defensive and said, "I received this notice from the fee department and . . . ." Ms. B. interrupted her and exclaimed, "And you had to bring it up! You couldn't control yourself, could you?" As Beverly was attempting to restore some calm in their interaction, Ms. B. walked out of the interview.

Ms. B. did not come for the next three sessions despite Beverly's calling her on the telephone several times "to come in and talk over" what had transpired. As Beverly was about to give up, Ms. B. called her and said she wanted to come in and make "a request." Beverly, glad to hear from her, made an appointment. With her fees unpaid and clad in torn garments, Ms. B. came into the interview obviously drunk. Beverly, again shocked, tried to have a normal interchange with Ms. B., but it was virtually impossible to do so. Ms. B. could not recall what "request" she had in mind. In her inebriated state, she alternated between laughing and crying, but it was too difficult to understand her.

Ms. B.'s drunken interview was her last with Beverly. In a phone conversation with Beverly, in which she appeared to be sober, Ms. B. told Beverly that she thought a clinic that worked with Alcoholics Anonymous would be "better" for her now.

In a staff seminar on work with parents of children in therapy, Beverly Yates was able to discuss the case of Ms. B. with her colleagues and to learn a great deal about herself and about her client. Although Beverly regretted that she was not able to present the case of Ms. B. to her peers when the client was in treatment, the lessons learned helped her to cope much better in the future with clients like Ms. B.

Beverly became aware of the fact that the parent's presenting problem of the child is usually a description of the parent (Aichorn, 1925). In telling Beverly that her son, Harold, was rebelling against controls, Ms. B. was unconsciously presenting a part of herself that needed help. As Ms. B. demonstrated later, she could not control her drinking, seemed rebellious in the way she talked and dressed, and obviously had a problem keeping appointments and paying bills.

For Harold to be helped, his mother needed help in mastering her impulses, not in having them gratified (Nagelberg, 1959). Instead of ignoring her latenesses, cancellations, and delinquent payments, Beverly should have addressed these issues and explored with Ms. B. what she was feeling and thinking when she found it difficult to adhere to these ground rules. Anger from Ms. B. may have come out in smaller doses had the client been confronted with her acting out earlier in the treatment. Instead, Beverly promoted her client's acting out and then abruptly questioned it. This made Beverly appear like an inconsistent, teasing, insensitive, and perhaps cruel parent. Hence, Ms. B. reacted with enormous rage and regressed further.

Because the therapist fostered regression and acting out rather than progression, mastery, and self-understanding, Ms. B. had little opportunity or desire to share her alcohol problem with Beverly. Instead, Ms. B. became in the therapeutic situation what Harold became at school—a rebel without cause.

In her further supervision and personal therapy, Beverly Yates was able to come to a better understanding and mastery of her own wish to rebel. She realized that just as Ms. B. derived vicarious satisfaction from identifying with Harold's rebelliousness, she unconsciously enjoyed Ms. B.'s rebelliousness. And just as she would have felt narcissistically insulted if her therapist had examined her wishes to fight controls, she protected her client from what seemed to her could be taken as an attack.

As Beverly became more sensitive to and more understanding of the Ms. B. and Harold in herself, she did not have to use her clients to fight voices in her own superego. Beverly realized that many of her counterresistances in her work with Ms. B. were resistances in her own personal treatment. She recognized that a constructive and helpful way to become more sensitive to her own counterresistances with clients was to review what she, herself, was struggling with in her own treatment.

Beverly Yates's insights can be profitably utilized by most clinicians, not only during the honeymoon phase of treatment, but also during the entire treatment process. As we have reiterated, clients' complaints about sons, daughters, mates, and significant others are frequently descriptions about the clients themselves. What clients criticize in others are frequently cover-ups for self-descriptions and self-appraisals. The therapist, in working with a nonconformist client, has to be in touch with his or her own nonconforming wishes; otherwise, the therapist will unconsciously collude with the client and promote regression and acting out.

These issues are particularly relevant when practitioners have to deal with their clients' resistances and their own counterresistances as they both encounter the first treatment crisis. We will focus particularly on the resolution of those counterresistances aroused by the first treatment crisis in the next chapter.

4

The First Treatment Crisis and the
Therapist's Counterresistances

"The honeymoon is over" is a frequent statement uttered by many individuals in many different circumstances. The phrase has its origins, no doubt, in describing the inevitable time in every romance when bliss recedes and reality asserts itself. However, the phrase has not been used only to describe the ebbing of bliss in a romance. It is not lovers alone who stop idealizing each other and begin to recognize their partners as mortals with limitations and vulnerabilities; the same phenomenon occurs between parents and children, teachers and students, and, of course, between therapists and their clients.

For the individuals involved, it is usually a very difficult time. Fantasies that were stimulated get punctured, hopes that were raised become frustrated, and expectations that were activated are not realized. As experts in the field of marriage note (Grunebaum & Christ, 1976; Segraves, 1982), after a few months of ecstasy, mates can become so disillusioned with each other that divorce during the first year of marriage is common. So too in psychotherapy—treatment relationships often end permanently after the honeymoon is over (Perlman, 1968).

There is a strong similarity between the behavior of marital pairs and therapy dyads as they try to cope with the disappointment, frustrations, hurts, and angers. Some husbands and wives become so disappointed with each other as they grapple with punctured fantasies, ungratified hopes, and unmet expectations that they demean the whole institution of marriage and vow never to marry again. Clients and therapists do something similar. There are many clients who appear like scorned lovers after several months to a year of treatment and vow they will have nothing to do with psychotherapy in any form again. Although only a small percentage of clinicians leave the field of psychotherapy after experiencing a series of disappointing and ungratifying therapeutic encounters with clients, many practitioners, particularly in their early days of practice, have many and frequent fantasies of abandoning their work and looking for greener pastures.

During their first major marital crisis, many husbands and wives spend a great deal of time complaining about each other. They are quite convinced that a much better partner is available somewhere. The much better mate will be more understanding, more gratifying, more supportive, more sensitive, and more and more of everything. Clients and therapists respond similarly. During the first treatment crisis, clients often accuse their therapists of depriving them of what they desperately need—more love, more understanding, more sensitivity, more support, and more responsiveness. And practitioners have their complaints, as well. They tell their supervisors, colleagues, friends, and sometimes even their clients that the latter are unmotivated, uncooperative, too narcissistic, quite psychopathic, very resistive, lack an observing ego, and have an infantile character structure with too much id showing and not enough superego in evidence. Like their clients, they yearn for a better therapy partner who will report and analyze more dreams more often, act out less, fantasy more, introspect more deeply, and relate to them in a more "object-oriented" fashion.

During the first marital crisis, partners often discuss changing their lifestyles and try to open up new dimensions of communication and relatedness. They may consider moving from a closed marriage to an open one, from a monogamous one to a marriage where each of them has other sexual partners. Of course, therapists and clients do the same. They discuss changing the therapeutic modality from one-to-one psychotherapy to couples therapy, family therapy, or group therapy. The frequency of sessions is reconsidered with some dyads wanting to see less of each other, while others believe that increased frequency might get them out of their therapeutic doldrums and dilemmas. Clients tell therapists to be more active, more responsive, and more interpretive, while therapists tell clients to be more verbal, more introspective, and more related.

Specialists in marital relations (Ackerman, 1958; Lloyd & Paulson, 1972) have noted that when partners undergo crises and experience much anger, sadness, and an array of other uncomfortable emotions, they are also quick to ascribe the source of their discomfort to their role partners. The same phenomenon tends to occur among therapy partners as well. Clients become quite convinced that the reason the therapy is not moving well is because of the practitioner's insensitivity and incompetence, and many practitioners become quite certain their clients are responding neurotically and irrationally because of their clients' negative transferences, which always have their roots in the latter's history!

Much of the literature concerning the first treatment crisis focuses on what occurs dynamically to the client. Not much attention is devoted to the therapist's role, activity, and subjective state. This is, of course, in consonance with everything we have noted about resistance in the therapeutic process. Much has been said about the client's resistances; little has been discussed that relates to the therapist's counterresistances.

Inasmuch as therapists are more similar to than different from their clients in virtually every dimension of living, and because we would like to focus this chapter on the psychological state of the practitioner during the first treatment crisis, it may be helpful to review first some of the major concerns of the client during this time. What we get to know about the client during the first treatment crisis can serve as a springboard for discussion of the therapist's role during this time.

When clients' expectations are dashed, their fantasies punctured, and their hopes unrealized, the therapist, instead of emerging as a loving partner to the client, begins to appear as a rough and tough taskmaster. Clients now begin to view the therapist as their own punitive superego. With a punitive superego figure as their therapist, clients feel unappreciated, unloved, and ungratified.

The first treatment crisis may be conceptualized as the first major resistance in therapy. Usually, if not always, it is accompanied by a negative transference, with wishes to terminate the treatment. The client's hostility at this time takes many forms—criticism of the therapist's office, dress, voice, diction, fee schedule, appointment time, and so on. According to Reuben Fine (1982), three major reasons account for the client's first treatment crisis, with its sudden shift from a positive to a negative transference:

1. The superego reasserts itself. Things have been going too well, and the client unconsciously is looking for punishment.
2. The id becomes too threatening. Sexual and aggressive fantasies create considerable anxiety.
3. The relationship becomes too close. The client feels frightened of warm, positive, and intimate feelings toward the therapist.

Glover (1955), who discusses the first treatment crisis but mainly from the perspective of the client, talks about a source of the client's anger at this time. Many clients become quite hostile when the practitioner "sits on the fence on all ethical issues" (p. 65). The client, feeling uncomfortable with the release of id material, wants the therapist to reward or to punish, and when the therapist does not comply, the client would like to punish the therapist.

THE THERAPIST'S SUPEREGO ASSERTS ITSELF

As we have suggested several times, the therapist is as vulnerable to mental stresses as is the client. Consequently, therapists can find themselves moving toward a negative countertransference from a positive one when the clients cease loving or admiring them. It is also possible for practitioners to become frightened of their own id wishes that have been stimulated by the honeymoon and begin to project their own superego injunctions onto their clients. Most practitioners who like to view themselves as freers of libido and champions of the id may find it quite difficult to accept the fact that they are frightened of fantasies to became symbiotic with their clients, to feed or be fed by them, to smear or be smeared by them, or to have genital sex with them. As we have seen in case examples from earlier chapters, therapists can resist facing forbidden id material and turn themselves and their clients into hard-working superego figures.

Furthermore, just as clients may fear an intimate relationship because it arouses unacceptable incestuous, homosexual, or other anxiety-provoking drives, a therapist can experience "the honeymoon" as something forbidden and unconsciously try to destroy it.

Jeremy Xerxes, a therapist in private practice, was treating one of his first clients in analytic therapy. Up until now he was seeing clients once or twice a week, but Ms. C., a single woman in her late twenties, was in treatment four times a week with Jeremy and had been using the couch for the last five months of her therapy. Altogether she had been in treatment with Jeremy for about seven months.

Ms. C. wanted to have intensive therapy because she was extremely frightened of relating to men. On dates with them, she suffered from gastrointestinal problems, was totally inhibited sexually, and she would become tongue-tied and sweaty.

In discussing her history, Ms. C. was able to share with Jeremy her conviction that her father did not love her but preferred her younger brother and that her mother did not love her either, preferring her older sister. As Ms. C. discussed her feelings of hurt, anger, and loss with Jeremy, she felt enormously relieved. "Feeling really loved and cared for for the first time in my life is a wonderful experience," said Ms. C. enthusiastically during the third month of treatment. She began to have one insight after another, her self-esteem rose by leaps and bounds, her anxiety with men diminished tremendously, and she was much more productive on her job. With each step forward that Ms. C. took, she attributed all of her success to her therapist.

As the treatment moved on and as Ms. C. continued to make progress in her love life and in her work, she began to have many erotic dreams that involved Jeremy. While she was turning Jeremy into a highly desirable oedipal father figure in her daily life, she was competing successfully with other women for their men. Jeremy began to view Ms. C.'s behavior as "destructive and self-destructive acting out." From a position of benign understanding and much tolerance for Ms. C.'s libidinal wishes, he began to make interpretations that, at least to Ms. C., sounded very critical. He told her that she seemed to be wanting "to take fathers away from mothers and was extremely involved in a war." Ms. C. felt crushed by Jeremy's interpretations and began to become very angry with him, telling him that in many ways she experienced him as if he were both her rejecting father and mother. From loving Jeremy, she became hateful toward him, criticizing his "rigid Freudian approach," his office, his clothes, and his "insensitive" attitude.

Although at first Jeremy attributed all of Ms. C.'s negative feelings toward him to her first treatment crisis, in which she was feeling like a "frustrated oedipal daughter," in supervision he was eventually able to confront his own fears of intimacy with Ms. C. As he analyzed his anxieties he discovered that Ms. C.'s therapeutic progress during the honeymoon phase of treatment was experienced by him as his own oedipal victory. Feeling too triumphant over the father figures in his life (his supervisor, his analyst, and some teachers current and past), he had to interfere with Ms. C.'s fantasied oedipal triumphs, punish her for them, and punish himself for his own "victories."

Although there was a lot of truth to the content of Jeremy's interpretations in that Ms. C. psychologically was involved in oedipal triangles and therefore was in a psychological war, Jeremy's timing of his statements was premature and his tone was much too harsh. Particularly with an inhibited client like Ms. C. it would have been helpful to her for Jeremy to remain neutral and quiet. This would have afforded the client the opportunity to reflect on her activity in an uncharged, relaxed, neutral setting. Eventually, through her dreams, fantasies, and transference reactions, Ms. C. might have moved toward more understanding of her oedipal conflicts. However, when her loving therapist emerged as a tyrannical superego figure, she could no longer examine herself but had to defend herself instead.

Ms. C., like all clients, would have eventually experienced disappointment and dejection in her relationship with her therapist. However, she was forced to face reality too quickly. The inevitable treatment crisis was provoked too abruptly and too early by her therapist, who was resisting facing his own oedipal conflicts. In effect, Jeremy Xerxes, acutely anxious because he had distorted his client's therapeutic movement and turned it into a grandiose triumph for himself, became very guilty in response to his fantasied transgressions. To ease his own guilt, he stopped his client from moving forward in therapy.

Jeremy Xerxes' behavior in his work with Ms. C. is reminiscent of a "Character Wrecked by Success" (Freud, 1916). Distorting the meaning of his real success with his client and using it to buttress his grandiose fantasies of being a triumphant oedipal winner, Jeremy had to stop his victorious escapade. His therapeutic work with Ms. C. was to him a forbidden sexual affair, and he had to become a superego figure to his client, rather than an understanding therapist. To Jeremy, being an understanding therapist felt like being an illicit lover. As we have reiterated, though the treatment crisis between Ms. C. and Jeremy Xerxes would have evolved, the therapist precipitated it out of his own anxiety.

What we appreciate more after reviewing the case of Jeremy Xerxes and Ms. C. is that one of the major ways of helping a client work through conflicts is through a benign and constructive therapeutic relationship. The client must see that the responses of the therapist are different from his own punitive superego. When that occurs, impulses are more readily acknowledged, and the need for resistances are less urgent. Reuben Fine's statement on this dimension of psychotherapy is pertinent.

> The patient produces material that contains forbidden impulses. True to his or her past, the patient punishes himself or herself for these impulses. The therapist . . . [the] new superego, does not give any punishment but merely understands the impulse. As this continues, the patient feels less and less threatened by his or her impulses. Eventually, the patient can talk about them freely, which gives him or her the possibility of rational choice; that is, the patient can now choose those impulses that can be given reality gratification and discard those that cannot. In either case, he or she makes choices on a conscious, rational basis whereas before the patient was driven compulsively to act in certain ways that were too often self-destructive. (1982, p. 240)

THE THERAPIST'S GRANDIOSE FANTASIES AND THE FIRST TREATMENT CRISIS

As we observed in the above case illustration, one of the major factors in the premature, abrupt, and tempestuous treatment crisis was the therapist's unresolved grandiose fantasies. As we have discussed other counterresistance problems in previous chapters, the clinician's difficulty with his or her own omnipotence has been a crucial variable in therapeutic impasses. It seems to be an important factor in the clinician's own contribution to many of the difficulties of the first and later treatment crises.

It has often been asked if psychotherapists have more problems coping with omnipotent fantasies than those individuals who work in other fields. This question is difficult to answer with certainty. However, if we understand more clearly some of the factors involved in sustaining grandiose fantasies, we may be able to become more aware of how and why psychotherapists cope the way they do.

We all feel omnipotent when we are infants. It is a time in our lives when we all want to be kings, queens, princes, and princesses (Freud, 1914b). Our cries are our parents' commands and we expect them and others around us to dote on us incessantly. It is a period of our lives when we are governed almost exclusively by the pleasure principle, and this period has been variously termed nirvana, oceanic bliss, and paradise.

Although psychosocial development requires that we slowly give up our kingdoms, take on some frustration, and accept the fact that we are not that special or unique, this is not an easy task for anyone to master. We all wish to return to the position of being a king or god, and the more difficult life is, the more we are desirous of returning to the infantile omnipotent state.

It is often overlooked that those individuals who refuse to appear vulnerable, who cannot admit mistakes or acknowledge limitations or inconsistencies in their character or behavior, feel quite weak but cannot face this fact. A dramatic example of this is the patient in the mental hospital who is suffering acutely from terror, paranoia, delusions, and hallucinations. This patient might insist that he is Napoleon, Jesus Christ, or God! Similar to the small boy who feels quite miniscule next to his big father but carries four guns and calls himself Superman, those clients who call themselves Napoleon and insist on their own supremacy are defending themselves against the humiliating feeling of being a "nobody."

If we can accept the notion that those individuals who are frequently bombarded by omnipotent fantasies really feel quite impotent and vulnerable, then the plight of psychotherapists becomes eminently more understandable. Psychotherapists, it would appear, feel weak and vulnerable much of the time but have to defend against recognizing this. Why should this be so?

In doing psychotherapy, clinicians, whether they realize it or not, are inevitably feeling within themselves their clients' anxieties, conflicts, doubts, terror, and shame. As we have stressed, the empathetic clinician is one who can put himself or herself in the client's psychological shoes and feel the client's pain. Often this pain feels overwhelming and stirs up painful memories as well as current conflicts of the therapist's. If the latter is supposed to help alleviate the client's distress, he or she may feel that it is imperative to deny his or her own psychological pains and aches and to make every effort to repress his or her identification with the client. A seemingly "helpful" way to deny one's similarity to the vulnerable and weak client is to become the client's opposite, a superman or superwoman, who has everything under control and feels nothing but strength.

As clinicians listen to their clients' associations and sense the complexity of their clients' dynamics, they feel baffled if they are at all honest with themselves. As a matter of fact, it has been noted that the more mature, sensitive clinician who achieves good results with clients allows for a frequent feeling of confusion and uncertainty in himself or herself (Fine, 1982). It is the less mature, less sensitive, and less successful practitioner who works hard to appear to be a "know-it-all."

Inasmuch as therapists feel baffled much of the time, confused and uncertain most of the time, and very clear about what is really happening in the therapeutic process only a small portion of the time, they have to mobilize defenses to cope with this ever-present state of acute discomfort. It is disconcerting, particularly for beginning therapists, to feel and act as experts when they do not know what is really taking place with their clients and within themselves. To ward off their feelings of impotence, ineptness, and ignorance, they are quick to offer "sure" advice, "accurate" and usually long interpretations, and, if necessary, show their clients how the clients are not doing their jobs properly.

If therapists need to appear like healthy, competent doctors who know it all and can always dispense the right medicine, then they are going to try to keep their clients in the position of the sick, incompetent patients who know little and are not equipped to come up with any of the correct prescriptions for their maladies. Therefore, if the client objects to the therapist's procedures, questions the wisdom of being in therapy, or has any negative reaction to the clinician's style, all of which usually occurs as the therapy honeymoon moves toward its end, the therapist is going to covertly or overtly obstruct the client's attempts to be critical, negative, or antagonistic.

One way in which the therapist's grandiosity surfaces toward the end of the honeymoon is to deny that the client is feeling less loving or admiring. To maintain the feeling of omnipotence, the therapist tries to maintain the conviction that the client is just as much in love with the therapist in the present as the client was during the initial period of the therapy honeymoon. This form of denial is very similar to the threatened spouse who cannot tolerate the fact that the marital partner is moving away emotionally from him or her and keeps reassuring himself or herself that all is just as blissful as ever. In effect, the frightened therapist, like the frightened spouse, denies that there is a treatment crisis and works overtime to keep the client on a perennial honeymoon.

Anita Witte, a social worker in a family agency, was treating Ms. D., a senior citizen in her late seventies. Ms. D. had been a widow for over five years and was finding living alone very difficult. She was often depressed, suffered from insomnia almost nightly, and found it very hard to enjoy being with her friends or family. Her physician referred her to the social agency "because she needed somebody to talk to."

During the first five months of twice-a-week treatment, Ms. D. made a lot of progress. As she was helped by Anita Witte to bring out her sadness, loneliness, and anger, she began to sleep better, eat better, and could begin to enjoy being with some of her friends and family. This included a son and daughter, both married with children, who lived in the same community as Ms. D.

Ms. D. easily acknowledged how much better she was feeling since she started working with Anita. She referred to her as her "stepdaughter" and told Anita how she "breathed life" into her, "saved" her life, and "made life worthwhile." Anita very much enjoyed the accolades coming from her client and returned Ms. D.'s laudatory remarks about her with praises of her own for the client. Therapist and client reinforced each other and created a blissful symbiosis, which was intense.

Inevitably, some of Ms. D.'s ambivalence toward her own daughter started to emerge in her transference relationship with Anita. The first sign of this was when Ms. D. told her therapist that the latter probably had better things to do than to spend time with her. Rather than explore Ms. D.'s mistrust and emerging ambivalence toward her, Anita offered reassurance and told her client "the truth," saying she "enjoyed" being with her. Although flattered, Ms. D. told Anita that she was "just being polite."

In an interview about a week later, Ms. D. told Anita that she really had some reservations about taking up her own time and Anita's time when "other people needed it so much." Again, Anita told Ms. D. that she "had every right to be helped and the time spent is well spent."

As the treatment continued, Ms. D. became more resistant, coming late for interviews and cancelling several. Anita did not explore with her client what was transpiring between them that sparked Ms. D.'s obvious negative behavior. Instead, she accepted Ms. D.'s rationalizations and kept pointing out that Ms. D. had "a right to be late" and "a right to take care of other business rather than feel pressured to come to interviews."

Early in her eighth month of therapy, Ms. D. told Anita that she felt much more comfortable with her own daughter now and wanted to discontinue her treatment at the agency. Anita, shocked and feeling rejected, blurted out spontaneously, with tears in her eyes and with her throat choked, "You mean you are going to leave me?" Ms. D. soothingly but patronizingly said, "You'll manage to get along without me. I did it by myself and you can do it, too." Anita was so upset about the possibility of losing Ms. D. that she became very helpless and could say no more. Ms. D., sensing her therapist's despondency, reassuringly said that she would come back for her last session next week.

Several supervisory sessions and help from her own therapist enabled Anita to get in touch with several of her own resistances that were interfering with her work with Ms. D. First, Anita was able to see that because of her very strong investment in maintaining a mutually positive relationship with Ms. D., she had deflected most of Ms. D.'s hostility. Second, Anita was able to become aware of her competition with Ms. D.'s children, particularly her daughter, and her strong wish to emerge as Ms. D.'s favorite child. Because of this she could not bear being rejected in any way by Ms. D. nor hear any of Ms. D.'s misgivings about treatment. Fourth, the basis of much of Ms. D.'s resistance to treatment was a fear of her stong dependency wishes. Because Anita wanted Ms. D. to be dependent on her, love her, admire her, and appreciate her, she could not relate to Ms. D.'s strong anxiety about being attached but instead tried to encourage her client to continue being passively dependent. This was very threatening to Ms. D. who did not wish to confront her desires to be a dependent little girl with her therapist. Therefore, she had to fight her dependency wishes and tried to project them onto her therapist and make Anita into a suffering little girl who would be bereft. Anita "cooperated."

Armed with more knowledge about herself and about Ms. D., Anita was able to restore a working relationship with Ms. D. She was able to tell her client that she, Anita, had the impression that she was pressuring Ms. D. too much to become more attached to her than Ms. D. felt comfortable with. Ms. D. acknowledged that this was so, and feeling more understood, she could then discuss some of her resentment toward Anita more directly. She told Anita that at first coming to see her was "wonderful," but after a while it "became too much." She said that she did not want to depend on anybody and that Anita was encouraging her too much in this direction. This time Anita was able to be more empathetic and therapeutic and asked Ms. D. what was worrisome about relying on her social worker a great deal. Ms. D. told her the answer: "Sometimes I think you want me to be a little girl and this is impossible. Sometimes I think you want to be my mother and this is also impossible. Sometimes I think you want to be my daughter and this, too, is impossible!"

As Anita continued to examine her counterresistances in more depth and breadth, she began to realize that there was a Ms. D. in herself that felt lonely, needy, and frightened. For many years Anita had fought her own strong dependency needs by appearing very independent and taking care of others. Her defense of reaction formation, that is, appearing independent and strong to ward off passive wishes to be a child, became punctured in her work with Ms. D. As long as Ms. D. was "the passive child" who relied on Anita, Anita could feel comfortable. However, when her client began to defend against her own dependency by striving for more autonomy, Anita was left feeling her strong wishes for Ms. D. who was a loving mother to her on one hand and a dependent daughter on the other.

Anita did not recognize how much *she* needed a symbiosis with her client in order to feel a sense of self-worth and competency. Her client's evolving negative transference threatened Anita's sense of omnipotence. Consequently, she had to keep deflecting Ms. D.'s hostility and fighting her own.

If therapists need a symbiosis with the client to feel a positive sense of self, then they are going to fight the client's expressions of hostility. If the client cannot discharge the inevitable hostility that is always part of the first treatment crisis, he or she may leave the treatment and act out the hostility. In the case of Ms. D., Anita became aware of what was transpiring before her client prematurely terminated. In some cases the client leaves treatment altogether before the therapist is aware of what resistances and counterresistances are at work.

WHY DO CLIENTS LEAVE TREATMENT DURING THE FIRST TREATMENT CRISIS?

If therapists feel compelled to protect themselves by maintaining a grandiose self-image, they are not going to be able to listen to their clients' anxieties, concerns, and transference reactions that are not in consonance with what they want to hear.

This is certainly what seemed to occur with Anita Witte in the above case illustration. As we have suggested several times in previous chapters and in this chapter as well, one of the most anxiety-provoking situations for therapists who have to maintain an image of one who consistently is loved and who is consistently competent is to be the recipient of the client's hostility.

As Ticho (1972) pointed out, when clinicians are the object of the client's negative feelings and thoughts, their own conflicts are activated frequently and they use their habitual defenses to deflect the client's hostility. Often the conflicts of the client's that spark the negative transference may be similar to the therapist's (Sonnenberg, 1991), and the therapist, to protect himself or herself from pain, may unconsciously arrange "to help" the client leave treatment before the first treatment crisis is resolved.

> Aaron Victor, a psychologist in private practice, had been treating Mr. E., a man in his early thirties, for about five months. Mr. E. came to see Aaron Victor because he was having marital conflicts. Seen twice a week, Mr. E. had been able to overcome severe impotency problems and to monitor angry outbursts, which led to drunkenness and depression. As he functioned much better sexually and interpersonally, and relied much less on alcohol to bolster his self-esteem, Mr. E. felt very grateful to Aaron Victor and commended him for his superb clinical skills and outstanding human kindness.
>
> As Mr. E. was extolling his therapist, he also began to compare Aaron with other father figures in his present and past. He referred at various times to his current boss as a "know it all," to the minister of his church as "arrogant and authoritarian," and to the golf pro at his country club as "smug." What Aaron Victor did not recognize was that his client was splitting the father transference, making his therapist "the good father" and all other paternal figures "the bad father." It is always important for the therapist to understand the splitting of the transference in order to help the client through the first treatment crisis. If the practitioner does not recognize that the client's constant negative references to parental figures are also references to the therapist, albeit unconscious ones, and must eventually be faced in the treatment, the client will be forced to act out his hostility. This is what happened with Mr. E.
>
> As Mr. E. disparaged his boss, his minister, and his golf pro, Aaron felt exempted from these character assassinations and therefore could not help his client face his negative transference toward him. On Mr. E.'s demeaning the father figures in his life, Aaron often found himself smiling since he enjoyed experiencing the contrast between himself and them. However, in one session during the early part of the seventh month of treatment, Mr. E. asked Aaron, "Have you ever disliked guys like my boss or like my minister?" Aaron, feeling uncomfortable at being questioned, unsure of how to answer, responded mechanically and asked, "What do you think?" Mr. E., very upset

at Aaron's response, stated vehemently, "You are pulling that Freudian crap! I thought you were a decent guy! What the hell is the matter with you? You know, I think you are something like those bastards I've been talking about." On hearing his client's critical comments, Aaron became speechless and to this Mr. E. became exasperated. Mr. E. said, "First you ask stupid and unrelated questions and then you give me the silent treatment!"

The temper tantrums that Mr. E. had been having previously with his wife now became manifest with Aaron. And, just as Mr. E. followed up his temper tantrums in his marital disputes with excessive drinking and depressive moods, this behavior occurred during his eighth and ninth months of treatment with Aaron. Feeling disgusted with himself and experiencing acute disappointment with his therapist, Mr. E. left treatment permanently.

Subjecting the premature termination of Mr. E.'s therapy to examination, Aaron Victor discovered the reasons for his counterresistive behavior with his client. Aaron was not able to see the split in his client's father transference and did not want to hear Mr. E.'s hostile criticisms because these were criticisms that Aaron was feeling toward his own supervisor. Just as Mr. E. could not face his negative transference toward his therapist, Aaron could not face his hostility toward his supervisor. Further, just as Mr. E. found it difficult to face certain resentments toward his own father, this was happening to Aaron Victor while treating his client.

During the time that Aaron was seeing Mr. E., his own father was very ill, suffering from terminal cancer. Aaron was so preoccupied with the loss of his father that he could not face his own death wishes toward him. Not able to face these feelings, he could not hear his client's death wishes toward him and unconsciously arranged for his client to act out his wish to kill his "therapist-father." By the end of their relationship, Aaron had placed his client in the same position as he was in—deprived of a father.

In reviewing the Aaron Victor–Mr. E. case, we recognize that the psychotherapist "does not lead a life of separate compartments: all experiences are, or can be, connected; those that are seemingly disconnected to current clinical practice potentially can be put to clinical use by the [therapist]" (Sonnenberg, 1991, p. 689). Consequently, self-analysis is a part of the clinician's life experience in and out of the consulting room (McLaughlin, 1981; 1991; Sonnenberg, 1991).

REEMERGENCE OF SYMPTOMS DURING THE FIRST TREATMENT CRISIS

As the bliss of the honeymoon phase of therapy recedes, as the client's positive transference ebbs and becomes more ambivalent, and as resistances return, the client's symptoms also reemerge and often become exacerbated. If the clinician, as part of his or her omnipotence, cannot tolerate the client's regression, he or she may not deal with the issues that need attending to, for example, current negative transference fantasies, current resistances, and/or negative therapeutic reactions. Instead, the therapist may try to cope with feelings of impotence by acting out his or her own negative countertransference feelings and distorting the meaning of the client's treatment crisis. The therapist may see the client as "borderline," "psychopathic," or as "an ambulatory schizophrenic" (Fine, 1982). Convinced that the client is too sick to introspect and/or form a therapeutic alliance, the therapist, out of desperation, may try to arrange for a different therapeutic modality (Strean, 1985/1990).

Stephanie Ure, a social worker who had been in private practice for a little over a year, was treating Mr. F. for his gambling addiction. After trying several self-help groups without too much success, Mr. F. found Stephanie Ure "to be very compassionate and helpful." Mr. F., a man in his mid-thirties, noted that he was about the same age as Stephanie; rather early in the therapy, he was free to express warm and loving feelings and fantasies toward her.

While in the honeymoon phase of treatment, Mr. F. discontinued his gambling and began to work steadily as a clothing salesman. Prior to his work with Stephanie, Mr. F. worked only intermittently, with his wife being the main financial support of the family. From the second through the eighth month of treatment, Mr. F. functioned well and consistently on his job, in his marriage, and he did not gamble.

In the ninth month of treatment when Mr. F. was offered the opportunity to become a manager in the department where he worked, he became very agitated. Although he wanted to prove to himself and to Stephanie that he was capable of assuming a leadership position, he became sweaty, had severe heart palpitations and gastrointestinal problems, and was very phobic almost every time he pictured himself in the role.

On noting her client's regression, Stephanie Ure began to regress, too. Rather than trying to understand Mr. F.'s fears of leadership and his possible phallic-oedipal conflicts, Stephanie began to give Mr. F. advice. She instructed him to agree to take the manager's job for two months and to see how it would go. This advice compounded the client's resistances. He began to arrive late for his appointments with Stephanie and was late at work as well. Eventually, Mr. F. became quite depressed, argued frequently with his wife, and resumed gambling.

When Stephanie observed that her client had resumed gambling and was functioning at a level even worse than at the beginning of treatment, she told her supervisor that she had changed her diagnosis of Mr. F. She now was "quite convinced" that her client was "a borderline personality with sociopathic traits." She further contended that Mr. F. would do better in group

therapy "so that his object relations could be improved." Stephanie did not
have much desire to study her own reactions to Mr. F. but obsessed about
her client's diagnosis and the need to change to group therapy.

Stephanie's negative feelings toward Mr. F. were detected by him. In the
tenth month of his twice-a-week therapy, he told Stephanie, "I think you've
lost confidence in me. You used to listen to me more. Now you tell me what
to do. I think you are afraid that I'm going to crack up." Stephanie could
not face hearing an accurate interpretation of her counterresistances. Instead
of listening to her client's thoughts and exploring them further, she tended
to deny the validity of Mr. F.'s observations. Soon after that, Mr. F. left
treatment.

After Mr. F. left treatment, Stephanie was better able to examine some of her
counterresistances. She could not tolerate her client's regression because she could
not face what triggered it. Rather than help Mr. F. talk about his fear of progressing,
she squelched him to protect herself. Stephanie learned both from supervisory discussions and her own personal therapy how frightened she was of progressing in
life because of the hostile fantasies stimulated by thoughts of surpassing her older
sister. Similar to her client who was afraid to progress, she colluded with him by
not working out his fears and unconsciously arranged for him not to move ahead.

BODILY SYMPTOMS AND THE FIRST TREATMENT CRISIS

During the course of the first treatment crisis, clients who do not feel comfortable
in verbalizing their wishes and resentments often communicate them bodily
(Fenichel, 1945). Although somatic symptoms may be expressed during any phase
of the treatment process, many clients unconsciously resort to them during the first
treatment crisis. If these somatic symptoms are not properly understood and attended
to by client and therapist, the client may leave therapy.

Because a client's bodily ailments can conjure up frightening associations in the
therapist, there is often limited agreement among clinicians about diagnosing these
dysfunctions. For example, most dynamically oriented therapists would agree that
repressed affects and unresolved conflicts are at work in such bodily problems as
migraine headaches, insomnia, and asthma; yet, many clinicians find such a notion
unpalatable. For the therapist who has to know all, cure all, and cannot live too
easily with uncertainty, the idea of the client having bodily symptoms that should
be the therapist's concern, but which he or she is not affecting much, if at all, can
puncture the therapist's narcissism and diminish his or her self-esteem.

Therefore, rather than consider how to use himself or herself with more disci-
pline, the therapist denies the psychic components of the client's bodily ailments.
On the other hand, some clinicians insist that physical problems such as appen-

dicitis or athlete's foot are caused by psychic conflict. Apparently, these therapists have difficulty acknowledging that perhaps there are certain phenomena they cannot affect through psychotherapy.

Even among psychoanalytically oriented theorists and therapists who share many beliefs about personality functioning, psychopathology, and treatment, there has been strong disagreement about the nature of psychosomatic problems. Some psychoanalytic writers contend that psychosomatic illnesses are merely expressions of dammed-up excitation and tension and do not express a unique set of psychodynamic conflicts. Glover (1949), for example, averred that psychosomatic disorders have in themselves "no psychic content" and, consequently, do not present stereotyped patterns of conflict. He would, like many other psychoanalytic theorists, explain the particular zone of the body that is dysfunctional as a constitutionally vulnerable area. Yet, Fenichel (1945) concluded that the particular bodily zone selected reflects a unique psychological conflict. Bronchial asthma, for example, according to Fenichel and many other psychoanalytically oriented therapists, expresses a passive, receptive longing for the mother that manifests itself in pathological changes of the breathing function. The asthmatic seizure is an anxiety-equivalent cry for help directed toward the mother, whom the client tries to introject by respiration, in order to be permanently protected. Similarly, Fenichel and others with a similar orientation would explain dermatitis as crying out through the skin.

If therapists are rigidly wedded to one or another of the perspectives described, they will tend to fall into a position in which they will make many diagnostic errors. Adhering tenaciously to a stance like Glover's puts clinicians in a position in which they may avoid considering and empathizing with the specific painful feelings and conflicts a client with a grinding stomach, severe headache, or upsetting ulcer is experiencing unconsciously. By the same token, if the therapist is absolutely convinced that a particular somatic symptom has only one specific meaning to the client, the therapist will tend to overlook other possibilities that may be at work. For example, a severe headache may be a manifestation of one or more of the following possibilities: repressed anger, undischarged tears, part of a postconcussion syndrome that follows physical injury, self-punishment for anxiety-provoking and guilt-producing sexual or aggressive thoughts and feelings, and a host of other possibilities. The responsible therapist who wants to help the client resolve conflicts should be open to any possible set of etiological factors. Therefore he or she should monitor biases while carefully listening to the client's associations. In doing so, the clinician may learn that a common cold can at times express a wish to avoid sexual intimacy, that a migraine headache can be an overdetermined symptom, and a peptic ulcer can be a manifestation of much acidity in the stomach, a poor diet, and unresolved dependency wishes and unacceptable passive fantasies, that is, also an overdetermined symptom.

One of the most difficult psychosomatic ailments to diagnose is hypochondriasis. The client who obsesses about the body and avoids facing interpersonal and psychological conflicts can be quite irritating, particularly to those therapists who want to hear a great deal about fantasies, dreams, history, and transference reactions. Therefore, it has been tempting to see these clients as "medical problems" exclusively so that they can reject them and refer them to physicians for treatment.

Other defensive responses are often summoned up by clinicians when assessing these clients. A popular one is to label the hypochondriasis a defense against psychosis and to point out to the client that the latter is better off going untreated by a psychotherapist. Sometimes it is quite difficult for therapists to consider the possibility that hypochondriasis may be viewed as an attempt on the part of the client to have the therapist and/or others become alert to his or her shaky body, comfort it, and hold it (Fenichel, 1945).

In making a comprehensive diagnostic assessment of a client's somatic problems, one common countertransference problem is a tendency to overidentify with the client and to accept all too readily the client's own diagnostic impressions, which may be made to defend against overwhelming anxiety. For example, a client with a severe prostate condition was able to convince his therapist that the problem was psychosomatic so that the therapist would agree that the client did not have to undergo surgery. Another client who had pruritis ani (itchy anus) was adamant about the fact that "nothing bothers me and nothing is a pain in my ass" because he wanted to avoid entering psychotherapy. He did convince his therapist that he was not suffering from any psychological difficulties and that psychotherapy should be ruled out.

In accepting a client's diagnosis, it is always important to try to understand the client's motives for making it. Many clients cannot cope with the finality of certain diseases such as cancer and therefore call the condition psychosomatic. By the same token, some clients cannot cope with the fact that they have unresolved psychological conflicts and would like to label conditions like ulcers or asthma as purely organic. It is conceivable that the perennial debates on such illnesses as epilepsy may be more indicative of the perennial biases of therapists that are part of counterresistive issues than they are reflective of issues such as insufficient research on the subject. Sometimes when therapists adamantly argue about whether epilepsy is an organic disease or an expression of intense frustration and anger whereby the client thrashes, kicks, and screams like an angry child, they themselves appear like angry children who are "protesting too much."

Because bodily hurt may be used at times by both children and adults to evoke sympathy, many clients and therapists have improperly diagnosed some organic diseases as forms of malingering. At times a severe case of multiple sclerosis, or lung cancer, or even a brain tumor has been diagnosed by both clients and therapists as psychosomatic illnesses, with the diagnosticians averring that the clients are "arranging to get sick" and appear like children who are trying to attract attention so that they will receive the tender ministrations of a parental figure. Most therapists, at one time or another, have met clients who suffer from real organic problems but feel guilty because they believe they have duped others into believing they need care and sympathy; their illness is nothing more than a psychological manipulation. These clients have internalized into their punitive superegos the notion that all bodily illnesses are attempts to exploit others and therefore they cannot accept the proper medical treatment: they are convinced that they are malicious gainers of attention and nothing else!

In diagnosing clients with bodily symptoms, it is crucial for therapists to be aware of their own biases and allow for many possibilities. The mind and body are in constant interaction and few human events when appraised can eliminate the contribution of both the psyche and the soma.

Clients with psychosomatic problems appear to induce in many therapists a wish to alter treatment procedures. In their overidentification with their clients' bodily distress, therapists often remove themselves from the psychotherapeutic situation. Instead of exposing their clients' psychic conflicts to them, they may become anxious, overzealous, overprotective parentlike figures. For example, when a therapist finds himself or herself prescribing or giving aspirins to a client with a migraine headache, he or she may be wishing to overlook the client's hostile transference, the client's extreme fear of expressing feelings to the therapist, and his or her own fear and discomfort in hearing the client express painful thoughts and feelings.

Once it is clear from the client's productions that certain psychological conflicts are at work, it is the therapist's responsibility to help the client feel and face these conflicts as they emerge through his or her transference reactions and resistive behavior. When therapists find they are frequently prescribing medication, making constant referrals to other professionals, or offering advice repeatedly, they can be quite certain they are trying to ease their own anxieties rather than to help their clients resolve the conflicts that have created their somatic problems. Further, when the therapist finds he or she is switching from one therapeutic modality to another, one theoretical perspective to another, vacillating from overactivity to withdrawal with the client, the therapist can be readily alerted to the fact that he or she is overly anxious about the client's bodily problem, so much that he has to abdicate from his role as an empathetic, neutral psychotherapist.

From time to time therapists in their overidentification with clients who somatize fail to recognize that many clients use psychosomatic ailments as a resistance. When the client is in a lot of pain, the therapist can overlook the fact that the client is frightened to face such issues as intense rage, infantile sexual fantasies, strong dependency yearnings, or wishes to spite and defeat the therapist. When unacceptable wishes and overwhelming anxieties are converted into psychosomatic symptoms, this is always an unconscious process. Consequently, clients who suffer from psychosomatic symptoms often find it difficult to take responsibility for their plight and instead tend to believe their ailments are imposed on them. Failing to see this behavior like any other form of resistance and waiting for the expression of the derivatives of unacceptable wishes, fantasies, memories, and so on, therapists can either prematurely tell clients that their somatic symptoms are psychologically based or abdicate from the possibility of helping the client face himself and herself.

Neither of the above therapeutic responses helps clients. When the client with a migraine headache, chronic backache, asthma, or ulcer is prematurely told he or she is suffering from psychological conflicts, he or she may become resentful and leave treatment, or as often occurs, repress and suppress his angry reactions toward the therapist and become worse. To join the client in never facing his or her inner conflicts is to indulge the client in a way that is destructive for the client and the therapy. The therapist who performs disciplined, effective, and empathic therapy with clients suffering from somatic problems always has to tread carefully between not ignoring the client's inner life with its often disturbing feelings, memories, fantasies, and thoughts and not imposing the client's dynamics on the client when he or she is not ready to confront his or her inner life.

A real difficulty in working with individuals who have psychosomatic problems is that they derive considerable secondary gain from their ailments. The client with an ulcer unconsciously relishes the ministrations of a physician, the client with migraine feels less guilty after experiencing much suffering, and the client with gastrointestinal disorders receives masochistic gratification on fretting over a bland diet. As we have reiterated throughout this section, it is only by having a therapist who is extremely patient and nonjudgmental that clients with psychosomatic problems can feel some comfort. Particularly during the first treatment crisis, if clients sense the therapist is subtly depreciating their real pains, is pointing out dynamics they do not want to hear, or is not sufficiently tolerant of their doubts, they are quick to leave treatment.

Morris Taubman was a psychiatrist in psychoanalytic training, treating Ms. G. four times weekly. Ms. G., a married woman in her forties, sought treatment because she was continually arguing with her husband, had temper tantrums with her daughter, felt an inability to enjoy her part-time job, and suffered from many phobias (she was afraid of flying, of heights, and of being in elevators).

Ms. G., from her first visit to Morris Taubman, responded well to the therapy. By sharing many of her hostile fantasies toward her husband and child with her therapist, she found that she was not acting out her rage in her daily interpersonal life. In response, her family members and friends began to relate to her more positively and, in turn, she began to like herself more. She attributed her gains to therapy and began to feel more and more positively toward Morris Taubman.

Around the sixth month of treatment, Ms. G. started to have numerous dreams and fantasies that centered on her therapist. She found herself deeply desiring to leave her marriage and have an affair with Morris, idealizing him a great deal to the point of considering him "the greatest man on earth," and finding her therapy "the most wonderful experience in the world."

Morris listened attentively to Ms. G.'s erotic and loving fantasies, encouraged their expression, but maintained his therapeutic posture and did not become seduced or manipulated by his client. Morris's therapeutic attitude was very frustrating to Ms. G. because he did not respond to her "in kind" (Schafer, 1983). She handled her hurt and resentment somatically, beginning to have severe migraine headaches during the eighth month of treatment along with insomnia and loss of appetite. By the tenth month of treatment, Ms. G. had lost 10 pounds and was very depressed.

Morris Taubman became alarmed as he saw his client move rather quickly from feeling happiness in her life and pleasure with her therapist and therapy to becoming a sad, sick woman who was in much pain. From a neutral, empathetic therapist who monitored his biases, Morris became an anxious, overprotective, parental figure who appeared less like a professional and more like an overwhelmed worrywart. Bypassing the possibility that Ms. G.'s somatic symptoms were expressing her unacceptable transference feelings of rage and disappointment with Morris, he began to try to lessen her symptomatology as quickly as possible. He prescribed medication for his client's headaches and insomnia and suggested certain foods for her to eat. Disregarding the possible transference reactions to giving his client something to take into her body and seeing himself exclusively as "a benign parental figure," Morris's acting out of his good intentions made his client worse. On one hand, Ms. G. felt cared for and stimulated by Morris's beneficent acts; however, once again she felt frustrated by not really being very fulfilled. In effect, she felt teased and her somatic symptoms became exacerbated as she had no outlet for the hostility toward and disappointment toward her therapist.

As we pointed out several times, when the practitioner is excessively benign, it inhibits the client's opportunities for dissent. Instead of verbalizing the rage she felt, Ms. G. had to be thankful for her doctor's prescription of pills. Consequently, she inhibited herself from talking about what she felt. When the client is blocked from expressing intense feelings, particularly of rage, somatic reactions are a very likely consequence (Fenichel, 1945; Nagelberg, 1959).

When Morris Taubman finally faced his counterresistances and saw that he had not really considered the meaning of Ms. G.'s somatic symptoms nor related to them therapeutically, it was too late. Ms. G., by the end of her first year of treatment, had become more involved with physical remedies than with her psychotherapy. Unable to vent her hostility toward Morris because he did not have an affair with her, Ms. G. had an affair with her physician instead. Although she was trying to get Morris jealous, she was unsuccessful in doing so. Feeling abandoned by him, she abandoned him in retaliation.

Morris not only overreacted to his client's somatic symptomatology, feeling that he had to cure his client pronto without understanding her resistances and transference reactions, but he also did not want to consider seriously that his client was feeling like a rejected lover. He did not appreciate that a woman could love him as much as Ms. G. did and therefore he could not relate to her deep disappointment in him. From not identifying enough with his client's erotic transference, and her eventual disappointment with him, he overidentified with Ms. G. and lost his sense of professional boundaries when he saw that she was suffering much bodily pain. Naterson (1991), who demonstrated how very well-trained clinicians often lose their sense of professional boundaries, pointed out that "the more ample the therapist's awareness of his subjective experience and its extended meanings, the less is the likelihood of destructive developments" (p. 177).

THE THERAPIST WHO CAN'T SAY "NO" AND THE FIRST TREATMENT CRISIS

When a honeymooner senses that the partner is not quite the omnipotent being that he or she was expected of being, there is a tendency on the honeymooner's part to deny the reality that is dawning. Instead of confronting reality directly, which is too painful for them to do, marital partners look for reassurance. Newlywedded individuals ask their partners repeatedly, "Do you love me?" If their mates respond, "Of course!," their requests for verbal reassurance are frequently followed up by requests and even demands for proof of love. Clients in psychotherapy, although not always as explicit in their demands for reassurance from the therapist, nonetheless make them frequently. Clients may seek reassurance by calling the therapist on the telephone in-between sessions. They may ask for extra sessions, seek reductions in their fee, pressure their therapists for advice, a handshake, or even a hug. Some clients ask for more verbal activity from their therapists such as for more interpretations, clarifications, or explanations. Others ask for more nonverbal activity such as for more frequent smiles or nods. Most clients want something in addition to therapeutic neutrality and therapeutic understanding.

If practitioners feel compelled to respond to their clients' requests for reassurance by giving them what they want, the treatment will deteriorate. Not only will clients fail to master their infantile wishes for an all-giving parental figure, but they will keep wanting more signs of reassurance; their wish to be a needy child is not being faced in the therapy. Clinicians, like many husbands and wives who do not want to offend, frustrate, anger, or hurt their mates, keep on trying to gratify their clients. They fail to realize that when their clients are not helped to face the fact that they are chasing a rainbow, no amount of reassurance will placate them.

One of the main reasons practitioners try to reassure their clients during the first treatment crisis, rather than to help them face what infantile fantasies are propelling their wishes for reassurance, is to maintain the honeymoon atmosphere whereby their own narcissism is reinforced. If instead of indulging their clients' wishes for more time and attention, they subject their clients' requests to examination, clients will not hold them in the same esteem as they did during the peak of the honeymoon. Rather than being resented, demeaned, and have their narcissism punctured, clinicians can "give in" to their clients' manipulations.

Finell (1985), in dealing with this issue in psychoanalytic treatment, stated,

> Idealization of the personal analyst, with the analysand experiencing personal grandiosity through identification, can be highly gratifying to both partners. The analysis has an overall positive aura and may continue interminably as long as nothing disturbs this folie à deux. (p. 436)

Although gratifying a client's requests usually does not provoke the client to leave treatment, it almost always leads to an interminable treatment process with little growth taking place in the client.

Joan Simmons, a social worker in a child guidance clinic, was working with Ms. H., the mother of Ellen, an eight-year-old girl. Ellen was in treatment because she responded very poorly to limits, whether they were placed on her by her teacher or her parents. Ellen had constant temper tantrums at home and at school, was very provocative with her peers, and appeared very negativistic with almost everyone with whom she came in contact.

As Ms. H. could vent her hostility and despair in her sessions with Joan Simmons, and faced how much of a burden she felt Ellen was to her, Ms. H. felt much more confident and relaxed. She also found that her weekly sessions enabled her to relate to Ellen without feeling as intimidated. In turn, Ellen's attitude toward her mother and others became more cooperative and less belligerent.

During the fifth month of their work together, Joan Simmons and Ms. H. directly recognized with each other how much their mutual efforts had paid off. They both felt that they were a good team and the recognition of this fact was mutually gratifying. As their work continued, Ms. H., reinforced by Joan Simmons's laudatory remarks, wanted more of them. During the sixth month of treatment, after telling her therapist how she had successfully limited Ellen and did not feel as intimidated by her temper tantrums, Ms. H. asked Joan, "Do you think I did the right thing?" Joan responded, "Of course." This kind of interaction persisted between them for many sessions. What neither party realized was that it progressively weakened Ms. H.'s sense of competence. Feeling that she needed Joan's reassurance to feel secure in coping with Ellen, Ms. H. could not respect herself for her extreme dependence.

In effect, she became more and more of a little girl to an overprotective mother.

It was not until Ms. H. began to call Joan many times on the telephone in-between sessions and tried to prolong the interviews at the clinic on several occasions that Joan realized that Ms. H. was not moving forward in her therapy.

In subjecting her own role in the treatment to examination, Joan was able to realize that she was afraid to limit Ms. H. in the same way that Ms. H. was reluctant to limit Ellen. Just as Ms. H. was intimidated by Ellen's anger, Joan had the same worry about Ms. H. On recognizing that she was recapitulating the same mother-daughter neurotic interaction with Ms. H., Joan concluded that she would have to be a different kind of role model for her client. Instead of gratifying her client incessantly, she began to subject Ms. H.'s requests for reassurance to mutual examination. As Ms. H. began to respond with anger, hurt, and shame, Joan could begin to face her own narcissistic overinvolvement in the case. In effect, Joan was projecting the part of herself that could not take "no" for an answer onto her client and then overidentifying with what she felt was her client's misery (Finnell, 1984).

In order to help a client resolve the first treatment crisis, and accept that the honeymoon is over, practitioners not only have to accept the notion that they cannot be eternally idealized, but they must also acquire the ability to take "no" for an answer in their own lives. Clinicians, like all human beings, feel anger and hurt when life's events do not provide them with what they want or think they deserve. However, if clinicians cannot master their reactions, and accept reality as it is, they will not be able to help their clients take "no" for an answer in and out of the treatment situation. Instead, they will find themselves conducting a prolonged treatment but one that will not yield productive results. It is now a virtual axiom in psychotherapy that therapists cannot help their clients resolve issues that they have not resolved themselves.

One sign that the honeymoon is ebbing and a treatment crisis is in sight is when the client wants to lessen the frequency of treatment and/or lessen the fee. Sometimes clients want to have "telephone interviews" because they are "too busy" to take time out to come to the therapist's office. This request also indicates the honeymoon is ending.

Although illnesses and other reality factors do occur, usually when clients want to lessen contact with their therapists, diminish the fee, plan a termination date, or ask questions about these possibilities, they are indirectly voicing their dissatisfaction with the therapy and the therapist. If the therapist cannot face the client's indirect rejection for what it is and study his or her motives for the wish to withdraw, it is usually because the therapist feels weakened and threatened. To cope with punctured narcissism when clients idealize them less, practitioners can utilize one of several counterresistances.

As we observed at the beginning of this chapter, practitioners can deny the reality of the client's negative transference and not face the fact that a treatment crisis is emerging. In fighting the truth of the client's negative feelings toward the therapist and the therapy, therapists can gratify their clients' wishes to lessen the frequency of the treatment, have phone calls instead of face-to-face sessions, or lower the fee. In colluding with their clients, under the guise of being "a benign parental figure," they undermine the therapy. What practitioners often overlook is that when clients observe that their therapists are willing to lessen the treatment's frequency, they can infer that the therapy is not that important to the therapist and then terminate treatment.

> When David Richmond, a psychologist in private practice, was told by his client Mr. I. that the latter would like to see him every other week rather than weekly, David Richmond picked up his appointment book and scheduled an appointment in two weeks. Although Mr. I. did not comment on his therapist's response, toward the end of the session the client asked, "Aren't you going to ask me why I wanted to shift the appointments around?" David responded, "I'm sure you have a good reason." Mr. I. stated, "I sure do. I wanted to see how much I can get away with. I see I can even quit if I want to and you won't mind. Although you can appear as a permissive guy, I'm not sure the treatment is important to you." Despite David's protests, Mr. I. left treatment.

The above vignette reaffirms for us that *every* request of a client's should be investigated. Some questions such as what time it is, or whether the therapist is working on a national holiday, or where he or she can be reached in case of an emergency seem so logical and pertinent that therapists answer them without thinking of their meaning. If practitioners genuinely accept the fact that their job is to help clients understand themselves, they do not feel so squeamish when they ask, "Let's see if we can understand better why the time of day [my vacation, an emergency] occurs to you now?" Although some clients do feel frustrated and respond with anger when their motives are investigated rather than their demands gratified, if the therapist does not feel too deserving of the client's anger, that is, does not feel that his or her question was provocative or unkind, the therapist can probably help the client make some self-discoveries.

The case of David Richmond and Mr. I. also helps us recognize that when clients want distance from their therapists it is important for the practitioner to keep an open mind and be receptive to other possible meanings of the phenomenon. Though clients are frequently aggressing toward the therapist when they express the wish for distance, often they are also trying see how involved the therapist is in the treatment. This was certainly true with Mr. I. in the above vignette. He was testing the therapist and concluded that if the latter did not mind lessening the frequency of treatment, it seemed quite appropriate to him to consider terminating the therapy.

LECTURING A CLIENT

During a treatment crisis, when clients are demeaning the importance of treatment, threatening to leave, and criticizing the therapist, the therapist sometimes finds the situation extremely unbearable; rather than exploring the client's feelings and fantasies, the therapist lectures the client to cease and desist complaining. Not patient enough to live with the client's uncertain status, feeling too threatened to hear why the client is angry and uncomfortable with the therapy, the therapist orders the client to continue business as usual. This rarely has positive consequences.

Pauline Quirk was a psychologist in private practice, treating Gilbert J., an 18-year-old college student who had been referred to her by college personnel. Gilbert was failing several of his courses in his first semester at college, felt very depressed, lost his appetite, and was suffering from severe insomnia. Gilbert, who had been an outstanding student in high school and well liked by peers and teachers, was finding that being away from his warm home and community was very trying for him. In his first consultation with Pauline Quirk, he was well aware of being "very homesick."

In his treatment, Gilbert was able to articulate how lonely he felt being away from home and how angry he was at teachers and peers who did not respond to him the way he was accustomed to being treated at home. "At home I was a big shot and everybody loved me. Here I am a nobody and I hate it," said Gilbert in one of his early interviews.

Seeing Pauline three times weekly and experiencing her as a woman who appeared very empathetic, nonjudgmental, and supportive was extremely helpful to Gilbert. In effect, his therapeutic experience was helping him feel "at home" and provided him with the nurturing atmosphere that seemed absent at the university. Consequently, by the end of his first semester, Gilbert was doing quite well in his courses, was no longer depressed, made some friends, and his "old self-confidence" returned.

At the end of four months of treatment, Gilbert told Pauline that he would like to try "going it alone" and terminate treatment. He felt that "talking things over" with Pauline had helped him master his problems quite well so that he could now function without her help.

On hearing Gilbert's desire to end treatment, Pauline did not wait to hear her client's associations nor did she explore his motives for wanting to discontinue therapy. Instead, she told Gilbert that she thought it was "a premature decision" and that he should allow himself more time before he "left" her. Pauline went on to tell Gilbert that he was demanding too much of himself and that she could help him sustain his therapeutic gains if he "stayed" with her longer.

Although Gilbert followed Pauline's advice and remained in treatment, his resentment toward his therapist's lecturing him manifested itself in a variety of ways. He started to come late to his sessions, his enthusiasm for school waned, and his poor grades returned. In addition, some of his depression also reemerged.

Noting Gilbert's resistance to treatment and sensing his negative transference, Pauline Quirk decided to evaluate her work with Gilbert in a peer supervisory group. Fortunately, her colleagues almost immediately were able to help her see how her failure to explore with her client what his wish to end treatment was about, and instead ordered him to stay, was strongly contributing to Gilbert's negative therapeutic reaction. Pauline became aware of how much she felt she "needed" Gilbert—to bolster her self-esteem, to maintain her private practice, and to sustain a relationship with a young man she loved and admired.

As Pauline Quirk accepted the fact that she was trying desperately to sustain a honeymoon with an ambivalent partner, she began to relate more empathetically and less narcissistically to Gilbert's resistances. She helped Gilbert verbalize his resentment about continuing to be in treatment and told him she felt that he must have been "damned annoyed" to be pressured to stay in treatment when he had some good reasons to at least consider terminating.

Feeling better understood by Pauline Quirk and less controlled by her, Gilbert was able to rally once more and to begin to function much better in his courses and in his relationships. Pauline, more sensitive to Gilbert's wishes for autonomy and independence, became less active in the therapy. As Gilbert took more initiative in the treatment, his self-confidence not only returned, but he became more assertive in many of his activities and took on some leadership roles in the university community.

Toward the end of the academic year, Gilbert again initiated the idea of ending treatment. This time, Pauline was more alert to her counterresistances and therefore encouraged Gilbert to air his thoughts and wishes. Without taking a stand on his idea of terminating, and maintaining her therapeutic neutrality, Pauline enabled Gilbert to get in touch with his own ambivalence to termination. During the month of May in his eighth month of treatment, Gilbert reported a dream to Pauline: Gilbert was saying goodbye to Pauline, but concomitantly was playing a childhood game with her called "May I?" At first Gilbert associated "May I?" to the month of May but was eventually able, without prompting from Pauline, to recognize that "May I?" also pertained to securing her permission to end treatment.

Instead of being admonished, Gilbert was helped by Pauline to explore why he needed her permission to end treatment. This brought into consciousness his strong ambivalence toward his parents and parental figures in general. On one hand, he wanted to please them and, on the other hand, he resented his dependence on them. He concluded that this conflict, which had endured for most of his life, needed further exploration. He suggested to Pauline that they continue their work for another semester, which they did. When treatment ended, Gilbert was an A- student and a leader on campus; but more important, he liked himself and others more than he ever had.

THE CLIENT'S SIGNIFICANT OTHERS AND THE THERAPIST'S COUNTERRESISTANCES

A phenomenon that takes place in most psychotherapy, particularly when the honeymoon is ending and the first treatment crisis is pending, is one where the client reports that family members and other close associates are being critical of the treatment and the practitioner. This phenomenon, as we have suggested in earlier chapters, is a rather complex and overdetermined issue. First, there is no doubt that when the client shows enthusiasm towards the therapy and the therapist, particularly during the honeymoon phase, the client's marital partner and significant others can feel displaced, threatened, and unloved. Second, if the client makes changes and becomes, for example, less masochistic and more assertive, family members and others may feel forced to make an accommodation. Often they resent the client's changes and resist adapting to the client. The client, threatened by the loss of love and possible abandonment by those considered near and dear, rarely can accept the criticisms of the therapy and the therapist by significant others without feeling some ambivalence. On one hand, he or she wants to protect the therapy and feels like attacking those who castigate it. On the other hand, the client also is angry at the therapist for forcing him or her to have to take verbal onslaughts from others.

Whenever clients report that someone in their social milieu is criticizing the therapy, the wise clinician should recognize that these clients are subtly attacking the therapist, feeling ambivalent about the treatment, but using others to do the job. However, if the clinician's own narcissism needs protection and/or he or she cannot acknowledge his or her hostility toward the client and those demeaning the therapy, the clinician may help the client to attack significant others, oblivious of the fact that the client's latent negative transference and the therapist's latent negative countertransference are not being recognized by either of them.

Occasionally, when clients have had one or more previous treatment experiences, they may contrast their former therapist's insensitivity and lack of empathy with the current therapist. What the clinician should always remember is that the ongoing transference is being split and the client is using other therapists to discharge negative thoughts and feelings that he or she feels toward the current therapist.

Greenacre (1971), in discussing this issue as it pertained to psychoanalysts, stated:

> It is not only the narcissistic needs of the analyst but his failure to recognize his own hostile aggressive drives which seem to make trouble by dovetailing with the problems of these analysands. He may then too readily identify with his patient and accept the latter's splitting of the transference with projection of negative transference onto others, especially accessory members of the patient's family or of the analytic community. (pp. 210-211)

Whether the client idealizes the therapist and attacks family, friends, and other practitioners, or demeans the therapist and idealized other helpers, the client is always involved in a split transference. If the clinicians cannot endure their clients' ambivalence toward them, they will not be able to help them move toward a resolution of the treatment crisis.

Dick Paley, a psychologist in private practice, was treating Ms. K., a divorced woman in her forties who had numerous therapists before she came to him. In her previous treatment encounters, she tended to follow the same pattern with each of her therapists. At first she would idealize them, tell them how understanding and helpful they were, slowly become disillusioned, and then leave treatment in anger. This sequence was similar to her behavior in her two marriages and in many of her friendships.

In her twice-a-week treatment with Dick Paley, Ms. K. repeated her usual patterns. Initially she told Dick how kind, sensitive, and fair he was, and how much she enjoyed working with him. Without saying too much about her previous treatment, she repeatedly told Dick how superior he was to her previous therapists. Although Dick enjoyed Ms. K.'s laudatory comments, he did not respond verbally to them.

During the fifth month of treatment, after Dick was away from his office and missed a session with Ms. K., his client told him how much she missed him—more than she had ever missed any of her previous therapists! She also told Dick how insensitive most of them were to her "separation anxiety" and "loneliness," and by contrast she was most appreciative of Dick's "keen understanding." Slowly Ms. K. began to ridicule her previous therapists and contended that several of them had told her to "shut up" and "control" herself. Tending to exaggerate her previous therapists' sadism, Ms. K. related one incident after another in which she was "accused and abused." Eventually, she manipulated Dick into joining her in her injustice collecting and he told her how her previous therapists were either "neurotic," "untrained," or had "psychopathic" tendencies. Ms. K. was gratified to hear Dick's assessments and went on to contrast his more benign attitude with the sadism of the other practitioners.

Although Ms. K. continued to idealize Dick for close to a year, after he returned from a summer vacation, he found that Ms. K. was in a deep depression. She had lost a lot of weight, was unable to sleep for more than an hour at a time, and could work only sporadically at her job. While Dick was on vacation, she visited a psychiatrist who gave her medication and told her to come into treatment with him. Although Ms. K. was ambivalent about the psychiatrist's recommendation, when Dick told her she had "acted out" her hostility toward him, Ms. K. felt so infuriated that she left treatment.

When clients repeat the same pattern with several therapists, it is easy enough to infer that their wish to defeat treatment is sufficiently strong that this will occur with virtually any practitioner. In many situations, this contention has a great deal of validity. Just as there are certain paranoid spouses who collect injustices as they go from one marriage to another, there are paranoid clients who repeatedly divorce their therapists in a similar manner. However, just as angry husbands and wives have a colluding partner who unconsciously aids and abets their distortions, therapists can do the same with their therapy partners.

Dick Paley's responses to Ms. K. were quite typical of many clinicians when they work with paranoid clients. These clients usually try their best to manipulate the therapist to join them in an attack on their enemies. The therapist, sensing that these clients are vengeful and sadistic, welcomes the idea of not being in the line of fire. What they overlook, however, is that a paranoid client cannot sustain the idea of loving or being loved for too long. Consequently, in the long run it never helps the therapeutic process to join a paranoid client in collecting injustices.

What does help a paranoid client feel safer in the therapy is when the practitioner is not easily manipulated by anything the client says or does. If the therapist maintains a comfortable distance and listens without supporting too much and explores without interpreting too much, the client may begin some self-exploration, however limited and inconsistent. To do this, the practitioner has to feel secure enough to be the object of the client's slings and arrows, have enough self-esteem to tolerate not being too appreciated, and have his or her competition toward colleagues under reasonable control. Dick Paley, in the case illustration, was intimidated by Ms. K.'s anger and therefore helped her become angry toward others, rather than toward him. His competition was not well monitored and his narcissistic investment in being extolled by his client was too strong. As a result, he colluded with Ms. K. and helped her destroy the therapy.

ON ADMITTING MISTAKES

A very frequent happenstance toward the end of a honeymoon in marriage is when the spouses constantly point out to each other how the partner's problems, insensitivities, oversights, and pathology are the main cause of the deteriorated bliss. During the first treatment crisis, as we have shown, clients and therapists do the same. And, just as marital counselors frequently suggest that spouses take responsibility for their parts in marital conflicts, it is often asked, "Should therapists, on realizing that they have erred either through commission or omission, admit to clients that they have made a mistake?" This question has been debated by clinicians for decades, yet it is still a difficult question to answer with certainty.

If we conceive of the psychotherapeutic process as one in which the client is helped to mature by accepting reality as it is, and moves toward renouncing his or her childish wishes for an omnipotent parent, then it makes perfect sense for the therapist to acknowledge mistakes when they have been made and perhaps even to discuss with the client how and why the errors evolved. In certain situations, at least, this would seem to be the correct procedure.

However, admitting mistakes can be motivated by many causes, and the client, on hearing the therapist's confessions, can have many different reactions. For example, just as there are husbands and wives who cannot bear to be the recipient of their mate's hostility and cannot tolerate feeling guilty and/or hostile themselves, and will try to wipe the slate clean by constantly declaring, "Mea culpa," there are clinicians who do likewise. Sometimes, without realizing it, clinicians can indulge themselves in masochistic orgies to soothe their own psyches, and by doing so, they may not help their clients move on in the therapy.

One of the possible reasons for the controversy about therapists disclosing to the client the nature of their counterresistances is because there is no definite answer to this issue. Sometimes the therapist's admission of mistakes can move the therapy forward; on other occasions, it can retard it.

When does it help a client to hear about a therapist's mistakes? Usually, it is when hearing about the mistakes leads to therapeutic growth, that is, the client learns more about himself or herself and is able to master a conflict with more certainty and less anxiety. In addition, if the therapist's error reinforces a neurotic perception of the client's, acknowledging the error can be of therapeutic value. Further, if the client in the therapist's judgment will not use the information in the service of just venting his or her hostility or in reinforcing his or her masochism, then the therapist's acknowledgment of error to the client may be appropriate. Although not always predictable, the best way to know that admitting mistakes will help the client is to ask one's self first, "Will the client use the admission for self-understanding or to berate me?" If it's more of the latter, admitting the mistake is probably not a good idea.

Earlier in this chapter in the case of Pauline Quirk treating Gilbert J., it seemed quite helpful to Gilbert to hear from Pauline that she had made a mistake in admonishing him to stay in treatment without exploring with him his own thoughts and feelings on the matter. Why do we say it was helpful? First of all, one of Gilbert's major problems was to rely too much on outsiders to make his decisions and to buttress his self-esteem. For the therapist to tell Gilbert what to do was clearly not in his best interest. Therefore, a mistake had been made.

It is always important for the therapist to ask, "Have I really made a mistake?" Some clients are often quick to see mistakes where they have not been made and other clients have to deny flagrant mistakes of their therapists because the truth will be too devastating for them. Some clients, like little children, feel too alone and vulnerable unless the parental figure is omniscient.

After recognizing that she had erred, indeed, Pauline Quirk had to ask herself what disclosing the error might induce in Gilbert. Although she could not be sure, and rarely can a practitioner be absolutely sure how the client will respond to an intervention, she did believe that after facing his disappointment and anger, Gilbert would be helped to rely less on Pauline and more on himself. Finally, Pauline was quite sure that the degree of Gilbert's hostility toward her was not that intense. Consequently, he would not use the disclosure just to vent hostility.

Some clients love to torment practitioners with the therapeutic blunders they have made. As was suggested above, if acknowledging mistakes compounds the client's resistances, fuels his or her neurotic hostility, and merely gratifies childish fantasies, it is probably not a good idea to disclose mistakes, even if the therapist recognizes that a mistake has been made. Rather, the client might need help in exploring why he or she finds it to be crucial to focus that persistently on the therapist's errors. Doing this might not placate the practitioner's superego, but it might help the client grow in therapy.

Eileen O'Shea, a social worker in a mental health clinic specializing in the treatment of addictions, was treating Ms. L., a young woman in her twenties, for alcoholism. During the course of the first four months of the three-times-a-week treatment, the therapeutic relationship became a very positive one. Ms. L. realized that much of her excessive drinking was a reaction to her parents who, as she experienced them, gave her many tangible things like food, clothes, vacations, and cars but did not seem available to her emotionally. Ms. L. also discovered in therapy that when she felt angry and lonely, alcohol would put her in an elated mood and she could temporarily forget her troubles.

Gaining insight and feeling supported by Eileen helped Ms. L. give up the alcoholism, start working at a responsible job, and move toward establishing more mature relationships with men and women.

During the fifth month of treatment, Eileen had to be away from a session but could only give her client a few hours notice. Feeling abandoned, angry, and unsupported, as she had felt so often vis à vis her parents, Ms. L. went on a binge and then missed her next two appointments with Eileen.

Upon the resumption of the therapy, both client and therapist immediately recognized how very disruptive Eileen's absence had been for Ms. L., and

Eileen was very apologetic for having to be away. As the weeks went on, Ms. L. damned Eileen at every and any opportunity she had. She called her "unkind," "selfish," "untherapeutic," and cursed at her repeatedly. Slowly it became obvious to Eileen that Ms. L. was using the missed session to vent hostility and avoid facing all that the absence meant to her. Eileen realized that Ms. L., like an angry baby, was having one temper tantrum after another, but was not profiting from her outbursts.

In the seventh month of treatment, Eileen confronted Ms. L. with her persistent outbursts and asked her, "What does it do for you to hang onto your anger at me for the missed session?" Ms. L. became indignant and told Eileen that she had her "nerve" for "questioning my legitimate right to have rage." Ms. L., with much self-righteousness in her voice declared, "You like to victimize people and that's what you are doing to me."

Eileen was able to maintain her firmness, and had sufficiently worked through her own guilt about the missed session, so that she did not have to say or do very much except try to continue the exploration of why Ms. L. needed to demean her constantly. As the client saw that her therapist could not be easily manipulated, she calmed down appreciably.

In the eighth month of treatment, Eileen had to tell Ms. L. that she would be away during the following month for a vacation. Ms. L. again resumed her belligerent attitude, castigated and demeaned Eileen severely, and then said, "Last time when you did this to me, you apologized. How come you are not admitting your mistake this time?" To this Eileen responded, "Why is it important for you to get me to confess guilt?" Ms. L. became infuriated once again and threatened to walk out of the session, shouting and cursing at Eileen. Finally, Eileen told Ms. L, "When you don't get what you want, you have to attack and try to get the other person guilty."

Although Ms. L. found Eileen's attitude difficult to cope with, it was very helpful to her. In effect, Ms. L. needed a weaning experience from a maternal figure who did not vacillate and did not feel guilty. This helped Ms. L. better master some of her own oral cravings and oral sadism.

Often clients like Ms. L. who need limits and structure are the ones who try to get the therapist to emerge as a guilty parental figure: they enjoy feeling sadistic while watching the therapist cringe. When therapists admit their mistakes to these clients, more often than not, they are doing so to placate these clients and appease the voices of their own superego, that is, diminish their own guilt. This is usually not in the service of sound therapy.

By contrast, clients like Gilbert J., who worked with Pauline Quirk, often are too ready to accept the therapist's word as gospel and are the ones who can profit from the therapist's admission of mistakes. With these clients the therapist has to be on the lookout for the client's latent resentments and determine whether it was the therapist's commissions or omissions that may have played a part in the client's evolving depression, psychosomatic problem, verbal inhibitions, or exacerbation of symptomatology. This sort of determination usually becomes more frequent during the middle phase of treatment to which we will turn in the next chapter.

5

---◆---

The Middle Phase: The Therapist's Resistances to Comply with the Ground Rules

Even after the first treatment crisis has been resolved, resistances and counterresistances constantly reappear—and sometimes with more frequency and intensity. As we have reiterated throughout this text, assessing and trying to help clients resolve resistances and assessing and trying to resolve their own counterresistances is an ever-present task for practitioners throughout the therapy.

The therapeutic work perfomed after the treatment crisis and before termination has been referred to as "the middle phase" (Fine, 1982). It is a somewhat arbitrary term in that the middle phase can endure for a short period of time like four or five months, or it can go on for many years, even for a decade or more.

It is difficult to generalize about the behavior and activity of clinicians and clients during this phase. Not only do we see reappearances of resistances and counterresistances discussed previously, such as fears of intimacy, problems with omnipotence, conflicts with sex and aggression, but often new client resistances and therapist counterresistances emerge for the first time. Practitioners and their therapy partners might begin to have difficulties with the fee, with the frequency of appointments, and one or both of them may start to arrive late for sessions, cancel several, or wish to switch the current therapeutic modality, for example from one-to-one long-term treatment to short-term family therapy.

In this chapter we discuss some of the therapist's difficulties in coping with ground rules. In doing so, we examine some of the practitioner's counterresistances when clients do not pay fees, arrive late for sessions, do not talk very much, or do not comply with other requests made of them. We also examine situations where therapists arrive late for sessions, cancel appointments frequently, overcharge or undercharge, or do not comply with other ground rules.

LATENESSES

Every practitioner, usually early in his or her career, works with clients who repeatedly arrive late for sessions. Although practitioners are not unaware of the many and complex reasons for clients arriving late, there has been little consideration in the professional literature and in other professional circles regarding how therapists feel when their clients are late and how they personally cope with this resistance.

It is well known that some clients arrive late for appointments because they are mistrustful of the therapist and/or angry toward him or her. Most therapists have heard more than once from the client who arrives late, "You don't care anyway! You are only interested in making money. You are not interested in me!" Other clients experience punctuality as yielding and submitting, and they worry that by arriving on time, they are surrendering to the therapist. Also, there are clients who are so frightened of intimacy that they arrive late for sessions in order to maintain a distance. They do not want their therapy to become too important in their lives, and they do not want the therapist to think that he or she is important to them (Strean, 1985/1990).

Although there are many reasons for clients coming late for sessions, how do therapists react? Some react very personally and believe that they are being rejected—and maybe for "good" reason. "Perhaps I am not doing my job right?" reasons many a therapist and begins to worry if the lateness is an omen for further rejections, including premature termination. Feeling unloved, disparaged, and unappreciated when their clients are habitually late, therapists can become angry and punitive in order to protect their injured narcissism. Some therapists handle their anger by lecturing the client on how the therapy is being sabotaged and that the latenesses must cease and desist! And a few practitioners even threaten to end the therapy if the client does not behave appropriately.

Although some practitioners handle client lateness by becoming quite punitive, there are others who become too indulgent, either by ignoring the lateness and not exploring the client's reasons for it, or by accepting too readily the client's rationalizations for the resistive behavior. There are a few therapists who handle their own anxiety by making up the time lost and do not face what the client's resistances and their own counterresistances are all about. Usually these practitioners are so worried about losing their clients permanently that they try to placate them by ignoring what is going on between them.

Perry Norman, a therapist in private practice, was treating Mr. M., a man in his early forties, for marital problems. Mr. M., married for three years, sought treatment because he found himself feeling indifferent toward his wife most of the time. He had little interest in sex, found talking with his wife a burden, and longed for the days when he was a happy bachelor. Mr. M.

was particularly bothered by what he referred to as "the requirements of commitment."

Finding Perry Norman to be a quiet, empathetic professional, Mr. M. overcame some of his initial suspicions of therapy. Although he raised questions from time to time about the gains that could evolve from psychotherapy, his resistances to the therapy did not seem too intense.

During the fifth month of once-a-week treatment, Mr. M. started to arrive late for his sessions. At first, he was only five or six minutes late. However, as time moved on, his tardiness extended to as much as 15 and 20 minutes. Not realizing that Mr. M. was behaving toward him in the same way that the client behaved toward his wife—creating distance—Perry rationalized his not commenting on his client's resistance by telling himself that Mr. M. "needed his autonomy preserved and his independence unquestioned."

Mr. M.'s latenesses not only continued but he started to cancel several of his appointments. Again, Perry did not feel it was appropriate to confront his client and try to explore what was going on, but persisted in ignoring Mr. M.'s resistive behavior. As often occurs when therapists choose to ignore a client's resistance and/or their own counterresistance, Perry did not discuss the case with a supervisor or with anyone else. Consequently, he was very surprised when Mr. M. did not return to therapy after a vacation break. Perry had concluded that there was "a good working relationship" between Mr. M. and himself, and he could not understand why his client would not come in for even one appointment but, instead, "was all through with treatment."

As we suggested, if clients do not reveal the habitual defenses in the transference relationship with their therapists that they utilize in their day-to-day functioning with their spouse and significant others, there are usually strong resistances and counterresistances that are being ignored. Inasmuch as Mr. M. arranged to create considerable distance between himself and his wife, Perry Norman should have expected the same phenomenon to occur in the treatment with him. The fact that he was surprised by Mr. M.'s desire to "divorce" him suggests that this was an issue that created anxiety for Perry.

Whenever a therapist ascertains that a client is not recapitulating in the transference relationship with the practitioner defensive behavior that the client shows in his or her daily interpersonal relationships, he or she should ask: "What am I possibly doing to prevent the emergence of this behavior in the transference and why do I not want to see it?" If Perry Norman had asked himself this question, he might have realized that by not confronting his client with the latter's latenesses (and subsequent cancellations), he was resisting facing the why's and wherefore's of Mr. M.'s rejection of him.

In order to do successful treatment, practitioners have to be able to tolerate their clients' rejecting behavior. Not only must they be able to withstand their clients' indifference and contempt, but they must be prepared to subject themselves to their clients' rationale for rejecting them and give their clients plenty of opportunities to verbalize what is on their minds. Usually when a practitioner does not provide the client with these opportunities, as was true of Perry Norman, the client has been made some figure of the practitioner's present or past with whom the practitioner does not want to deal. Also, the client may remind the practitioner of parts of himself or herself, which the practitioner does not want exposed.

> When Jill Martini, a social worker in an outpatient clinic of a general hospital, found that she was not helping her client, Mr. N., to discuss his habitual lateness to the sessions, she discovered that by avoiding hearing her client's negative thoughts about her, she could avoid facing her negative transference toward her own therapist. To Jill, aggressing toward anyone was "for men only." Consequently, she had to inhibit her anger. If she helped Mr. N. aggress toward her, it would appear to her as if through identification she were a man aggressing toward her female therapist.
>
> When Jill recognized the distortion in her thinking and traced it back to her relationship with her older brother, she was able to confront Mr. N. with his resistive behavior and explore some of his negative feelings toward her. Recognizing that she was not her brother when she was assertive helped her to deal much better with her clients' and her own aggression.

THE THERAPIST IS CHRONICALLY LATE

A subject that has received scant attention is the clinician's lateness to sessions. As suggested in Chapter 1, clinicians are much readier to accept their own rationalizations for being late for sessions than they are ready to accept their clients' rationale for the same behavior. Yet, when practitioners are late for sessions, they are resisting the therapeutic process and they are obliged to look inward. It is an insufficient explanation to tell their clients and themselves of their "emergencies," "busy schedules," or "important calls."

For some practitioners, their lateness is confined to one or two clients; other practitioners find that they are late with practically all of their clients. Whether the lateness is confined to one or two clients, or extends to most of them, this counterresistance should be examined carefully.

> Gerald Lenox was a psychoanalyst in private practice seeing Mr. O. four times a week. Mr. O. went into intensive treatment for several reasons. Although he was approaching the age of 50, Mr. O. had never been able to sustain a relationship with a woman. Despite his always dating women, "it never worked out." Either the woman would reject him, which happened most of the time, or he would do the rejecting. In addition, he found himself depressed a great deal and would occasionally think about suicide. On his

job he was often bored with his work and, in addition, he frequently felt alienated by his peers.

Mr. O. had tried various forms of treatment prior to seeking out analysis with Gerald Lenox. He had been in group therapy, sensitivity and encounter groups, and Gestalt therapy. His experience with therapy was the same as it had been with women and work—there was a great deal of mutual rejection.

With Gerald, Mr. O. was an enthusiastic client. He reported his dreams and fantasies conscientiously and examined his history carefully. Gerald did not have to say very much because Mr. O. did much of the analytic work. During much of the first six months of the treatment, Mr. O. described feeling better and reported that he was more relaxed on the job, with women, and with himself.

Around the seventh month of treatment, Gerald Lenox found that he was starting several of the sessions with Mr. O. 5 to 10 minutes late. Although Mr. O. never mentioned that Gerald was late, Gerald was very aware that his lateness was becoming a pattern and he felt very guilty about it. To compound matters, when Gerald noticed that he had begun the sessions late, he would remind himself to extend the sessions at the end of them, but invariably he would forget to do so.

In trying to come to grips with this counterresistance, Gerald told himself that Mr. O. had managed to antagonize many people before he came into treatment with him. "Perhaps," Gerald wondered, "I'm irritated with him and do not recognize it." As Gerald tried to expose and examine his latent resentment toward Mr. O., at first he was dumbfounded. "The guy comes for all of his sessions, free associates, does most of the work, accepts my occasional interpretations, and pays on time. Why should I resent him?" Gerald asked himself. As he let his mind wander some more, Gerald began to have further thoughts about Mr. O. "He's such a good boy! He's such a nice guy! He never does anything wrong! He acts like a teacher's pet. He's Mr. Superego himself," Gerald exclaimed one day after a session in the eighth month. Slowly it dawned on Gerald that Mr. O. reminded him of a youngster from his elementary school years "who did everything right." And Gerald was finally able to say to himself, "The bastard had a supercilious grin, looked down at all of us, and I really hated him."

Gerald Lenox's ability to be honest with himself and to acknowledge his own anger toward Mr. O. was very helpful to him in overcoming his resistance to beginning sessions on time. Gerald realized that despite Mr. O.'s "very correct" behavior in and out of therapy, the client, by always being proper, was also very demeaning of those around him. Although his friends and colleagues could not consciously be aware of Mr. O.'s thinly veiled contempt and their own wish to retaliate, this seemed to be what was happening. Furthermore, this is what was happening in the treatment. Mr. O., by being "a very good client," was telling his analyst that he, Mr. O., really knew all of the answers and was a superior human being.

Gerald not only felt much more liberated by the release of his resentment toward Mr. O, but he could use his understanding to help Mr. O. in treatment. Not needing to act out his resentment by coming late to sessions, Gerald could look more actively and with less guilt for signs of Mr. O.'s contempt. As often occurs when a practitioner is freed of a counterresistance, the client becomes unconsciously aware of it, and is better able to explore some of his or her own resistances. In the ninth month of treatment, Mr. O. reported a dream: "I arrived at a session a few minutes early. You greeted me in the waiting room and you said, 'Let's begin the session early. I'm not angry at you anymore.'"

Although it took many sessions for Mr. O. to acknowledge that his "neutral analyst" could harbor negative thoughts toward him, he eventually believed that it was a possibility. From there, Mr. O. could be helped to consider what it was about his way of relating that provoked Gerald and others.

The case of Gerald Lenox and Mr. O. is an excellent example of how a practitioner's willingness to face his counterresistive behavior helped to turn the therapy into a much more mutually constructive experience. When Gerald did not have to act out his anger by coming late to sessions, but accepted the fact that his client reminded him of a supercilious classmate from his past, Gerald's counterresistance was weakened. Then he could face the fact that Mr. O. was his vulnerable client, not his obnoxious classmate. Realizing this, he could help his client, rather than reject him by acting out his hostility.

When clients like Mr. O. are provocative and invite rejection, it is extremely important for therapists to monitor their wishes to retaliate. When they arrive late for sessions, they are usually acting out retaliatory wishes without being consciously aware of them.

Sometimes practitioners find themselves arriving late for most of their sessions with most of their clients. When this occurs, something in the practitioner's life, personal and/or professional, is usually not being faced, but is being acted out instead. Often when habitual tardiness takes place, clinicians are resenting their work and resenting their clients. In addition, their constant provocative behavior arouses anger in their clients. Their clients' anger can sometimes serve as a punishment that they, the clinicians, feel they deserve.

When practitioners habitually start their sessions late, sooner or later clients threaten to quit and some do terminate. With fewer clients and diminished income, the therapist then feels sufficiently castigated and may relax and arrange to be prompt. However, if the issues that precipitate the lateness are not faced, the same sequence of events will be resumed.

Sue Katsouros was a psychotherapist working privately. During her third year of a rather successful practice, Sue found herself starting her sessions late with many clients. At first, she was off schedule by only four or five minutes, but then the lateness increased to as much as 15 or 20 minutes with most of her clients.

Sue's problem went from bad to worse. Feeling guilty and ashamed, she would make up the lost time at the end of sessions with several clients. However, compensating some clients made her late for others and before long most of her clients had only a slim notion of when their appointments began and ended. She was just as confused as her clients were.

Because the situation was overwhelming and caused her enormous embarrassment, Sue found it extremely difficult, virtually impossible, to discuss the problem with her supervisor or with her therapist. She walked around for months feeling like a criminal who felt guilty and humiliated but could not confess her problem to anyone. As a result, her concentration with clients weakened, her judgment became impaired, and she began to feel like a severe emotional cripple.

As clients became indignant, as some threatened to leave, and as a few did terminate, Sue still could not talk to anyone about her vexing problem. What eventually did "help" her face herself was something that occurred with her own therapist. Sue began to arrive late for her own therapy sessions.

When Sue's therapist commented on Sue's lateness, it took Sue many sessions to discuss her counterresistance with her clients. Eventually she got in touch with her enormous resentment toward her own therapist who kept her "waiting" in the waiting room and kept her "waiting" in between sessions and on vacations. Although her therapist was never late for appointments, Sue experienced waiting for her at any time as a powerful deprivation that put her in an intense rage.

Sue was recapitulating something from her history in her own therapy and in her contact with clients. She was able to recall, and with a great deal of affect, how much she hated her mother for keeping her waiting on many occasions. As a young girl Sue had to wait for hours until her mother came home from work. As the only financial support in the family—Sue's father was dead—Sue's mother had to leave home early in the morning before Sue went to school and did not return home until about 6:30 P.M., Mondays through Saturdays. Sue had to do a lot of waiting as a child but never felt she could let her mother know how she felt, in fear that her mother would abandon her forever. This was why the matter of lateness could not be easily discussed with anyone in the present. Sue feared the same kind of retribution from supervisors and from her therapist that she anticipated from her mother when she was a child.

When Sue could discharge her rage at her therapist "for all the waiting" her therapist made her endure, Sue could subsequently begin to face and master the rage toward her mother for the nondeliberate negligence. Doing this enabled Sue to resolve her counterresistance of lateness with her clients. She began to see that by being late for appointments with her client's, she was placing them in the same psychological position in which her mother put her. This maneuver, "identification with the aggressor" (A. Freud, 1946), helped Sue discharge her resentment toward her mother and therapist in an indirect way, but it also caused her clients to suffer much more than anybody else did.

By acting out her hatred toward her mother and therapist in the manner she did, Sue suffered much pain and guilt. Not only did the pain and guilt serve as punishment for the way she mistreated her clients, it also served another purpose. Sue discovered that making money and being successful professionally were unconsciously experienced by her as a hostile triumph over her mother as well as an attempt to compete with her therapist. As she unconsciously provoked her clients to leave her, Sue was arranging to destroy her practice and in this way she would not be the threat she thought she was to her mother and to her therapist.

Sue Katsouros's lateness with her clients is an example of how an unresolved problem from childhood can seriously interfere with a practitioner's ability to conduct sound therapy. Sue's hatred toward her mother was displaced onto her clients and became a disabling counterresistance until she could examine it in her own transference relationship with her therapist. Although there are many counterresistance problems that do not require intensive therapy, Sue Katsouros's problem with lateness did.

CANCELLATIONS

Particularly for beginning practitioners, clients cancelling appointments can be a most disturbing event. If clients are late, at least they are demonstrating that they have not forgotten about the therapist completely. However, when clients don't show up, particularly without notice, practitioners can feel wiped out!

Clients, as we know, cancel appointments for many reasons. They can be ill or called away on some emergency. Most of the time, however, when the practice becomes repetitive, the client is trying to get away from the therapist. Frequently, repetitive cancellations suggest that the client is frightened to reveal sexual or aggressive fantasies, painful memories, or shameful acts. More often than not, repetitive cancellations are an expression of defiance toward the practitioner who transferentially embodies many features of a punitive superego. Occasionally, clients cancel to ascertain whether the therapist will show concern, worrying meanwhile that he or she feels indifferent toward them.

Although practitioners are usually aware of the many unconscious reasons that prompt a client's persistent cancellations, they are not always able to cope with their own reactions to this event. As we suggested above, not only do many practitioners feel wiped out emotionally, but they also fear that they will be wiped out economically. It is many a practitioner who obsesses about his or her income for long periods of time when a client has not been present for appointments.

Cancellations in many ways can be experienced like "broken dates" and, consequently, many practitioners react like rejected lovers. Those clinicians who turn their aggression inward can become depressed, masochistic, and feel unlovable. Other therapists who are freer with their aggression can become irrate, punitive, and rejecting. Few stay emotionally neutral.

Despite the fact that the majority of therapists tend to lean toward the side of feeling disappointed and rejected, when clients habitually cancel, there are some who are quite relieved and even pleased. Work with some clients presents such drudgery that when they cancel appointments, the therapist can breathe a little easier.

One of the ways that therapists reveal their feelings about cancelled appointments is how they handle the payment of fees when a cancellation occurs. Although there are exceptions, usually when professionals take the psychotherapuetic work seriously, they are eager for their clients to be present for all sessions and are eager to be at the sessions themselves. To insure this, the well-motivated therapist charges for all missed sessions. By doing do, the transference implications and the resistances at work when a client cancels have a better chance for exploration and exposure. If the therapist does not charge for missed appointments, clients are apt not to think too much about being absent, and as we indicated in earlier chapters, the client can infer that the therapist condones absences if he does not charge a fee when they occur.

In the middle phase of treatment when shameful memories, guilt-provoking thoughts, and forbidden wishes all create intense anxiety for the client, cancellations are more frequent. Many clients feel that their troubles will disappear, if they disappear from the therapist's office.

What is also important to keep in mind about the middle phase of treatment is that as the client experiences more pain and anxiety, and therefore produces more resistances, therapeutic work for the practitioner arouses more counterresistances. Therapists, too, may want to get away from it all!

When therapists cancel appointments, they usually do it more subtly than their counterparts. For example, if practitioners choose to be away for a few conferences during the course of the year, they may find that when they make up lost time for clients, they manage to exclude the same client or clients persistently. Sometimes therapists find themselves taking short vacations and arrange not to see the same clients each time they go away. The same phenomenon can take place when practitioners must see a dentist, doctor, or attorney—they manage to cancel appointments with the same clients and always manage to keep appointments, or make them up, with others.

Therapists' motives for cancelling are usually quite similar to the motives of their clients: they harbor resentment that they cannot face; impulses, memories, fantasies, and superego injunctions become aroused in their therapeutic work and they react the same way their clients do—they do not want to face their therapeutic partners; other people and other events in the practitioner's life offer more pleasure and comfort; and the intensity of therapeutic work and the anxiety it induces prompts the practitioner sometimes, in desperation, to want to get away from it all.

When a client cancels appointments persistently, it is not only important for the clinician to assess the meaning of the client's absences and try to help the client resolve the resistances when they become apparent, but the clinician should also try to determine how he or she is feeling about the client's constant absences. Sometimes practitioners learn that they are colluding with the client to help the resistive behavior persist.

Tyrone Jones was a psychologist in a clinic that specialized in work with senior citizens. He was working with Ms. Q., a 77-year-old widow who was referred by a physician for psychotherapy because she was frequently depressed, suffered from insomnia, often drank alcohol to excess, and felt acutely hostile toward her two children who lived nearby but did not visit very frequently.

Ms. Q. was in weekly treatment with Tyrone Jones for about five months and came to each appointment faithfully and on time. She used her appointments to vent anger toward her children, discussed how most people that she had met were untrustworthy, and lamented about the loss of her husband who had died about five years before.

Talking to Tyrone was very helpful to Ms. Q. She clearly felt individualized, supported, and cared for. As a result, her depression diminished, as did the intensity and frequency of other symptoms.

During the sixth month of treatment, Ms. Q. started to miss appointments quite regularly. Sometimes she would call in ill; on other occasions, she did not even call Tyrone and just failed to show up. Occasionally, Tyrone would phone to find out where Ms. Q. was when she did not show up; sometimes, he "forgot" to do so. This ambivalent pattern on the part of client and therapist continued for about three months, into the ninth month of treatment.

What Tyrone Jones defended against recognizing was Ms. Q.'s anxiety as she began to feel closer to him. Her cancellations were her way of trying to renounce her sexual and affectionate feelings toward her therapist. Not only did Tyrone not want to face the fact that a woman old enough to be his own mother wanted a sexual liaison with him, but he did not want to face feelings of his own when his client wanted closeness with him.

Unaware of the nuances of the transference-countertransference collusion, not able to understand that Ms. Q.'s staying away from appointments was psychologically equivalent to her feeling like a frightened virgin, and reluctant to explore his own inhibitions, Tyrone, in effect, colluded with his client to keep them away from each other. The treatment deteriorated with Ms. Q. becoming more depressed and resorting once again to alcohol. Eventually, she terminated therapy altogether.

Sometimes therapists overlook the fact that senior citizens are sexual people, and as a consequence, some therapists cannot fully appreciate nor understand the transference responses and resistive behavior of their older clients. Usually when practitioners counterresist by denying the reality of the senior citizen's sexual capacities and sexual interests, they are reliving parts of their own childhoods when they felt compelled to view their parents as nonlibidinal people. When children perceive their parents as asexual, the youngsters are usually afraid of their own incestuous feelings toward their parents. The same is true of therapists who deny that clients over 70 years of age are sexual beings.

Just as a therapist can help a client resist (which occurred when Tyrone Jones colluded with Ms. Q.), clients are equally adept in "helping" their therapists protect themselves from facing psychological truths and staying away from the treatment.

Alice Ingersoll was a psychiatrist in private practice who saw clients from a variety of socioeconomic groups. Thus, she often agreed to see certain individuals for low fees. Most of the time the psychic income derived from work with less affluent but creative individuals seemed quite acceptable to Alice.

When Alice was seeing Mr. R., an unemployed artist, at a low fee, she repeatedly told herself that the therapeutic work was going well and that both client and therapist were very satisfied with each other. Although Mr. R., from time to time, would suggest that Alice must resent "working for next to nothing," she always handled her client's doubts by interpreting to him that unconsciously he wished to feel rejected by her. This tended to reassure Mr. R. for only a short while. He constantly returned to voicing his doubts, never trusting Alice's accepting demeanor.

Although Mr. R. gained some confidence during the first seven months of treatment, he did not gain very much income. His inability to make money was only superficially explored by Alice, similar to the kind of therapeutic neglect that she showed when she reassured Mr. R. that it was quite acceptable to her if he paid a lower fee.

Around the eighth month of treatment, Alice wanted to enroll in a seminar, which necessitated changing the time of Mr. R.'s appointment. Mr. R. readily complied with Alice's wishes. Not only did he "cooperate" with Alice in changing the schedule, but he began to arrive late for his sessions. Alice accepted Mr. R.'s rationalization for his latenesses and did not see them as resistances.

In the tenth month of treatment, Alice had to do some lecturing out of town and again asked Mr. R. to change his appointment time. This time he suggested to Alice, "It will be all right if I miss my sessions because you won't be out too much money." At last, Alice was able to get the message. Because she was treating a "low-fee patient," she felt she could ask him frequently to comply with her changes in schedule. When Alice realized that she singled out Mr. R. for this, she became aware of her resentment in taking the low fee, which, of course, ignited her counterresistive behavior. Of equal importance, Mr. R. colluded with her and both tacitly concurred that a "low-fee patient" should be indebted to his altruistic therapist and feel obligated to accommodate to her schedule.

The case of Alice Ingersoll and Mr. R. helps us realize that when we reassure clients about any of their doubts, there is usually something we do not want to face. Often the client is speaking a truth that we want to deny. When we reassure our clients and deny the client's right to a full exploration of his or her feelings, a counterresistance is usually at work. Alice did not want to hear about Mr. R.'s concerns about paying a low fee and reassured him instead. She reassured him because she did not want to see the part of herself that resented collecting a low fee.

When practitioners are not in touch with their resentments toward their clients, they are more apt to act out with them. Alice Ingersoll acted out her resentment toward Mr. R. by asking him frequently to accommodate to her schedule. And, when a therapist acts out, self-effacing clients often conclude that they must join their revered doctor who always knows best.

Just as some therapists are habitually late with many clients, there are also some who habitually cancel appointments with many or all of their clients. As we have already suggested, doing psychotherapy is tedious and the wish to get away from it all is understandable—hence, the wish to cancel is ubiquitous.

It is one thing for practitioners to accept the fact that their work arouses all kinds of intense countertransferences and counterresistances. It is quite another to act out one's feelings toward clients by saying goodbye to them frequently, rather than understanding one's hostility, boredom, and revenge, and mastering the issue. Sylvia Teitelbaum (1991) points out:

> The new advances in the use of countertransference have given rise to the potential of destructive application. Freed from the restraints of classical neutrality, the misuse of the [therapist's] countertransferential feelings has loomed as more prevalent in today's [psychotherapeutic] arena.

It is quite possible the notion of "tabula rasa" and "blank screen" could prove, at times, sterile and unproductive, but the abuse of the therapist's induced countertransference feelings can have more overt potential of inflicting emotional damage to the patient. (p. 271)

When practitioners abandon their patients several times during the year, particularly for long periods, they should eventually be able to tell themselves that they do not wish to make their clients too important to them. Just as clients who are habitually absent from sessions wish to demean the therapy, therapists who take off frequently are doing the same thing.

Some very charismatic practitioners who charge very high fees can afford to take frequent and long vacations. Their clients, financially burdened by the high fees, welcome the therapist's frequent and long absences. Again, we have a collusion between practitioner and client whereby they both reinforce a resistance—counterresisistance interaction. Usually this kind of collusion goes undetected because the charismatic therapist is rarely in supervision or in personal therapy. Furthermore, because the idealizing, masochistic client of the charismatic therapist is usually too inhibited to complain, this type of folie à deux can continue indefinitely.

There is more of a possibility to resolve the problem of constant therapist absences if the therapist involved is not charismatic or wealthy. Eventually, clients of a less affluent and less prestigious therapist begin to protest.

Ernest Hilson was a social worker in private practice. After working in social agencies for many years, he very much welcomed the idea of being an independent practitioner. Not only did he like the idea of selecting his own supervisors, attending seminars of his own choosing, and arranging his own schedule, but he was particularly pleased with the idea of doubling his income within two years after he started working privately.

With his increase in income and with no agency policies to adhere to, Ernest began to take more and more vacations. By the end of his third year of private practice, Ernest was taking a week vacation after every five or six weeks of work.

When Ernest's clients eventually became angry at him for his constant absences, Ernest became quite defensive, making interpretations to them regarding their wishes to be infantilized, their chronic dependency, and their refusal to permit him to be human. If these interpretations did not give Ernest the kind of response he wanted, he would remind his clients that they were saving money when he was away, so he was really doing them a favor.

Slowly Ernest's clientele began to dwindle and soon he could just not afford to go on that many vacations. As he was forced to stay with his clients in order to make a living, he began to get in touch with some of the feelings that were contributing to his counterresistance. Ernest began to feel controlled and dominated by his clients, much the same way he felt dominated and controlled by his supervisors and administrators at the agency where he previously worked. Eventually Ernest had to face the fact that continued commitment to anybody aroused anger in him and he had to move away from anybody who desired a continued commitment from him.

Ernest returned for more personal psychotherapy and was able to realize that the form his counterresistance took—frequent absences from his clients—was reliving a childhood relationship that he had with both of his parents. Each in his or her way demanded a great deal from Ernest. Unable to let them know of his anger, he would withdraw from them for periods of time, only to be reprimanded and punished. As Ernest faced the fact that he was making virtually all of his clients into his demanding parents, he was able to stop punishing them as much and could get to enjoy his work with them more.

FEES

One of the ways clients express their dissatisfaction and disappointment with the therapy is by requesting a reduction in the therapist's fee. Although this request can occur during any phase of treatment, it frequently happens during the middle phase when resistances can become strong and therapeutic impasses can become frequent. Sometimes clients do not merely request a reduction in the fee; they demand it. And a few threaten to leave treatment unless the fee is reduced pronto!

Equally as frequent as the request or demand for a lower fee during the middle phase is the client's reported inability to pay the fee on time. Some clients, if permitted, can go for many months without paying anything.

As we suggested in Chapter 2, practitioners show a variety of attitudes toward fees. Some are very firm, demand payment immediately, and refuse to ever lower a fee. Others are just the opposite: they are quick to lower fees and are lax about commenting about overdue payments.

Although financial crises do emerge in a client's life, quite often when a client wants to reduce the fee and/or accumulates a debt with the therapist, he or she is covertly trying to reduce the importance and value of the therapy.

In responding to a client's nonpayment of fees and/or wish to lower the fee, it is of paramount importance for both therapist and client to understand fully what the client is really expressing through this behavior. What is going on in both the client's external and internal lives that prompts the request is something that should always be investigated. Unusual expenses and debts of clients have to be evaluated carefully. Are they expenses that were quite necessary or has the client acted out something that appears self-defeating? Quite often, incurred debts and unusual expenses signal that psychological problems are at work; these need to be addressed in the therapy. As we implied earlier, clients through their financial indebtedness to the therapist are indirectly expressing transference problems that have to be unearthed.

Those clients who accumulate debts and demand lowered fees are usually the ones who want to be treated as beloved children who should be indulged. They cannot see why their therapists who seem to love them, respect them, and understand them, also want to take money from them. For such clients, these seem like two very incompatible ideas. Furthermore, the idea that the therapist makes a living from them seems demeaning. It feels like a parent asking for an allowance from a son or daughter.

The practitioner's unconscious views toward money, as well as the state of his or her current countertransference, will in many ways determine how the practitioner will respond when clients wish to have their fees reduced or cannot pay the amount they had agreed to at the start of the treatment.

Lisa Gallo, a psychotherapist in private practice, had been treating Ms. T. for close to a year. Ms. T., a graduate student in anthropology, sought help because she was rejected by her female lover with whom she had been living for over a year. At the time of her application for treatment, Ms. T. was acutely depressed, had lost her appetite for food, did not want to have anything to do with anybody, and could not concentrate on her academic work.

Seeing Lisa Gallo three times a week aided Ms. T. enormously. The client was helped to verbalize her deep resentment and hurt about feeling abandoned by her lover, and she was able to recall memories from her childhood when she felt abandoned by her father who left the family when she was five, never to return. Lisa was able to show Ms. T. that not only was she deeply mourning the loss of her lover, but she was reliving the loss of her father and all that loss represented to her.

Ms. T. experienced her therapist as warm and understanding, a "perfect role model," and "a great facilitator." As a consequence, Ms. T.'s depression lifted, her appetite returned, and she was able to concentrate once again on her studies. Although she resumed some social life, she did not find another lover and referred to this ever so faintly and quite infrequently in the therapy. It was quite obvious to Lisa that Ms. T. experienced her therapist as a substitute for her lover.

Toward the end of the first year of treatment, Ms. T. told Lisa that because she was not sharing household expenses anymore with her lover, her expenses had gone up. Ms. T. did not want to cut down her sessions with Lisa, nor did she want to consider other living arrangements—all she wanted was to reduce her fee per session to half the amount. Ms. T. told Lisa that although she realized her fee of $15 a session was a reduced one, she just could not afford it.

Despite the fact that up to now Lisa Gallo had been able to explore her client's many fantasies in depth, had skillfully confronted her with her resistances over the year, and had helped her investigate transference issues, when it came to handling Ms. T.'s financial request, Lisa abdicated her therapeutic role. Instead, without investigating anything, Lisa told Ms. T. that she would grant her request. She did inform Ms. T. that if the latter were able to increase her income and/or reduce her expenses, she would like to return to the old fee. The client agreed.

Ms. T. was very grateful to Lisa and told her how she could always trust her "and without any qualifications." "You are the mother and father I've always wanted," said Ms. T. rather wistfully during the thirteenth month of therapy.

After the reduction in fee, Ms. T. began to make more requests of Lisa. She called her on the phone in between sessions to ask for changes in appointment times, prolonged the sessions after the ending time, and tried to elicit information on Lisa's personal and professional life.

During the fifteenth month of treatment, as Lisa became keenly aware of her client's increased demandingness, she confronted Ms. T. with her behavior. Commented Lisa in one session, "I've noticed you'd like more contact with me," and alluded to the phone calls, prolonging of sessions, and so on. Ms. T. somewhat indignantly and very surprised said, "Well, of course! Isn't that what psychotherapy is all about? Aren't you here to give me a corrective emotional experience and be the mother, father, and lover that I never had?" Lisa was speechless when she heard her client's self-righteous proclamation. On noting this, Ms. T. said, "By your silence, I think you don't agree with my point of view?" To this Lisa was able to ask, "What do I disagree with?"

Ms. T. in later sessions told her therapist that she was "shocked" and "amazed" that Lisa had different goals for her than she had for herself. Ms. T. wanted "a real friend, lover, and parent," while Lisa just wanted "to give intellectual understanding."

Evidently, Lisa Gallo's reduction of the fee stimulated a strong regression in her client. Symbolically it seemed to give Ms. T. permission to make many childish demands on her therapist without examining her motives for doing so.

When therapists act without reflection, they tacitly encourage the client to do the same. In effect, Lisa Gallo acted out a wish to infantilize her client and the client became more infantile in and out of the treatment situation.

Had Lisa not been so ready to gratify her client's wishes, Ms. T. might have been able *to talk about* her fantasies to have a symbiosis with her therapist. Talking about her wish for an enduring breast might have led to more ego mastery by the client. Instead, Ms. T. emerged as more and more of a baby and it took Lisa a long time to help her client accept the reality that Lisa was, indeed, her therapist and not a friend or relative.

Very often if practitioners act impulsively when their clients wish to be gratified, they are overidentified with the clients and cannot feel comfortable in assuming the role of a weaning mother. Some practitioners, like some parents, view weaning and imposing other limits as being "too cruel." Thus they do not feel relaxed about exploring requests of their clients, convinced that their clients will have to endure too much frustration.

Although many therapists tend to behave as Lisa Gallo did in the above vignette and reduce a fee too quickly, there are other practitioners who can use the fee as a weapon and punish their clients by raising fees often and without preparing the client.

Despite disagreement on the subject (Langs, 1976), it does seem appropriate for therapists, from time to time, to raise their fees. Like anyone else, as their expenses go up and as their expertise increases, clinicians are entitled to enhance themselves economically. It can even be argued that when their clients come to view them more as struggling human beings who do not "have it all," clients are helped to renounce their wishes for an omnipotent parent, and through identification with their therapists, they begin to diminsh some of their own grandiose fantasies.

However, clients need preparation when they are asked to pay a higher fee. They need time to respond to the therapist's request, face the transference fantasies that have been activated, and confront the resistances that have been mobilized. When clients are given this opportunity, most of them are willing to cooperate, providing, of course, that their therapists are not too ambivalent about making the request and also feel their request is legitimate.

ASKING FOR INCREASES IN FEES

When practitioners find themselves not giving their clients sufficient time to react to a request for a higher fee, and/or ask for frequent raises in fee, there are usually counterresistances at work. Clients need at least three or four weeks to discuss their reaction to the increase in fee before it goes into effect, and it would seem reasonable that they should not have to increase their fee more than once a year, unless there are special circumstances involved.

Roy Ferrar was a psychologist in private practice who had been treating Mr. U. for about two years. Mr. U., an attorney, had come into treatment because he had severe anxiety attacks, particularly when he had to defend a case in court. His treatment with Roy Ferrar was going well and Mr. U. felt that his twice-weekly sessions with Roy had given him a better self-image, more self-confidence, and reduced his anxiety attacks more than he thought "they ever would be reduced."

On the day he resumed working with Mr. U. after a month's summer vacation, Roy asked his client for an increase in fee. Replying to Mr. U.'s question as to when the raise in fee would begin, Roy said matter-of-factly, "Ten dollars more per session starting today." Mr. U., after a long silence, said with scorn, "You don't even wait to listen to how my summer went! You don't even want to know if my practice is okay! All you are interested in is yourself! What happened? Did you buy a new house?" After a long silence, Mr. U. went on, "I don't mind considering a raise in fee. However, I think your timing is all off. Wait awhile and show a little bit of human compassion and I might consider it!"

Roy then told Mr. U. that his anger was excessive and wondered, "What childhood issues do you think my request is stirring up?" At this query Mr. U. became very indignant and bellowed, "That question is a shrink's defense. When you are against the wall, you call your patient a child! I think *you* are behaving childishly, and if you were in court, the judge and jury would think you were an amateur!"

Mr. U. refused to pay the fee immediately and threatened, "If you want it right away, I'll quit treatment! Is that what you want?"

Inasmuch as Roy had attempted to raise the fees of other clients in the same manner, his clients, in a way, gave him some supervision. Several told him how selfish and narcissistic he was and one or two left treatment. Consequently, Roy had to face himself and the financial policies he was using in the treatment situation at the time.

Roy realized that after being on vacation for a month and having no income during that time, he was feeling "pinched." Furthermore, during the summer he had spent a lot of money for his family's vacation and this made him feel even more "pinched." Further reflection helped him to see that he deeply resented going back to work after a vacation that was quite pleasant. All of this prompted Roy to "pinch" his clients and displace his anger onto them. In effect, he wanted them to feel the way he was feeling, "out of money."

Roy also recognized that the way he asked for the increased fee, "right away," provoked his clients into negative transferences. In doing so, Roy received the punishment he felt he deserved.

When practitioners feel they are making reasonable financial requests, do not feel guilty for wanting to make more money, are not feeling particularly deprived, angry, or vulnerable, they can ask their clients for an increase in fee and wonder out loud with their clients, "Is this manageable?" Their clients are then given several weeks before the raise is implemented. If clients are not rushed, if their reactions are given empathetic attention, most of them are usually willing to cooperate with the new financial arrangement.

SILENCE

Clients and therapists can be silent in therapy sessions for many different reasons. In assessing the meaning of their respective silences, it is important to note the obvious fact that because of their different roles, the silence of each can have different meanings and may be interpreted by each in vastly different ways.

Most if not all clients are encouraged by their therapists to talk, and many are directed "to say everything that comes to mind." Saying everything is called "the fundamental rule" in psychoanalytic psychotherapy and most of the other therapeutic perspectives endorse the rule. Consequently, when clients do not talk, in one way or another, they are having difficulty complying with a major ground rule.

By not talking, a client may be acting out defiance toward the practitioner. As one client stated, "I know you like it when I talk and all you have to do is listen. I'm not going to talk so you can feel frustrated. Then I'll feel triumphant."

A client, through silence, may be acting out strong passive wishes. Said another client about being silent, "I really hate to work here. I feel like doing absolutely nothing. If *you* want to talk, it is okay with me."

When fantasies seem dangerous and stir up anxiety, clients can become silent. Their silence may make them feel very uncomfortable and consciously they might want to rectify the situation, but they feel helpless and frightened to do so.

Occasionally, clients may believe that their therapists are not interested in them or in their productions. By being silent, they can determine if the therapist will be sufficiently concerned to ask them to talk. Said one client, "I'll be silent so that sooner or later you might say, 'What comes to your mind?' Then I'll know that you care."

A client's silence is almost always a resistance, but as important as it is for the client to get to what activates the resistance, it is equally as important for the therapist to know how he or she is experiencing the client's silence. Does the therapist feel wiped out by the client's silence and in retaliation become silent too (Greenson, 1967)? Or does the practitioner react with discouragement, hopelessness, and helplessness and believe that any intervention will be ineffective so he or she gives up (Fenichel, 1945)? Or does the therapist view the silence as a welcome respite and just lets his or her own mind wander to his or her private concerns. All therapists respond in their own idiosyncratic manner to the client's silence, and then conduct themselves in their own unique way, usually telling themselves that whatever they do is "therapeutic."

For a little over a year, Ingrid Erikson, a social worker in a family agency, had been treating George, an 18-year-old college freshman. George came to the agency because he was finding it very difficult to feel comfortable living in the coed dormitory at the college. An only child from a very religious family, George found his colleagues' liberal attitudes toward sexuality difficult to reconcile with his rather puritanical background.

During the one year of treatment with Ingrid Erikson, George made a lot of progress. He learned to talk freely about the anxiety he felt as he related to young women. Although he had a great deal of reluctance to have sex with them, he did come to recognize that everybody is sexual, despite his parents' rather rigid attitudes. With the lifting of some of his repressions, George became less frightened and inhibited and more self-assured.

As the relationship between therapist and client became closer, and as George shared more of his sexual fantasies, masturbatory routines, and painful memories with Ingrid, he became more reluctant to talk in the sessions. Sometimes a silence of three or four minutes occurred as many as four times during a 45-minute session.

Although Ingrid had been a patient, empathetic practitioner with George throughout most of the treatment, she seemed to lose her objectivity and neutrality in responding to George's silence. Instead of continuing to be patient and to realize that George's silences reflected a current resistance emanating from a shift in his transference position, Ingrid began to pressure her client to talk. As usually occurs when a client's resistance is not being respected, and the anxiety and pain that precipitates it is ignored, George became more silent!

What Ingrid did not appreciate as she was pressuring her client to talk was that George experienced Ingrid as a woman who was badgering him to have sex with her. The more she pushed him to open up and talk, the more he resisted. To George it was perceived as a command to undress and to perform sexually. His silence in the sessions was equivalent to a form of sexual impotence.

In many ways the child who is isolated from the sexual dimension of life is a child who has been sexually abused. Just as the youngster who has been exploited to perform sexual favors for a parent or for some other adult grows up to believe that sex is something dangerous, the child who has been forced to deny sexuality to please his or her parents also grows up to avoid discussion and participation in sex. It becomes too frightening a prospect to consider. Consequently, Raphling (1991) points out:

It is especially difficult for patients whose bodily and psychic integrity, autonomy, and sense of self have been betrayed in abusive relationships to allow themselves to relax their defenses enough to participate in the shared work of a psychodynamic inquiry . . . . The patient experiences the therapeutic situation as most perilous when any of its realistic aspects or those created by the patient's enactments of transference and resistance resemble the original traumatic experience. (p. 2)

On recognizing that George was not responding to her exhortations to talk, Ingrid did bring the case to supervision. To her surprise, she saw that she had not been able to recognize that George was in the middle of a growing erotic transference. She also had to admit that she had not permitted herself to accept her own sexual fantasies toward George. Paradoxically, she viewed her excessive badgering of George to talk as if she were a concerned teacher and he was a delinquent student.

A client's silence usually cannot be resolved unless the therapist demonstrates to the client that the latter is deluged with anxiety and feels in danger. When the client feels understood and not pressured, he or she might consider with the therapist what the current dangers are that interfere with talking in the sessions.

On recognizing that they are pressuring their clients to break the silence rather than understand the silence, practitioners can tell themselves that they are probably not in touch with one or more counterresistances. In Ingrid Erikson's case, not only was she complying with George's unconscious mandate to become his asexual, inhibiting mother and father, but also she was distorting the therapy and turning her client into an obstinate student. In reality he was a young man terrified of his sexual fantasies toward her.

As we have already suggested, the role of the therapist, particularly the psycho-analytically oriented therapist, as an essentially silent listener and observer is generally assumed (Aull & Strean, 1967). The effect of the clinician's silence has been viewed as promoting the therapeutic process by allowing the client to talk, to follow his or her own associations, and to use the ambiguity of the therapist for projections and fantasies. As the client regresses, he makes the therapist the object of his fantasies, an ultimate aid in the lifting of repressions.

THE THERAPIST USES SILENCE AS A WEAPON

It has also been recognized that nonresponsiveness and silence of the therapist might frustrate the client too severely, causing the client to feel ignored, excluded, or disapproved of, provoking unnecessary anxiety and resentment (Menninger, 1958). As previously said, the therapist's silence in the face of the client's silence can be a form of retaliation, annoyance, or hatred. However, because the practitioner's silence has often been regarded by both clinicians and clients as something that is sacrosanct and therapeutically beneficial, its role in counterresistive behavior has not always been apparent.

Graham Doyle, a psychiatrist and psychoanalyst in private practice, had been treating Ms. W. four times a week for over a year. Ms. W. sought intensive treatment because she had many problems that were causing her much pain. In her forties and unmarried, Ms. W. was very concerned about never getting married and having children. Occasionally dating men, she found herself wanting to form a symbiosis with them. Her clingingness and demandingness alienated them and in response she perceived herself as "a social misfit." After Ms. W. was rejected by a man, she would gossip angrily about him. This self-destructive cycle was something she wanted to resolve in her therapy. During Ms. W.'s first year of treatment she began to realize that her clinging behavior with men was a defense against her competition with them. Basically she was reliving on her dates the intense sadomasochistic relationships that she had with her parents and two older brothers.

Toward the end of her first year of treatment, Ms. W. recapitulated in her transference with Graham Doyle her experiences with men. After sharing many sexual fantasies that she had toward him and seeing that he did not respond beyond empathically listening and trying to understand her, Ms. W. began to gossip negatively about her therapist to many of her friends and relatives. Instead of helping Ms. W. to see how revengeful she was feeling toward him, Graham became very silent. In response to his silence, Ms. W. gossiped even more. However, she also began to feel rejected and alienated by him. In response, she sought out other therapists for consultations, acting out even more revenge.

When Graham saw that he was becoming more and more silent in the sessions, he realized that his silence was his way of retaliating. Ms. W.'s acting out was experienced by him as a narcissistic injury, and he in turn tried to injure her with strong doses of silence.

Silence, if used prudently, tactfully, and carefully by the therapist, can promote the forward movement of the treatment. When used for long periods of time, the client can feel rejected, misunderstood, and rageful. Almost always, the prolonged silence of a practitioner suggests that he or she is feeling rejected, misunderstood, and in a rage—usually in response to the client but often unconsciously aimed at others as well, such as ungiving parents in the therapist's present or past.

GOSSIPING

Although clients and practitioners usually agree to keep the therapy a private and confidential matter, this ground rule is often broken by both parties. In many ways it is quite understandable! The anxiety, resentment, excitement, and other intense emotions aroused in the treatment situation are often too much to bear alone. Consequently, clients and practitioners gossip about each other to many friends, colleagues, and relatives.

Therapists, of course, can mask their wishes to gossip about their clients by attending seminars, going to supervision, writing books and articles, and partic-

ipating in conferences. All of these activities are "professional" and provide practitioners a legitimate outlet to discharge feelings and sometimes resolve conflicts
that center around their work with clients.

Clients usually do not have legitimate outlets to talk about their therapists, and
most of the time the kind of discussions they have about their therapy partners is
labelled by professionals as "acting out." Although clients do not routinely attend
conferences, meetings, or supervisory sessions to discuss their feelings about their
therapists, their gossiping sessions with friends, relatives, and colleagues are not that
dissimilar from their therapists' activities at professional meetings.

Some group therapists encourage their clients to have "alternate sessions" where
the therapist is not present and the clients often gossip about the therapist (Ormont
& Strean, 1978). However, there still remain few legitimate gossiping outlets for
clients in most therapeutic settings.

When clients or clinicians talk about each other away from each other, they are
usually not able to face certain issues in the therapy sessions. What cannot be faced
can span many possibilities, including all kinds of transference and countertransference reactions and all types of resistances and counterresistances.

Learning that clients are frequently talking about the therapist and the therapy,
the mature practitioner attempts to help the client consider what the dangers are
in discussing inside the therapy what is being gossiped about outside. The practitioner tries to help the client resolve those resistances that impede the discussion
of sexual and aggressive thoughts, fantasies, and impressions of the therapist or any
other issues that seem to feel forbidden and/or dangerous to the client.

Therapists cannot help their clients face the meanings of their gossiping if they
are unduly uncomfortable about the act of gossiping or its content, or perhaps too
involved in doing the same thing themselves. When therapists learn that a client
is gossiping about them, they can feel demeaned, criticized, overlooked, rejected,
or no longer in control of the therapeutic process. No clinician is exempt from personal reactions when the client gossips. However, every clinician should know what
he or she feels about the specific client's gossiping and should be aware of how he
or she feels about the content of the gossip.

Mary Cooper, a psychiatrist in private practice, had been treating Mr. X.
for over a year on a twice-weekly basis. The client sought psychotherapy
because at the age of 35 he had been divorced three times, was suffering from
alcoholism, drug addiction, and a gambling compulsion. Although he was
an excellent salesman, Mr. X.'s drinking and gambling interfered with his
working consistently. He was also quite concerned about his "abusive" behavior with his wives as well as with other women, in that he found that he would
yell at them, insult them, and then physically hurt them.

Mr. X. responded very positively to Mary Cooper's empathetic, nonjudgmental, caring demeanor. Feeling accepted by a woman that he thought

was "very bright and very compassionate" increased his self-esteem and self-confidence and enabled him to give up a great deal of his self-destructive behavior. His work habits improved and in his relationships he stopped acting out much of his belligerence. With an improvement in Mr. X.'s functioning came a growing positive transference. He began to tell Mary Cooper constantly that she was the tender mother he always wanted, and if she were not his psychiatrist, he would think seriously of "making [her] a friend."

While Mr. X. was in the midst of his positive transference, he began to try to learn more about Mary's professional and personal life. He called professional organizations, consulted medical directories, and enlisted the help of some of his friends who were in the mental health field.

With a large amount of information about his therapist at his disposal, Mr. X. used the data to demean Mary in front of his friends. He told several of them that she went to an inferior medical school, did not have a solid psychiatric training, and was in personal analysis with a man who should have retired long ago. In response to his constant criticisms of Mary, Mr. X.'s friends told him that he should seriously consider leaving treatment.

When Mr. X. mentioned rather casually during the early part of his second year of treatment that his friends were questioning Mary Cooper's credentials, Mary asked him how he felt about that. He told her that his friends had their reservations about psychotherapy and, therefore, their questioning Mary's qualifications was understandable. As Mary slowly moved into asking her client about his own reservations about her, Mr. X. eventually acknowledged how he had investigated her background and then gossiped about her with his friends.

Without consciously realizing how irritated she was with Mr. X., Mary told him, "You are acting out your voyeurism, hostility, and wish to defeat me!" Mr. X. denied what he felt were "accusations" and told Mary, "I think you are much too angry for a psychiatrist and it is unlike you and does not become you."

Inasmuch as Mary was in therapy herself as well as in supervision, she had several opportunities to discuss her counterresistances in her work with Mr. X. She realized that she experienced Mr. X.'s "snooping" into her life as a rape. Furthermore, when she vehemently called her client a voyeur, it was as if he had broken into her bedroom, undressed her, and gazed at her while she was in the nude. Although Mr. X. may have been expressing some hostility of his own, Mary recognized that calling him "hostile" was a projection of her own hostility, because she was furious with Mr. X. and had fantasies of ending the treatment.

When Mary Cooper could better understand her own overreaction to her client's excessive curiosity as well as her anger at his gossiping, she could begin to consider the real meaning of his behavior. The client was like a young boy in love who could not face his intense wishes to "eat up" his partner. Instead, as a substitute, he devoured data about her personal life. But because he felt a great deal of guilt and anxiety about his wish to be extremely dependent on his kind, maternal therapist, he arranged to have his friends rebuke her.

Mr. X. could eventually face some of his resistances to discuss his transference reactions when Mary Cooper could face and resolve some of her counterresistances.

Although practitioners have many opportunities to discuss their feelings about their clients in many professional circles, they often find themselves discussing certain clients repetitively and with many different colleagues and friends. When this occurs, certain counterresistances are not being faced or worked through.

Peter Bayliss, a therapist in private practice, was treating Mr. Y. in intensive therapy, seeing him four times a week. Mr. Y. came into treatment because he was very depressed, worked sporadically, had several psychosomatic symptoms, and was sexually impotent much of the time. In addition, Mr. Y. was very paranoid and refused to give Peter Bayliss his name until the eighteenth month of treatment.

Despite Mr. Y.'s acute distrust of Peter Bayliss, he formed a good working alliance with him and made a lot of progress. By the end of the first year of treatment, Mr. Y. began to work consistently in his chosen field. In addition, his depression lifted and he overcame most of his sexual and psychosomatic problems. However, he continued to be unwilling to tell his therapist his name.

Peter Bayliss found himself discussing the case of Mr. Y. wherever he went. Initially, he told himself and others that a client who did not want to give his name was a most interesting case and the exhibitionistic pleasure that was derived, Peter rationalized, was why he gossiped so much about Mr. Y. However, as Peter discussed the case in seminars and conferences, he began to note that many of his colleagues responded in a paranoid manner. For example, more than one colleague cautioned Peter that he may be treating an "unsavory" character, one who was not "trustworthy" and could be a "criminal." Furthermore, as Peter began to consider his colleagues' reactions more seriously, he realized that many were reacting, not only with anger and paranoia, but felt very teased by Peter's renditions.

What Peter was overlooking in his work with Mr. Y. were several counterresistances. He had not allowed himself to experience how teased he felt by his client, nor was he aware of his own paranoid reactions to Mr. Y.'s unwillingness to give him his name. Peter was unconsciously arranging for his friends and colleagues to feel what he, Peter, was repressing—anger, paranoia, and teased. When Peter could better understand what he was acting out by repetitively discussing his client with others, he became more determined to keep his feelings about Mr. Y. to himself. As a result, he began to experience anger, paranoia, and being teased in the sessions with his client. As Peter studied his reactions more carefully, he could use them in the therapy. Slowly he could confront Mr. Y. with the latter's wish to tease Peter, make him angry, and get him uncomfortable.

The more Peter could confront his own reactions to Mr. Y. and use some of them in the therapy, the more the client could verbalize his strong homosexual fantasies toward Peter as well as his own wish to be raped by the therapist. When these fantasies became more conscious, Mr. Y. could then reveal his name to Peter.

PERSISTENT DEMANDS

As therapy moves on and deepens, most clients begin to experience more intense fantasies, more powerful transference reactions, and more anxiety. One way that clients cope with the acute discomfort that frequently emerges during the middle phase of therapy is that, instead of keeping all of the attention focused on themselves and confronting their own internal demands, they place demands on their therapists. Although this resistance is used during other phases of therapy, it is quite prevalent during the middle phase.

In lieu of responding to their therapists' questions about their own feelings, thoughts, memories, and reactions, clients ask their therapists questions about their fantasies, memories, and thoughts. Instead of interacting with the therapist solely in the consultation room, clients call the therapist on the phone in between sessions, at home, or elsewhere. Some ask for home visits or meetings at their own office in lieu of the therapist's. All of these demands are usually attempts of the client to make the relationship with the therapist less professional, less frustrating, less painful, and more friendly, more equal, and more gratifying.

In previous chapters, we pointed out that many practitioners have difficulty coping with their clients' demands. Most practitioners prefer to ask questions rather than answer them and to hear fantasies rather than report them. They would rather direct the treatment than be directed.

If practitioners cannot empathize with nor understand the nature of their clients' resistances when the latter make persistent demands, they can become quite punitive. Directly or indirectly, they can command their clients to stop reversing roles and/or respond to their clients' questions and demands by coldly and mechanically asking them, "Why do you ask?" or, "What is your need to know?" Rarely are clients helped when they are given responses devoid of empathy and understanding.

What clients usually do need when they make unusual and persistent demands is a genuine attempt on the practitioner's part to try to understand what the client is feeling and thinking when he or she stops the process of self-examination. When the therapist is sincerely interested in what is transpiring in the client's internal and interpersonal life that prompts the demands, most clients eventually return to the self-inquiry that is part of their role-set as a client. Although some clients initially respond with anger when the clinician tries to investigate without being ambivalent about his or her stance, or hostile in his or her tone, what the client is feeling and thinking, the client usually tries to cooperate with the therapist and master the real tasks at hand.

Nonetheless, practitioners can experience their clients' demandingness as put-downs, castigations, castrations, and wipeouts. Consequently, they can get annoyed and handle their annoyance through the use of one or more counterresistances.

> Shirley Adams, a psychologist in a mental health clinic, had been treating Ms. Z., a young woman in her early twenties, for a year and a half. Ms. Z. was in twice-weekly treatment for alternating attacks of anorexia and bulimia nervosa. As is true with many clients who suffer from eating disorders, Ms. Z. frequently defended herself from the impact of the therapeutic interventions because she feared becoming engulfed or merged with the therapist (Bruch, 1984). During the first year and a half of the therapy, Ms. Z. was frequently critical of Shirley Adams. Her criticisms ranged all the way from derogatory remarks about her attire to Shirley's lack of professional discipline. Often the demeaning remarks were contradictory. Sometimes Ms. Z. told Shirley that she was too warm, too verbal, too friendly, and not sufficiently "professional"; on other occasions the client damned her therapist for being too withholding, too cold, too silent, and too "classically Freudian."
>
> Shirley Adams weathered the storms and the client never left treatment, although she often threatened to do so. However, when Ms. Z. ceased voicing criticisms and lessened her power struggles with Shirley, she began to make many demands on her. She asked for didactic information on eating disorders, wanted to know if Shirley had ever had bulimia, anorexia, or any other type of problem with food, and she raised questions about the training of psychotherapists, wondering if they had sufficient training in physiology and biochemistry.
>
> Although Shirley had recognized up until now that Ms. Z.'s criticisms had been attempts to create distance and to prevent intimacy between them, she was not able to realize that Ms. Z.'s persistent demands served the same unconscious purposes. Thus, she found herself responding quite coldly and mechanically to Ms. Z.'s demands with questions such as, "Why do you ask?" or "What's your motive?" When Ms. Z. noticed that Shirley was not particularly responsive to her requests, she became more insistent—and more hostile. When Shirley felt overwhelmed by her client's intense affect, numerous

demands, and sense of entitlement, she became quite punitive and author-itarian and said to Ms. Z., "You are using the therapy inappropriately. You are here to understand yourself, not to understand me. You have to stop the demands and start working!"

Ms. Z. did not accept her therapist's cease and desist orders with much equanimity. On the contrary, like many other clients who suffer from bulimia nervosa, she "vomited back" the therapist's interventions (Zerbe, 1990) and told Shirley that the treatment she was getting was "not the right stuff." Exclaimed the client, "I'd like to take all of the shit that comes out of your foul mouth and dump it on you, instead of having to take it in myself. You are a very hurtful person!"

What was happening with Ms. Z. is something that very frequently occurs in the middle phase of psychotherapy. The client was working overtime to get her therapist to become the same unresponsive, inattentive, unloving mother of her past. If the therapist succeeded in complying with this mandate, the client could victoriously exclaim, "See, closeness and intimacy with another person is a waste of time! You just get hurt all over again."

Although Shirley had unconsciously complied with Ms. Z.'s attempts to make her "a nonnurturing mother," she also felt uncomfortable as she observed and examined herself behaving in a hostile fashion. Slowly but surely she began to realize that her client's persistent demands reminded her of her own mother's demands during her teenage years. As Shirley told one of her colleagues, "I could always deal with my mother's criticisms and therefore Ms. Z.'s knocks didn't get to me. But I never could deal with my mother's persistent demands. I felt weakened by them and that's what happened to me with my client."

When the practitioner gets in touch with the dynamic and genetic causes of a counterresistance, the counterresistance usually dissolves. Therefore, as Shirley stopped making Ms. Z. the demanding mother of her past, she did not have to resist being an understanding therapist as much and eventually stopped giving her client cease and desist orders.

THE PRACTITIONER IS VERY DEMANDING

Although much attention has been given in the professional literature to the client making persistent demands on the therapist, little has been said about the therapist being very demanding of the client. The intensity of the therapeutic process and the anxiety it engenders for practitioners can cause them to be equally as demanding of their clients as their clients can be of them. We have already alluded to therapists raising fees frequently as a possible sign of their feeling overworked. But practitioners can urge clients to dream more, fantasy more, accept interpretations with more cooperation, and get better sooner and faster! Practitioners can demand of their clients to have more transference reactions, particularly sexual fantasies. They can demand more aggressive responses, too.

Just as it is when their clients become too demanding, it is important for practitioners to understand what is happening when they themselves become too demanding.

James Zimmer, a therapist in private practice, had been treating Ms. A., a woman in her mid-thirties, for close to two years. Ms. A. was being seen three times a week during most of that time. She had sought therapy primarily because of her consistent failures in relationships with men. Each time she began a relationship with a man there was much mutual excitement and adoration. Within a few weeks, the romance would deteriorate and, almost always at the man's instigation, the relationship would end.

During her two years of treatment, Ms. A. got in touch with strong masochistic fantasies which played a large part in her chaotic relationships with men. In her fantasies she was raped, demeaned verbally and physically, and abandoned. The more she was abused in her fantasies, the more sexual excitement she derived. Orgasm was attained when she fantasied that she was "beaten to a pulp."

Although Ms. A.'s self-esteem improved while in treatment, and although, she had received less abuse in her relationships with men, Ms. A. did not make substantial progress. She had few transference reactions, rarely discussed fantasies or dreams, but instead focused on concrete issues such as how much work she did on the computer at her job.

Feeling that Ms. A. needed more help in moving ahead both in and out of therapy, Jim started to put some pressure on her. He told her in a strong voice that she was "not sufficiently involved" in the therapy, that she "did not examine" herself enough, that the material she presented was "superficial," and that she "better get to work" if she wanted to improve her life.

Essentially agreeing with her therapist, Ms. A. told him that she realized that she was an "unrewarding client" and that just like her relationships with her boyfriends, Ms. A. could see that she was "not bringing very much into the relationship." Jim, obviously pleased with his client's remarks, praised her for her insight, particularly for her ability to recognize how her patterns in relating to Jim were similar to the way she related to other men.

Despite Ms. A.'s "insight," she soon began to have migraine headaches, could not concentrate at work, and had to spend a lot of time in bed trying to sleep in order to shake off a depression and get rid of her painful headaches. What neither client nor therapist recognized is that they were both caught up in the same kind of intense sadomasochistic interaction that Ms. A. had with her boyfriends. Ms. A. had succeeded in getting her therapist to demean her and to induce her to suffer from much pain—although under the guise of trying to help her therapeutically. Her going to bed with migraine headaches was not too different psychologically from her having orgasms when she fantasied herself as "beaten to a pulp."

Jim Zimmer's behavior with Ms. A. is an excellent example of a therapist complying with the client's transference wishes (Racker, 1968). Ms. A. unconsciously wanted to be treated sadistically and her therapist cooperated with her! However, what precipitated Jim Zimmer's provocative behavior was his overactive therapeutic ambitiousness. Unable to understand and empathize with his client's masochism, he experienced her resistance to getting better as a personal affront to him. Rather than helping her to see that improving her own life was experienced by her as a sadistic attack on others, he pressured her to get better.

Most clients, particularly self-hating clients, usually use the practitioner's demands to buttress their self-hatred. Ms. A. agreed with Jim Zimmer's "interpretations" but used them to suffer more pain. Because Jim Zimmer was unaware of his own sadism in the therapy as well as his narcissistic injury because the client did not improve, he made unnecessary demands on her, which only strengthened her resistances and exacerbated her symptomatology.

Whenever clinicians want to make many demands on their clients and/or find themselves doing so, they can usually tell themselves that they are experiencing their clients' resistances as personal affronts and are not able to empathize with the anxiety and other issues that are sustaining their clients' resistances. Very often when the practitioner is making excessive demands on the client, the practitioner is experiencing himself or herself as a frustrated lover, parent, or child, and has turned the client into an important figure of the past.

EXTRATHERAPEUTIC CONTACTS

A phenomenon that occurs during therapy but which has received very limited discussion is the extratherapeutic contact—a contact between client and therapist outside the consultation room that is not planned by either party. There are probably many reasons to account for why there has been little discussion in the professional literature (Strean, 1981).

Many, if not most psychotherapists, tend to model themselves after the "abstinent, anonymous surgeon who is an opaque mirror" for the client (Freud, 1912). Thus this demeanor can create anxiety, embarrassment, shame, or guilt for a therapist when a client observes him or her shopping at a store, chatting with a friend, eating at a restaurant, walking with a spouse, or using the facilities of a restroom. It is difficult, if not impossible, for a therapist to sustain a surgeonlike countenance when the client observes him or her outside the consultation room.

Because treasured unconscious transference and countertransference positions risk being altered, regressive wishes can be stimulated, and new and different behaviors are often expected when the client is not in the therapist's office, the extratherapeutic contact can assume a phobic and neurotic quality for both client and therapist (Tarnower, 1966). Particularly if client and therapist meet in the presence of others, both may fear that the confidentiality of their relationship is in danger of being violated. Even if they go unobserved, therapist and client may become unduly concerned about the injunction to avoid acting out. Finally, the parties are often caught unprepared, a situation that usually provokes anxiety (Strean, 1981, 1985/1990).

The extratherapeutic contact also has the potential of releasing hidden anxiety, thus provoking transference and countertransference fantasies such as primal scene conflicts, oedipal and homosexual desires, sadistic and masochistic urges, and oral incorporative yearnings. However, inasmuch as the extratherapeutic contact is a clinical reality for many clients and therapists, it is incumbent upon both parties not to try to avoid or stimulate such contacts, but to investigate their dynamic meaning when they do occur. If the extratherapeutic contact is viewed as an interpersonal experience that is not to be encouraged or discouraged but is to be thoroughly understood, it can then be used in the treatment to promote understanding of transference and countertransference phenomena, as well as to clarify the meaning of unresolved resistances and counterresistances.

Two major counterresistances tend to emerge when therapists meet their clients outside the consultation room. One counterresistance is to attempt to avoid facing the issues that emerge for both parties and to try to pretend nothing is happening or has happened. Some therapists feel so squeamish about the extratherapeutic contact that they will not only do everything to avoid it—and not analyze the dynamic issues if a contact does occur—but also go so far as to prohibit the client from going anyplace where he or she might meet the therapist.

The second type of counterresistance that is common in coping with the extratherapeutic contact is to use the contact for gratifying client and therapist wishes that should be understood and mastered rather than acted out. Here we are referring to intellectual exchanges, sharing interests, or even participating together in social, political, or community projects. Most often these extratherapeutic contacts are unconsciously arranged to gratify wishes such as symbiotic hunger, voyeuristic and exhibitionistic fantasies, genital fantasies, and other libidinal desires. Occasionally they are used defensively to ward off such issues as mutual hatred or power struggles.

Sometimes the two types of counterresistance can be observed in the same therapist at different times with the same client or with different clients.

Angela Yates, a therapist in private practice, had been treating Ms. B. on a three-times-a-week basis for close to two years. Ms. B., a woman in her middle thirties, came to Angela for treatment after she had become separated from her husband to whom she had been married for over 10 years. What precipitated the separation was Ms. B. learning that her husband had been engaged in an extramarital affair for over four years.

When Ms. B. sought therapy with Angela Yates, she was extremely depressed, had lost much weight, was full of doubts about herself, and lost a great deal of interest in her work. Ms. B, who was living alone after the separation, occasionally had suicidal fantasies but had not acted on any of them.

Ms. B. did very well in her therapy. After Angela showed her how she was turning much of her hatred toward her husband against herself, Ms. B. could freely discharge a lot of rage. This diminished her depression, increased her appetite, and improved her self-image. As a result, Ms. B. began to date men. Not only did she derive much pleasure from her dates, but also her pleasure in her work was greater than at any previous time in her career.

Ms. B. and Angela grew very fond of each other. Ms. B. was very grateful to Angela for the many positive changes that accrued through her treatment, and Angela made it very obvious that she considered Ms. B. a most gratifying client. The two women were roughly the same age and there was an implicit assumption that they had a lot in common.

Toward the end of the second year of treatment, Ms. B. and Angela found themselves at a meeting devoted to feminist issues. In greeting each other, both of them spontaneously blurted out that it was not a surprise to find each other at the meeting.

Angela was able to recognize, even at the meeting, that she derived a lot of pleasure being with Ms. B. outside the consultation room. In many ways it felt as if she were with a close friend or relative at some festive occasion.

Analysis of some of her own dreams helped Angela see that she felt a sexual attraction toward Ms. B. The extratherapeutic contact, she eventually concluded, was like a date and both parties were excited about the rendezvous. It also intensified a latent but strong homosexual transference-countertransference relationship. Angela had become a substitute for Ms. B.'s husband, and Ms. B. had become for Angela the daughter, younger sister, and female lover that Angela had always wanted.

Although the extratherapeutic contact had helped therapist and client to fall in love with each other, this did not help the therapeutic process. On the contrary, Ms. B. tried to change the nature of the relationship with Angela from treatment to chit-chat and from self-examination to mutual gratification. As Angela began to realize that Ms. B. had stopped dating men and was participating in activities that were more exclusively feminist-oriented, it dawned on her that this shift had something to do with the intensely positive transference-countertransference relationship between Ms. B. and herself. She further realized that the extratherapeutic contact had not been analyzed—fantasies, transference reactions, and dreams connected with it were not forthcoming. Consequently, it occurred to Angela that not investigating the meaning of the extratherapeutic contact gave Ms. B. the impetus to turn more and more of their interaction into something more social and less professional.

As Angela was working on her counterresistances in her work with Ms. B., and trying to restore their work into something more therapeutic and less social, Ms. B. and Angela again met outside the consultation room. It took place about three months after their first extratherapeutic meeting, at a theatre during the intermission of a play. Angela, aware of the difficulties that had transpired after the first extratherapeutic contact, appeared very detached and said only one or two words to Ms. B. The contrast between Angela's previous behavior at the first meeting and the one at the theatre was so great that Ms. B. in the conversation at the theatre asked, "Are you okay?" When Angela responded neutrally and asked, "Do I appear okay?" Ms. B. stomped off and cut the conversation short, obviously doing to Angela what she felt Angela had done to her—Ms. B. cut her off.

At the next several treatment sessions, Ms. B. was in a rage. She felt that Angela had led her on, became her friend, and then rejected her. She exclaimed, "Angela, you are a sick, ambivalent woman who doesn't know whether you are coming or going!" Ms. B. also told Angela that she reminded her of her former husband whom she could never trust.

Although Ms. B. threatened to discontinue treatment several times, she stayed and was able to work out her deep homosexual yearnings, oral cravings, and strong hurt and rage when she was frustrated.

The extratherapeutic contact, as we learned from Angela Yates's experience with Ms. B., always has the potential hazard of diminishing the practitioner's role as fantasied object, of forcing the client to deal with more frustration than he or she can bear, and of disrupting the work and resolution of the client's transference fantasies and his or her resistances. As in any other interpersonal event between therapist and client, it is imperative for the therapist to help the client explore associations to meeting the therapist outside the consultation room and make these experiences part of the treatment process. It is equally important for therapists to become aware of their own fantasies, wishes, and defenses when they meet clients outside of their offices. They should always consider not only their own internal responses, but also how much have they unconsciously played a part in arranging for the extratherapeutic contact to take place.

In sum, although extratherapeutic contacts are bound to occur, therapists should recognize that they have a responsibility to assess why they occur when they do, to help their clients understand their role in them and their associations to them, to understand their own internal responses when the contact occurs, and, what is most crucial yet very difficult, to behave like a human being but concomitantly safeguard the therapeutic relationship.

In the case of Angela Yates, she was insufficiently disciplined and abandoned her role as therapist in the first extratherapeutic contact. In the second extratherapeutic contact, she was overcontrolled and insufficiently human. Both of these responses are quite typical of many clinicians as they strive to help resolve their clients' resistances and their own counterresistances. Some of these resistances and counterresistances can be overt and observable such as the ones we discussed in this chapter. Others can be subtle and less observable and these will be discussed in Chapter 6.

6

The Middle Phase Continued: The Therapist's Reactions to Subtle Resistances and the Therapist's Subtle Counterresistances

In Chapter 5 we reviewed how clients and therapists resist the therapeutic process by not complying with the ground rules of treatment, such as by frequently arriving late for sessions or by cancelling them consistently. In this chapter, we examine the therapist's responses to clients whose resistances are not as apparent. We attempt to demonstrate how practitioners can obstruct the therapeutic process through the use of subtle, albeit unconscious counterresistances.

Quite often clients and therapists observe that although the client and the practitioner faithfully attend all treatment sessions, arrive on time, and focus conscientiously on the pertinent clinical material, the client does not progress. Neither practitioner nor client can be sure what is impeding the therapeutic progress. But they think about it and wonder if something not so easily recognized is taking place.

One of the first clinicians to comment on this phenomenon was a disciple of Freud's, Karl Abraham (1919). He referred to the compliant client who overtly cooperates but indirectly fights the treatment process. He pointed out that these clients, though dominated by a punitive superego and a powerful feeling of obligation to submit to most therapeutic requirements, secretly resent their therapists and rebel against them by not using the therapy constructively. They "grudge the physician any remark that refers to the external progress of their [therapy] or to its data. In their opinion he ought not to have supplied any contribution to the treatment" (p. 307).

As we briefly mentioned in Chapter 1, Freud (1926) discussed the *negative therapeutic reaction*. By this term, Freud referred to the many patients who could verbalize all the interpretations given to them but still maintained their symptoms. He inferred that there must be some force within these patients that prevents their using the insights gained. Freud identified this force as the superego.

Most clinicians now recognize that when clients resist getting better, their superegos are restraining them from receiving pleasure. The superego, which contains the prohibitive voices of parents and parental figures, forbids clients to enjoy their lives.

Since Abraham's and Freud's discoveries, much has been learned about subtle but negative reactions to treatment. Concomitant with experiencing superego pressure, the client with the negative therapeutic reaction is also trying to defeat the therapist. By calling attention to the fact that he or she never improves from therapy, the client is demeaning the clinician and not permitting the therapist to have any influence. In effect, the client is like the child who claims to want to be toilet trained but nonetheless has many "accidents." Similar to the youngster who persistently states he or she wants to learn to read or write but "can't," the client with a negative therapeutic reaction is unconsciously discharging a great deal of spite (Kesten, 1970).

As the reader can now appreciate, no client resistance can be viewed in isolation but must be understood as part of an interactional process between client and therapist (Boesky, 1990). Consequently, in this chapter we are first going to attempt to demonstrate that when subtle resistances emerge, there is often a collusion between therapist and client in which both are unconsciously wedded to maintain certain transference-countertransference patterns. In the following section, we attempt to study various types of untherapeutic collusions between clients and therapists, which, although subtle, interfere with the treatment's progress in a real way.

MAINTENANCE OF FIXED TRANSFERENCE-COUNTERTRANSFERENCE POSITIONS

Mutual Love

If psychotherapy is to be helpful to the client, the latter must have the opportunity to experience in the treatment situation a whole range of human emotions. Furthermore, in successful treatment, a great deal of the emotion should be directed toward the practitioner. The clinician who is truly helpful to the client invariably is the recipient of dependency yearnings, oral desires, sadistic and masochistic fantasies, oedipal rivalry, homoerotic wishes, competitive stirrings, and revengeful impulses, to name just a small number of possibilities. If the therapist has had few of these affects cathected in his or her direction, the therapy is probably a limited experience for the client and will have a limited impact on his or her functioning.

One of the ways that therapists and clients collude to mutually resist the treatment process is by trying to do everything to accommodate one another and to avoid any interpersonal transaction that may interfere with the maintenance of a love-and-be-loved relationship. Often this kind of "therapeutic symbiosis" has been given theoretical justification (Adler, 1967; Blanck & Blanck, 1979). However, when client and therapist must idealize each other like a mother and infant do during the early stages of the infant's life, client and therapist usually fear being autonomous and are frightened to deal with issues like genital sexuality, assertion, competition, and aggression. A consistent love and be loved relationship between client and therapist can offer both of them a passive form of narcissistic joy, but the client's hostile wishes go underground only to reappear in the form of symptoms after separation and termination. As we have suggested repeatedly, when the client is required to suppress and repress hostile reactions to frustration, the resistance against feeling and expressing the hateful parts of the psyche is, of course, maintained. However, when the client is helped to discharge hostile fantasies, the ego is freed of its excessive destructiveness and the creative parts of the personality are made available for healthier functioning (Nagelberg, 1959).

Despite the fact that most clinicians agree with the notion that clients should be helped to experience and articulate a whole range of human feelings, they are often frightened to receive anything other than warmth, love, admiration, and gratitude from them.

Sheng Xu, a psychiatrist in private practive, had been treating Mr. C., a man in his mid-thirties, on a twice-weekly basis for over two years. Mr. C. had been referred to Sheng by the courts because the client was involved in a series of thefts. The thefts were motivated principally by a wish of Mr. C.'s to maintain his drug habit. The court took the position that Mr. C. could be on probation and not be imprisoned if he agreed to be in psychiatric treatment for a minimum of two years.

Although Sheng neglected to explore with Mr. C. how he experienced being in the involuntary treatment, Mr. C. seemed to be a cooperative client who formed a good working alliance with Sheng. Mr. C. came to each appointment on time, hardly ever cancelled any of them, always greeted Sheng with a smile and departed with the same kind of enthusiasm. In addition, he paid his fees faithfully at the end of each month.

In the treatment sessions, Mr. C. told Sheng that he very much welcomed Sheng's warm and understanding approach and contrasted his therapist's demeanor with that of his parents' whom he experienced as "cold and rejecting." Furthermore, Mr. C. could understand how he had married the woman he did. Irene, his wife, was also described as cold and rejecting. "I guess that's what I felt I deserved," said Mr. C.

During the two years of treatment, Mr. C. consistently reported that his work as a computer specialist was going smoothly, and although his wife continued to be cold, he was able to cope with her. "What I really like about my relationship with you," said Mr. C. toward the end of the second year of treatment, "is that it has helped me to stay clean. I don't use drugs and I don't get into trouble with the law."

When Sheng asked Mr. C. to what he attributed his overall improvement,

Mr. C. was quick to answer. He declared, "It's because of our great relationship. You never criticize me, you seem to care about me, you are always friendly, and I feel good because of you."

Given Mr. C.'s strong positive transference as well as his apparent therapeutic progress, Sheng was very surprised to learn toward the end of the second year of treatment that his client was picked up by the police because he was caught stealing. Furthermore, Mr. C.'s drug habits had not really changed one iota.

What Sheng had overlooked in his work with Mr. C. were the implications of a transference relationship that remained consistently positive. For a man on drugs who had been in trouble with the law, it would be psychologically impossible to feel only love toward his therapist. Nobody on drugs who has consistently stolen, and is in treatment involuntarily, can possibly be exempt from frustrated dependency wishes, narcissistic injuries, and hostile fantasies. Furthermore, no man in a relationship with a woman whom he described as cold and rejecting can cope with life only by smiling.

In reflecting on the work of Sheng and Mr. C., we can infer that one of the best ways to assess progress of treatment is for the practitioner to ask, "What conflicts of the client's have emerged in the treatment relationship?" If, as was true of Mr. C., there are conflicts around unfulfilled dependency wishes, rage, impulse control, and narcissistic injury, these issues should emerge in the client's transference toward the therapist. Sheng should have been somewhat skeptical on seeing that all Mr. C. did with him was to speak positively of life, of the therapy, and of his therapist.

When a client copes with life through antisocial behavior and loss of impulse control, it is inevitable that the client recapitulates this form of modus vivendi in the treatment. Sheng should have expected Mr. C. to be dishonest with him, and he should have expected part of Mr. C.'s psychopathology to be part of the transference relationship. A deceptive person will always become a deceptive client.

As mentioned earlier in this section, effective therapy necessitates that the client be helped to feel and express a whole range of affects in the treatment. When this does not take place, effective treatment is not taking place. On noting that his client was expressing nothing more than warmth, gratitude, and admiration, Sheng Xu should have been alerted to the fact that the client was repressing and suppressing most of his feelings, thoughts, memories, and fantasies when with him. What was repressed and suppressed was acted out by Mr. C. in his continued stealing and drug use.

When practitioners aid and abet a consistently positive transference-countertransference relationship between the client and themselves, invariably they are invested in maintaining an omnipotent defense to protect themselves against some kind of danger. Usually the danger they fear is to be hated and/or rejected. To many practitioners, as it feels to many clients, to be hated and rejected seems like the end of the world. Rather than explore and understand how and why they distort the meaning of their clients' negative attitudes, they protect themselves by deflecting aggression being directed toward them. When clients and practitioners alike are protecting themselves against being the targets of hostility, they are usually afraid to feel like abandoned, helpless, and rejected children. Consequently, like Mr. C. and Sheng Xu, they work hard to maintain a love-and-be-loved relationship with each other. All that they really feel goes underground only to be acted out or discharged in symptoms and maladaptive character traits.

Supporting Marital Complaints

Mutual love as a resistance-counterresistance maneuver is frequently observed in the treatment of marital conflicts, especially when one member of the marital dyad is in individual treatment. Most individuals who experience marital conflicts see themselves as victims of their partners' insensitivities and immaturities. Rarely do individuals who come to therapy for help with their conflicted marriages say to the practitioner, "I am here to find out how and why I provoke my spouse and how and why I help to sustain my marital woes." On the contrary. Most unhappy husbands and wives say, "I'm here to find out why I live with such a disturbed person. I'd like your help in leaving my marriage or, at least, help me to change my spouse!"

Aware of the anger and frustration in the unhappy spouse, many therapists protect themselves against being the recipient of their negative affects. Instead, they join the unhappy spouse in criticizing the partner, maintain a positive transference-countertransference with the client, and the conflicted marriage stays conflicted or gets worse.

For a marriage to improve, the unhappy spouse must experience the therapist at some point during the therapy as similar to the marital partner. The best way for an unhappy husband or wife to recognize that his or her chronic marital complaints are really wishes is to experience them in the transference relationship with the therapist (Strean, 1981; 1985/1990). When, for example, an unhappy husband finds himself complaining in treatment that his therapist is cold and rejecting in the same way his wife is cold and rejecting, he may begin to wonder, "How come I'm finding some of the most important people in my life so unfriendly? Maybe I have something to do with it?"

> Beverly Wilson, a social worker in a family agency, was treating Mr. D. for about a year and a half on a weekly basis. Mr. D. sought marital counselling because he felt bored and irritated with his wife much of the time, had lost interest in having sex with her, and was seriously considering a divorce. In his late thirties, Mr. D. had been married for a little over 10 years. With the exception of the first year of marriage, according to Mr. D., "Life with my wife has been hum-drum." Although the client enjoyed his two daughters,

eight and six, he said many times to Beverly Wilson, "They are not enough to keep me in the marriage."

During the first year of treatment, Mr. D. came to his therapy sessions conscientiously and spent most of his time complaining about his wife. Discharging this aggression helped Mr. D. feel more energetic. His work as a high school teacher became more enjoyable to him and he found himself acquiring a sense of humor. However, his marital relationship did not improve at all.

Realizing that Mr. D. had been making no changes in his marriage and was complaining about his wife as much after a year of treatment as he did at the beginning, Beverly evaluated the treatment process more carefully. What became quite clear to her was that she found herself subtly supporting Mr. D.'s attacks on his wife and in no way had she been helping him to see his own role in the marital difficulties.

As Beverly decided to become less supportive and more neutral in her interaction with Mr. D., the transference relationship was modified. Mr. D. became irritated with Beverly and soon told her that she was "quite boring." "Like my wife, you don't stimulate me or turn me on," stated Mr. D. in one interview during the thirteenth month of treatment. A few weeks later he said to Beverly, "You give me next to nothing. I'm thinking of leaving you."

Beverly asked Mr. D. how it felt to be in two situations that seemed similar. Both with his wife and with her Mr. D. felt bored, unstimulated, and was tempted to end the relationship. In response to Beverly's question, Mr. D. became furious and said vehemently, "You are trying to do therapy on me! You think that you'll get me to say that I want women to take care of me. You think I want a mother, don't you?"

On Beverly's listening attentively to Mr. D.'s angry tirade without counterattacking, Mr. D. began to have some memories of his mother. He described her as being a woman who was "very engulfing" and "never minded her own business." As Beverly listened and gave Mr. D. much room to take the lead in their sessions and to talk about anything that came to his mind, slowly he began to reveal sexual fantasies toward his mother. He recalled how as a boy he often tried to watch her get undressed and was very interested in her body and bodily functions.

When it was clear to both Mr. D. and Beverly that Mr. D. had been repressing and suppressing incestuous fantasies for a good portion of his life, it also became clear that Mr. D.'s boredom with his wife as well as with his therapist was his way of defending against his sexual fantasies toward both of them. On being able to accept his incestuous fantasies with more equanimity and to express them with less anxiety, Mr. D.'s marital relationship improved enormously as did the rest of his day-to-day functioning.

Beverly's subtle counterresistance that interfered with Mr. D.'s therapeutic growth was her tacitly supporting his complaints about his wife rather than helping her client confront them. Whenever a practitioner does not see growth in the client, one question that should be asked is, "Am I supporting or in any way validating the client's complaints?" Although we have noted in previous chapters that supporting a client's complaints can be done actively and purposefully, Beverly Wilson seemed to support Mr. D.'s marital complaints covertly and subtly.

When clients complain constantly about a spouse or about anybody else in their social network, they are almost always masking feelings of warmth, disappointment, and hurt. Frequently, they are trying to defend against sexual feelings. When the complaints are directed toward someone of the same gender, the complaints are often masking unacceptable homosexual fantasies.

It is because chronic complaints usually defend against wishes that are unacceptable to the client, it rarely, if ever, helps the client to have them supported by the therapist. When therapists attempt to validate, legitimize, or support their clients' complaints, they provide rationalizations for them but hardly foster their clients' growth in therapy.

Practitioners who do not confront their clients' complaints and who do not help them understand the conflicts and anxieties that generate them are frequently frightened of some of their own aggressive and sexual fantasies. By trying to give their clients a means of escape from facing themselves, they are concomitantly attempting to avoid facing their own anxieties.

Sadomasochism in the Therapeutic Relationship

Although overt power struggles between client and therapist are relatively infrequent, subtle power struggles are ubiquitous. Inasmuch as all human beings have strong wishes to preserve the status quo, the treatment situation lends itself to power struggles because both parties are constantly being confronted by material that makes them anxious. When anyone is confronted by anxiety in a dyadic interpersonal situation, there is a tendency to want to put the other person down.

When clients reveal unacceptable dependency wishes, frightening symbiotic yearnings, homosexual cravings, oedipal fantasies, and all of the id impulses that emerge in productive psychotherapy, they frequently feel weak and vulnerable after doing so. Many, if not most, clients on exposing their primitive wishes to the therapist feel like guilt-ridden children who are also experiencing much shame and embarrassment. To ease feelings of weakness, vulnerability, and anxiety, clients often try to expose the therapists' weaknesses, limitations, and vulnerabilities.

It is often quite difficult for practitioners to have themselves viewed as weak, limited, and vulnerable. It is even more difficult for practitioners to have themselves analyzed by their clients and have their own latent homosexuality, oedipal strivings, or primitive aggression exposed. To cope with the anxiety generated, the therapist can try to "get even" by asserting his or her authority, knowledge, and expertise.

Inasmuch as clinicians do not feel comfortable when they engage in name-calling with their clients, they prefer to tell a client that he or she is narcissistic rather than labelling the client an S.O.B. Or, the practitioner may refer to the client's need for "one-upmanship" when the clinician would really like to "put down" the client.

Because overt power struggles go against most practitioners' therapeutic ideals and because most clients have difficulty overtly aggressing toward their therapists, subtle sadomasochistic power plays and low-level fracases between client and therapist are not uncommon during the middle phase of treatment.

In discussing a sadomasochistic relationship, we have to keep in mind that sadistic individuals are ones who have many passive, dependent, masochistic desires that they cannot tolerate. Their sadistic behavior defends against the anxiety that their passive-dependent wishes generate. By having someone to dominate, they can deny their own passive, dependent, masochistic wishes.

Masochistic individuals are usually those people who are very frightened of their sadistic and dominating wishes and they defend against them by being passive and dependent. They say to themselves and others, "It is you who is sadistic, not I" (Strean, 1985).

When one partner is dominant and the other is submissive, as we see in sadomasochistic marriages, neither partner maintains this equilibrium for too long. The dominant partner begins to feel guilty about his or her sadism and submits, while the submissive partner begins to feel resentful about being placed so frequently in a submissive position and begins to aggress. Consequently, when we talk about a sadomasochistic relationship, we are referring to two people who both have a great deal of sadism and masochism within themselves and who constantly alternate roles with one another (Strean, 1985).

In the sadomasochistic treatment relationships, the alternating of roles by clients and therapists, though usually subtle, is real. Neither of the partners feels secure or safe in the relationship; therefore both constantly vacillate between demeaning themselves and each other.

Tom Vigilante was a psychologist in private practice who had been treating Ms. E., a 40-year-old twice-divorced woman, for close to two years. Ms. E. sought treatment because she was depressed about her two unsuccessful marriages and what she felt was her dim future with men and the unlikelihood of her ever becoming a natural mother. Ms. E., a psychiatric nurse, was seen twice a week in psychotherapy.

During the first year and a half of treatment, Ms. E. spent much of her time demeaning and devaluing herself. She referred to herself at various times as "a social misfit," "a lousy sexual partner," or "an emotional idiot." When Tom listened and did not say very much as Ms. E. castigated herself, Ms.

E. would psychologically beat herself unmercifully. But when Tom tried to investigate with his client her investment in having masochistic orgies in the treatment sessions, she would bring out many sadistic fantasies toward her former husbands, her older brother, and her father. Yet, when Tom made reference to Ms. E.'s hostility, she would deny its existence and return to her masochistic position.

Without consciously realizing it, Tom was becoming frustrated with Ms. E. She did not show any progress in resolving her problems with men, she sounded like a "broken record" in the treatment sessions, and she was completely devoid of overt transference reactions toward him. In a session toward the end of the second year of treatment, Tom told his client that she was involved "in constant sadomasochistic relationships with me." Feeling criticized, Ms. E. began to weep and had another masochistic orgy saying, "I never do anything right. I feel like a social deviant." On noting his client's negative therapeutic reaction, Tom felt frustrated once again and told Ms. E., "You always manage to hate yourself. You must like it!" In response, Ms. E. wept intensely again and told Tom she realized that the treatment was "going nowhere" and maybe she ought to try medication, group therapy, or religion.

Not sensitizing himself to his client's latent hostility, fearful of losing her to another therapist, and guilty for having sadistic fantasies toward Ms. E., Tom began to castigate himself openly. He told Ms. E., "I think I've been insensitive to many of your issues. I'd like a second chance." Feeling upset about her own hostility toward Tom, Ms. E. tried to reassure him that he was "doing a good job." However, she soon resumed demeaning herself and told Tom, "I should appreciate you more. I'm not grateful enough." Tired of hearing her self-attacks, Tom became irritated with Ms. E. and accusingly told her, "You want to be a pussycat, don't you?"

Apparently, Tom did not recognize the thinly veiled sarcasm in his remarks to Ms. E., nor was he aware of his own self-hatred when Ms. E. voiced her threats to abandon him. Although client and therapist alternated roles, each trying sadism and masochism at different times in their relationship, it was not until the middle of the third year of therapy that Tom could really see what was gong on in the transference-countertransference transactions between Ms. E. and himself.

Tom had been unable to help Ms. E. with her wishes to defeat him because he was too angry at her to be in a position to observe and understand her subtle resistances. He also failed to recognize that Ms. E.'s masochism aroused his own sadism to such a degree that he became so busy coping with his own rage that he did not have the freedom to help Ms. E. with hers.

On noting his frustration and anger with Ms. E., Tom was eventually able to get in touch with the idea that he was making Ms. E. his older sister who taunted and teased him throughout most of his childhood and adolescence. When he emotionally accepted that some of his revengeful wishes toward his sister were being directed at Ms. E., he could begin resolving some of his counterresistances. Instead of being critical of his client's masochism and guilty and defensive when she became sadistic toward him, Tom began to help Ms. E. work on some of her revengeful feelings toward men.

As Tom became more accepting of his own sadism, he could be more helpful to his client in recognizing her own. As Tom lessened his need to defend himself against his own rage through self-blame, he was better able to help Ms. E. see how she was doing likewise.

When we see masochism in ourselves and/or in our clients, it is helpful to recall what Theodor Reik (1941) said of the masochist. Reik pointed out that this person always needs a witness because he wants someone to watch him suffer. The lambskin he wears hides a wolf. His yielding includes defiance, his submissiveness, opposition. Beneath his softness there is hardness. Behind his obsequiousness, rebellion is concealed.

Similarly, when we see sadism in ourselves or in our clients, it might be helpful to think of the obverse of masochism. Individuals suffering from sadistic fantasies and/or sadistic behavior need to compensate for their low feelings of self-worth. They try to overcome their deep self-hatred by making others suffer. Their wolflike façade hides a lamb. Their defiance obscures their wish to yield and be subordinate. Behind their hardness is much softness. Beneath their rebellion is much obsequiousness.

The Competitive Dyad

Closely related to the sadomasochistic therapist-client relationship is the one where the two subtly compete with each other. Although it is close to universal for clients to compete with their therapists—whom they often consider to be omnipotent, idealized parental figures, as we pointed out earlier in this book—therapists competing with their clients is rarely discussed among practitioners or in the professional literature.

Although the client's competition is often apparent and occasionally subtle, the practitioner's competition with the client is usually subtle and rarely overt. But, therapists can envy almost everything about their clients that their clients can envy about them. However, there is one form of envy that therapists can feel that clients do not feel, and that is the wish of the therapist's to become the client and be in treatment with the client, that is, to reverse roles.

Just as many parents would like to be children again and change positions with their sons and daughters, many clinicians would like to change places with their clients. If the professional views himself or herself as empathetic, sensitive, warm, and caring, why wouldn't he or she feel competitive and envious toward those clients who are the beneficiaries of such wonderful care?

Gail Underwood, a psychiatrist in private practice, had been treating Ms. F. for over a year on a weekly basis. Ms. F., a woman in her mid-twenties, sought treatment because she was unable to sustain relationships with men, was sexually inhibited, had trouble asserting herself, and lacked self-confidence. Although attractive and bright, Ms. F. did not appreciate her many virtues and skills.

Ms. F. grew by leaps and bounds in her treatment with Gail Underwood. She experienced Gail as "a very nurturing mother who was very accepting" of anything she felt or did. Responding very positively to Gail's nonjudgmental attitude, Ms. F. rather quickly overcame her sexual inhibitions and began to date men who were attractive and bright. As her self-esteem rose, she received increases in status and income at her place of employment, a publishing firm. She rose from copy editior to a senior editor in less than a year.

As Ms. F. proudly discussed her social and professional achievements in her therapy, Gail subtly began to compete with her. For example, when Ms. F. talked about having dates with three different men during the course of one week, Gail told her client, "You have fantasies of running a harem!" On Ms. F.'s mentioning that colleagues were complimenting her on her grooming, Gail told Ms. F. that she was trying to gratify exhibitionistic fantasies. When Ms. F. was promoted to a position that many of her male colleagues wanted, Gail told Ms. F. that her "penis envy was showing."

Ms. F. did not respond with overt anger to Gail's not-so-veiled criticisms. However, she did become subtly critical of her therapist. Ms. F., in one session, told Gail that she was glad to be in her profession: "It was much more challenging than being a psychiatrist." On another occasion, Ms. F. mentioned that it was "a shame" Gail had to wear "drab clothes" in her work as a psychiatrist. "Fortunately, in my profession," said Ms. F. "we are encouraged to look glamorous."

The "one-upmanship" dialogues continued between therapist and client—derisive, mildly contemptuous, but always controlled. Around the middle of the second year of treatment, Ms. F. had a dream in which she was a child and Gail was warmly feeding her and admiring her beauty. In associating to the dream, Ms. F. lamented, "I miss the good old days when you used to be a mother figure and supported me. Now I feel that you are a cold colleague competing with me."

Gail took Ms. F.'s message very seriously and began to wonder if her client's observations had at least some component of reality to them. "Maybe it's not all transference," thought Gail. As she associated further to her work with Ms. F., Gail had a dream about a week after Ms. F. reported the dream mentioned above. Gail dreamed that Ms. F. was her therapist and was giving her helpful interpretations about accepting herself as she was. At first Gail thought the dream was her own way of prescribing to herself how she should treat Ms. F. Though not discounting this possibility, Gail was able to realize that she was very hungry to have the kind of treatment she had been giving Ms. F. It helped Ms. F. grow in areas where Gail had aspirations for herself that were not being fulfilled.

As Gail studied her counterresistances carefully, she realized that she had put herself in the position of a mother who vicariously enjoyed her daughter's achievements, but after a while began to envy her daughter. Gail's envy of her client needed to be further explored in her own personal therapy, where she eventually learned that she had some unresolved rivalries with her own mother, as well as with both of her siblings.

Allphin (1982) discussed envy among clinical social workers who

often find themselves envying those with whom they work. Psychologists and psychiatrists have higher status and earn more money even when the quality of work is the same for all three disciplines. When people envy those above them in a social hierarchy, they may, in order to compensate, subtly encourage the envy of those beneath them in the hierarchy, so the clients of clinical social workers may have their own envy fanned and intensified, rather than understood and put in appropriate perspective. (p. 151)

In further considering envy in the therapy relationship, it is important to point out that it is often expressed by idealization (Greenacre, 1966). Denying their envy, clients and therapists by using the defense of reaction formation (saying the opposite of what they feel and think) lavish praise on each other and extol each other's virtues. As we suggested earlier in this chapter, if client and therapist have a strong wish to maintain a loving and admiring relationship and enjoy each other's idealization of each other, the positive transference-countertransference interaction may become so mutually reinforced that therapist and client may be unable to decipher its negative elements, particularly envy (Allphin, 1982).

Student and Teacher

A very common collusion between therapist and client is when they abdicate their therapy responsibilities and become student and teacher with each other. To this day, when a candidate in a psychoanalytic institute is in treatment, the process is from time to time referred to as "didactic analysis," implying that the candidate is not primarily a client or patient but is a learner of a technical process.

Inasmuch as psychotherapy is in many ways a process of self-discovery, teaching and learning do take place. However, if the treatment is to have an impact, the client should, as we suggested earlier in this chapter, have an affective experience in which he or she is involved in a unique relationship where a wide range of emotions is directed toward the therapist. When this takes place, the client learns how he or she disrupts relationships, modifies perceptions of people, and becomes familiar with his or her wishes, defenses, and superego commands that have been unconscious. One might define this process as "emotional learning," but it definintely is not an intellectual one.

When clients and clinicians are frightened of their own feelings and are made anxious by those of each other, they can intellectualize the therapy experience and turn the consultation room into a classroom. Many clients resist therapy by wanting intellectual answers to their emotional conflicts. Therapists often comply with their clients' requests and give definitions of such terms as "superego," "conflict," and "neurosis." From time to time therapists, who cannot comfortably relate to their clients' emotional life, turn the treatment into philosophical dialogues or monologues and subtly get their clients to support their counterresistances.

If the therapy becomes an intellectual experience in which client and therapist are colluding to avoid an emotional interchange, it can be inferred that the practitioner is exhibiting sexual and aggressive wishes of his or her own and needs to squelch the client's desires for intimacy and/or wishes to aggress toward the therapist.

Guy Taylor was a social worker in an outpatient treatment center designed exclusively to help alcoholics recover from their addiction. He had been treating Mr. G. for a little over a year on a weekly basis. A man in his early forties, Mr. G. sought treatment because his severe alcoholism prevented him from working steadily and had also alienated him from his wife and children.

In his work with Guy Taylor, Mr. G. initially questioned whether psychotherapy could help him. He had found that previous treatment had not been "of any value at all." On hearing from Mr. G. that mental health professionals "only want your money," Guy was able to help Mr. G. verbalize a great deal of resentment toward therapists and then move on to assist him in voicing his distrust toward his parents and parental figures in his past and present.

By the eighth month of treatment, Mr. G. was quite comfortable with Guy and looked forward to his sessions with him. He became very interested in the techniques of psychotherapy and curious about psychotherapists. He asked Guy technical questions about how the process works, the role of the therapist and the role of transference, countertransference, resistance, and counterresistance. In addition to his direct queries in his sessions with Guy, Mr. G. started to read articles and books on psychotherapy and psychoanalysis.

Guy Taylor reasoned that inasmuch as Mr. G. had been deprived of appropriate nurturing and had never enjoyed a dependable relationship with a parental figure, it would be important to answer his client's questions, including those queries about Guy's professional training. To try to establish "trust" (Erikson, 1950), Guy also answered Mr. G.'s questions about the therapist's countertransference reactions.

Mr. G. loved being the student and very much enjoyed and appreciated Guy as his teacher. The client talked about how his therapy was helping him to function much better on his job and also helping him to enjoy his relationship with his family and friends much more.

Although Mr. G. continued to appreciate his therapy and his therapist and frequently thanked Guy by telling him that coming to see him was the high point of the week because he really "learned a great deal" from "the best teacher" he ever had, his euphoria slowly diminished. By the fifteenth month of therapy, Mr. G. was drinking again, was fired from his job, and lost his driver's license.

Despite the fact that Guy was very surprised when he observed how much his client had regressed, he began to evaluate the therapy both with Mr. G.'s help and on his own. What seemed to occur in the treatment is that Guy's generosity was so appealing to Mr. G. that he began to look for it everywhere he went. He asked many questions of friends, family, and customers. When they did not give him the responses he thought he deserved, he became angry, and his questions turned into demands. If his demands were not responded to positively, and they were not inasmuch as most people do not welcome being the object of demands, he began to withdraw and resumed drinking.

One of the serious consequences of being a giving teacher to a client is that the client understandably begins to want the same kind of "treatment" from others. When family and friends do not emulate the benign teaching offered by the therapist, the client can become angry at his or her frustrating family and friends and wonder why they cannot relate the way the therapist does.

If the practitioner indulges the client in therapy, as Guy Taylor did with Mr. G., there is a strong possibility that the client will attempt to receive the same kind of treatment in his or her daily life. However, if the therapist focuses the treatment on the client's inner processes and helps the client take a major responsibility for what happens in the treatment, the client will be more enabled to take responsibility for his or her life outside the consultation room.

Just as the eminent educator John Dewey (1939) pointed out that education is more than a preparation for life, but "it is life itself," psychotherapy can be similarly conceptualized. The therapist is not only interested in helping the client cope with life after he or she ends treatment, but, in addition, how the therapist relates to the client in the current therapy very much influences his or her daily functioning.

In cases where the client wants to be a student and turn the therapist into a teacher, as with any other transference wish, the matter should be explored in the therapy. Just as students ask questions for many reasons, so do clients. Questions may be asked to gain attention, gratify voyeurism, provoke debate, or mask suspicion. As we pointed out in Chapter 2, clients who are distrustful, as was Mr. G. in the case above, often ask questions because they have real doubts about the therapeutic process, that is, they question it. If the therapist answers the client's questions, the latter's doubts, suspicions, anger, and latent paranoia go underground, only to be acted out or to become a component of neurotic symptomatology.

Just Friends

In his paper "Transference, Psychic Reality, and Countertransference," James McLaughlin (1981) points out that "transference is a matter of equal rights" for therapists and clients. Consequently, he argues that the term "countertransference" be laid to rest, and instead the term "therapist's transference" be used.

Perhaps no collusion in psychotherapy in which therapist and client better demonstrate that they are equally subject to transference reactions is when they become friends and mutually resist the therapeutic process. If practitioner and client become friends, both of them are usually frightened to face complementary transferences and mutual resistances. Rather than helping clients face the discomfort they feel when experiencing themselves as docile sons or daughters or struggling students with a powerful father or master teacher, therapists subtly encourage a friendship between them, fearing the client's aggression, as well as their own.

Although friendly feelings almost always emerge in a productive therapeutic relationship, this is quite different when friendship supplants treatment and therapist and client chit-chat, joke, and share anecdotes to ward off feelings of competition, sexuality, dependency, aggression, or any other affects that can stir up mutual anxiety in either or both parties.

Ellen Shore, a social worker in a mental hygiene consultation center at a university, had in treatment for over a year a 19-year-old sophomore, Mr. H. He had gone for treatment because he was very depressed, could not concentrate on his studies, felt very self-conscious in social situations, and was fearful that he might become homosexual. Although he had never participated in any homosexual activity, this possibility became a major obsession of his since he started college.

In his once-a-week treatment with Ellen Shore, Mr. H. rather quickly overcame his depression, improved his grades, became more comfortable socially, and lost his preoccupation with homosexuality. It was quite clear that the client, who very much missed his home and family and doubted himself when he did not have their support, found a wonderful ally in Ellen Shore. By listening attentively to him, encouraging him to talk about his strong symbiotic yearnings, and by showing him that his preoccupation with homosexuality was a defense against his anxiety about being a heterosexual adult male, Ellen became the nurturing parent that Mr. H. craved.

After about eight or nine months of treatment, Mr. H. told Ellen that she was the kind of person he'd like to keep as "an eternal friend." With enormous conviction, Mr. H. said, "With someone like you in my corner, I feel strong and competent. If I know you will always be there for me, I'll always be sure of myself."

Rather than try to understand her client's idealizing transference and help him with his wish for a symbiosis, Ellen was seduced by the client's transference fantasies and manipulated by Mr. H.'s wish for a symbiosis. In an untherapeutic response, she thanked Mr. H. for his "confidence" in her and told him that they made "a great team." Mr. H., in turn, was seduced and manipulated by Ellen's appreciative remarks, and continued to help create a mutual admiration society between them.

Although there was never any physical interchange between client and therapist, for the next several months they had very friendly, intimate, verbal exchanges. They discussed politics, religion, psychotherapy, education, and many other areas of mutual interest. Ellen justified her behavior in the treatment situation by telling herself and Mr. H. that she was providing her client with "a corrective emotional experience" (Alexander & Ross, 1952). When confronted consciously by the practitioner, most counterresistances are legitimized with a technical label or psychodynamic phrase.

However, Ellen began to listen to her "psychotherapeutic superego" and slowly realized that in contrast to her therapeutic work with most of her other clients, she found that she looked forward to her appointments with Mr. H. with "a special excitement," as if the contact were a date. It also dawned on her that she was particularly careful about how she appeared and what perfume she wore on the day of the week she saw Mr. H.

On acknowledging her "crush" on her client, Ellen was very critical of herself. She had prided herself on never "acting out" with clients and always putting their needs before her own. With Mr. H., she was "using him" to enhance her self-image and to be a lovable woman with an attractive man.

As Ellen subjected her counterresistive behavior to further analysis, she was able to derive a very valuable insight. She became painfully aware of the fact that she had been denying and repressing her libidinal fantasies toward most of her clients. Because Ellen had been working overtime putting pressure on herself to defend against her very human feelings, resentment grew, and her friendship with Mr. H. was really an expression of rebellion toward her strict superego (Blum, 1981).

Very often when clients and/or clinicians rebel against therapeutic rules, rituals, and requirements, they are more often than not very law-abiding people. Actually, they feel so very obligated to submit to the voices of a tyrannical superego that after awhile they cannot tolerate the pressure of the prohibitions they inflict on themselves. This is what happened to Ellen Shore. Always defending against pleasure in doing therapeutic work, she finally rebelled and acted out. In many ways, she was like a submissive, masochistic spouse to her partner, that is, her profession; after years of feeling tortured by the demands inflicted on her, she rebelled.

Although sustaining a friendship is one way that therapist and client can subtly but mutually resist the therapeutic process, there are other ways as well. One way is to collude to overemphasize or underemphasize certain clinical material. We will examine this issue in some detail in the next section.

Overemphasis and Underemphasis of Certain Material

A productive psychotherapy moves freely between past, present, and transference. The practitioner hovers equidistant not only from the three psychic structures of id, ego, and superego, but also between intrapsychic and interpersonal dynamics, the internal and external world, and transference issues and original objects. If therapist and client overemphasize or underemphasize any of these issues, the therapy is hurt (Rangell, 1981).

Transference Excesses

Some practitioners pursue and interpret transference too exclusively, going so far as to practically ignore reality events, history, and other clinical data. Although virtually all competent therapists recognize that an exploration of transference fantasies and transference wishes is an indispensable part of every worthwhile treatment, some therapists can push for transference material to such an excessive degree that they appear to be "monomaniacs" (Fenichel, 1945).

It should be mentioned that one of the main reasons we try to help our clients face transference reactions toward their therapists is to show them that they bring an inner script into all of their relationships. We want our clients to see that their transference reactions are based on childish wishes, defensive reactions, introjects, ego ideals, and superego pressures. As clients better understand their transference reactions in therapy, they begin to see how and why they distort their current interpersonal relationships and how and why their infantile wishes color their current perceptions. If studying transference reactions in therapy is not viewed by the therapist and client as a means to an end, and handled discriminatingly, the clinician will tend to emerge as a narcissistic parental figure who has to be in the center of everything. This kind of parental figure cannot foster growth in the client because he or she will be extremely resented.

Usually when practitioners overemphasize the study of transference reactions in the treatment, they cannot withstand being alone for too long. Without attention on themselves, they begin to doubt their own importance and/or feel devalued.

Since they feel neglected and isolated, their overemphasis on the transference is really an attempt to ask the client, "How about me? Why do you leave me out of this?"

Paradoxically, it is often the frightened client, who needs to defend strongly against transference reactions, who provokes the therapist to repeatedly ask, "How about me?" This client, on hearing the therapist's questions as demands, then feels all the more vulnerable and resists exploring the transference with increased tenacity. Feeling even more neglected, the therapist then intensively focuses on the client's resistance to the exploration of transference issues and a power struggle between client and therapist ensues.

Some clients who resist the exploration of the transference do their best therapeutic work and make their most progress when the therapist genuinely respects the client's resistances and does not pressure him or her. This is often a difficult lesson for therapists to learn.

John Ripple, a psychologist in private practice, had been treating Ms. I. for over a year. A woman in her mid-thirties, Ms. I. came for help after a painful divorce from her husband to whom she had been married for five years.

Ms. I., who was seen in therapy on a weekly basis, spent most of her time in her treatment expressing her sadness and anger at her husband for leaving her. As far as she was concerned, she had done everything for him that a wife could do, while her husband did nothing else but ignore her. He refused to have sex most of the time and rarely wanted to talk about anything personal or intimate.

Ms. I. described a cold family atmosphere in growing up as a child. Her parents had little to do with each other and got divorced when Ms. I. was 10 years old. After the divorce, her father moved far away and she hardly ever saw him. Her mother, an accountant, was busy with her work and also had little to do with the client.

Ms. I. had few friends, and although she did well in her work as a librarian, she rarely expressed much enthusiasm about it.

A brief review of Ms. I.'s past and present should have alerted John Ripple to the real possibility that she would not eagerly form a close, intimate relationship with him. Yet, after several months of feeling left out of the treatment, John asked Ms. I. why she ignored him so much. Ms. I. tried to respond to John's question but only felt very self-conscious and extremely anxious, and she could say little. When John pointed out her discomfort when confronted with the observation that she had been ignoring him, Ms. I. became very halting in her speech and withdrew from John even more.

John tried to get Ms. I. to tell him what she "didn't like" about him, but this got him nowhere. Ms. I. replied that she had "nothing against" him; she even thought he was "quite neat." However, notions like transference fantasies or wishes or discomfort with transference reactions were politely but firmly repudiated by the client. She kept on saying, "I think you are a nice man, but I have no feelings toward you."

John then went on a therapeutic rampage. He told Ms. I. that she was very stubborn and negativistic. When she denied this, John interpreted her defense of denial and told Ms. I. she did not want to face the truth. Experiencing this interpretation as an accusation that she was a liar, Ms. I. became less and less revealing in the treatment, somaticized, and felt helpless about communicating anything but superficialities to John.

After about a year of "trying to get the client to focus on the transference," John realized that he had reached an impasse with her. Not only did he become aware of the fact that focusing on Ms. I.'s resistances to exploring the transference exacerbated her need to withdraw (Gill, 1982), but John saw that his pushing for transference material was a major counterresistance in his work with her.

John experienced Ms. I. as a reluctant sexual partner who was rejecting him. Rather than face his feelings of being rejected, he kept pushing for a response. In many ways John was behaving like an insecure teenager who was trying to prove that he was sexually desirable. Ms. I. in turn felt that she was experiencing "date rape" and kept withdrawing from John. Her withdrawal provoked John to push more, and client and therapist were involved in a power struggle.

Putting his insights into action, John decided to try to avoid giving transference interpretations. He focused instead with Ms. I. on issues in her day-to-day life, work at the library, discussions with friends, the difficulties in finding a date, and other extratransferential issues (Blum, 1983). John began to see his client "thaw out." Her range of affect was widened in her sessions, she shared more intimate details of her life, and she began to improve her functioning in many areas of living.

After four months of staying away from transference interpretations, John saw further evidence that his changed attitude toward Ms. I.'s treatment was producing good results. In the sixteenth month of treatment, Ms. I. reported a transference dream: "I'm lying on a couch and you are lying next to me. I'm ambivalent about having sex with you. You say, 'We'll proceed at your rate.'" The dream reflected Ms. I.'s decreased fear of intimacy and demonstrated Ms. I.'s appreciation of John Ripple's more tender and less forceful attitude toward his client. As a result she could let him be a sexual man to her in therapy.

We wish to reiterate that the above case illustration is not an attempt to diminish the importance of studying transference reactions in treatment. The understanding of transference is crucial to every treatment. However, like any other important dimension of treatment, when the therapist is excessively preoccupied with it, the client feels misunderstood and neglected. Perhaps an overzealous use of transference interpretations, when the client wants distance from the therapist, can be the practitioner's unconscious way of seeking revenge. Having felt unappreciated and neglected by the client, the therapist behaves in such a way that the client is the one who ends up feeling neglected and unappreciated.

AVOIDANCE OF TRANSFERENCE ISSUES

As we pointed out in Chapter 1, transference is a universal phenomenon that exists in all relationships. We human beings never quite see our confreres as they are. We make them mothers, fathers, and siblings. We project our superego commands, id wishes, and other parts of our psychic structures onto them. We distort their comments and actions to buttress our defenses. We act out old problems in new relationships and bring new conflicts into old relationships!

Because transference reactions reveal much about a person, its study is extremely helpful to the therapeutic process. However, many therapists avoid studying transference wishes and fantasies and ignore its inevitable manifestations in the treatment.

In contrast to those therapists who love to be the center of attention are those who do not want to be confronted with their clients' feelings toward them. Consequently, they deflect their clients' aggression, ignore their sexual fantasies, and move away from having their clients' superego mandates, ideals, or forbidden id wishes projected onto them.

If a therapist is uncomfortable being the recipient of a client's wide range of feelings, extending all the way from intense love and wishes for a symbiotic merger to active hatred and desires to kill, the therapist will not be able to foster much growth in the client. When a client cannot be himself or herself with the practitioner, a corrective relationship is blocked, ventilation of feelings is inhibited, and the client's self-understanding will be limited.

Very often when a therapist cannot explore and listen to the client's transference reactions, he or she is threatened by them, often experiencing the client's remarks as personal criticisms. On being called inept or incompetent by the client, many therapists begin to regard themselves in this way. Criticisms become realistic appraisals, sexual fantasies become commands for action, and questions become demands that have to be fulfilled.

Therapists who ignore transference material often do so not only because its revelation makes them feel vulnerable and weak, but also because they cannot clearly distinguish transference reactions from realistic appraisals. In a way they are reacting in as narcissistic a manner as those practitioners who crave attention from their clients. They fear being the object of transference fantasies because they do not want to feel personally abused.

Dorothy Quentin was a psychiatrist in private practice treating Ms. J., an attorney. She had been referred to Dorothy by her physician who felt that her somatic problems were an expression of stress in her life. The client had been suffering from migraine headaches, insomnia, backaches, and asthma.

In her twice-weekly treatment, Ms. J. made a great deal of progress during the first six months. She realized that she had been very condemning of herself for the inevitable anger she felt on the job. In addition, she realized that she had been "chasing a rainbow" by trying to secure love from all of her clients, colleagues, and even from her adversaries. Ms. J., by the end of the seventh month of treatment, proclaimed, "I realize I'm a little girl in many ways in trying to get love from all adults who don't give it. It has made me furious and I didn't even know it."

Despite Ms. J's progress in her therapy, after about two months of being symptom-free, the client's migraine headaches, insomnia, and other bodily problems returned. Dorothy Quentin was stumped by the return of the symptoms inasmuch as Ms. J. was feeling much better on the job, not needing everybody's love and approval. Although Dorothy considered every possibility to try to determine what transpired to precipitate the return of her client's symptoms, she considered everything but the right thing, that is, the client's transference relationship.

What Dorothy Quentin overlooked is a truism in all of psychotherapy, which we have emphasized several times in this text: Every client recapitulates in treatment with the therapist the major interpersonal conflicts that he or she has experienced throughout life. Ms. J. desperately wanted the love of those who surrounded her, so she was going to experience the same yearnings with Dorothy. Just as she had to somaticize the conflict for not allowing herself to feel the rage when the love she craved in her personal life was not forthcoming, she had to cope with her therapist in the same way for not loving her the way she wanted to be loved in the therapy situation—she somaticized the conflict.

The return of Ms. J.'s bodily symptoms was her only way of exhibiting her rage toward Dorothy. When Dorothy was eventually helped by her supervisor to become aware of the nature of her counterresistance, she was able to see how much she wanted to appear different from Ms. J.'s colleagues, clients, and adversaries. To Ms. J., these people were unloving parents and siblings from her past. In effect, Dorothy wanted to be loved by Ms. J. as much as Ms. J. wanted to be loved by her colleagues and others.

Very frequently when therapists are frightened by the emergence of transference material and stay away from it, they justify their counterresistive behavior by pointing out to themselves and to their colleagues that they are trying to be the loving mother and/or father that the client never had. What is missing from this "treatment plan" is the notion that a loving therapist who aspires to be a loving parental figure is emotionally available to be the recipient of the client's rage, hatred, envy, and competition, as well as the client's more positive emotions such as love, admiration, affection, and sexuality.

Usually when the client is not afforded the opportunity to experience basic emotions toward the therapist, he or she eventually withdraws and quits treatment. For the therapist who resists participating in intense emotional interchanges with clients, this is often the desired, albeit unconscious, result.

OVEREMPHASIS OF THE PAST

As we already suggested, when clients are experiencing difficulties in the present such as in marriage, on the job, or with relatives and friends, there is a strong tendency on their parts to ascribe their pains and aches to individuals in their current environment. Wives ascribe their marital difficulties to their husbands, and husbands blame their wives for the marital woes. The same phenomenon occurs with parents and children, teachers and students, and of course with therapists and clients.

If life in the present is difficult, most individuals try to modify their current circumstances. It usually takes quite a bit of time and hard work for clients to become convinced of the fact that they bring an inner script from the past to current relationships. It is not easy for them to accept that they are provoking their spouses, children, or colleagues to become figures of their past. They resist, strenuously at times, facing the child in themselves that distorts the present and "makes" the present the past.

Because clients frequently try to diminish the saliency of their pasts, practitioners find themselves trying to weave it into the therapeutic work. Sometimes their zealousness is so great that they forget about the client's present reality and instead help the client exclusively to study the past to ascertain how it affects current functioning.

Usually when therapists overemphasize their clients' pasts in their therapeutic work, they are anxious and conflicted about facing and discussing with their clients their current reality. For example, instead of helping a distressed husband see how he has some responsibility for his own contribution to his marital difficulties, the therapist can spend almost all of the therapeutic time discussing with the client how he has been the victim of a tyrannical mother. Of course, this approach is antitherapeutic. Not only does the approach compound the client's resistance to dealing with his marriage, but also the client goes nowhere by just talking about his tyrannical mother. What the client needs to see is how he *makes* his wife his tyrannical mother and why he wants to keep himself in the role of son with his wife.

When practitioners observe their clients obsessing about their horrible current circumstances, they can—if they are not careful—"help" their clients convert the obsessing about the present into obsessing about the past.

Bill Patterson, a social worker in a child guidance clinic, was working with Mr. K., the father of 10-year-old Joe, who had been referred for therapy because he was extremely belligerent in school and with friends. Both in school and in the neighborhood, Joe provoked adults and peers into arguments, power struggles, and even into physical battles.

In studying Joe's dynamics, the clinic staff became convinced that Mr. K. was deriving a lot of vicarious gratification from Joe's provocative behavior. Therefore, they thought it would be advisable to get him to participate in the treatment plan.

Mr. K. responded positively to Bill Patterson's invitation. In many interviews, he voiced his tremendous anguish about Joe's behavior. He could not understand why Joe was belligerent; both he and his wife were "peaceful people who never challenge or provoke a soul." Mr. K. further pointed out that he was brought up as a boy to conform; hence, he was mystified by Joe's nonconforming behavior.

When Mr. K. referred to his past, Bill Patterson thought it might be a good idea to help Mr. K. talk about this and eventually to help him see how his constricted background probably made him want to rebel. Then, he would be able to show Mr. K. how and why he was aiding and abetting Joe's provocative behavior by inducing him to rebel.

Although Bill Patterson was well-intentioned by helping Mr. K. to look at his constricted past, he joined his client in wallowing in it. Each interview consisted of the client telling vignettes of how his parents controlled and dominated him, squelching his aggression and limiting his spontaneity.

Bill found himself feeling very empathetic toward Mr. K. and commiserated with him. Mr. K. enjoyed Bill's concern and continued to tell more stories about his painful past. Bill was aware of the fact that no client can alter his present reality merely by talking about the past. However, his behavior in the sessions did not seem to indicate that he knew that Mr. K. had to get to the point of seeing how he was turning the past into the present in order to progress therapeutically.

Bill Patterson, like many practitioners, became so interested in Mr. K.'s childhhood, and so identified with "the slings and arrows" of his client's "outrageous fortune," that he overlooked some of his responsibilities as a clinician. Why did this happen to Bill and why does this happen to many practitioners?

Bill, like many individuals who become psychotherapists, had a background similar to Mr. K.'s (Burton, 1972). He, too, had parents who were very rigid in their child-rearing attitudes, and he, too, had a strong need to rebel against them, but he did not do so. As Mr. K. talked about his past, Bill derived so much vicarious gratification from the experience that he lost sight of his therapeutic tasks to gratify his voyeurism.

Just as Mr. K. abdicated some of his responsibilities as a father and aided his son to act out rebelliously so that he could derive vicarious gratification from his son's behavior, Bill abdicated his responsibilities as a therapist to Mr. K. It was not until Bill could see how he was using Mr. K.—however subtly—to express his own frustrations with his parents that he was able to show Mr. K. how Mr. K. was using his son Joe to act out his own problems with his parents.

The "parallel process" (Sigman, 1985) observed in the above case often occurs in therapeutic work with parents of children who have emotional difficulties (Feldman, 1958). It is also observed frequently in the supervisory process when the practitioner behaves with the supervisor in the same way that the client relates to him or her.

UNDEREMPHASIS OF THE PAST

In the 1990s, since short-term therapy is in vogue and other therapies that emphasize the "here and now" are popular, the client's past is often given limited attention. Actually, it is probably more prevalent now for clinicians to neglect using the past in their treatment plan than it is to overemphasize it.

One of the main reasons that practitioners overlook their clients' pasts in their treatment plans is because they do not want to relate to the child in their adult clients. This is usually because they do not want to face the child within themselves.

As we have reiterated, many clients and therapists would rather engage in "problem solving" in the present or in "manipulating the current environment" than in facing the fact that they, like all individuals, are recapitulating their histories in their current adaptations and maladaptations. Many clients and therapists resist facing the idea that to resolve a serious problem in the present usually involves becoming aware of the genetic antecedents that precipitate the current conflict. When they do not want to face the child within themselves, their pasts will often be ignored.

Nicole Orr was a psychologist who worked in a clinic that specialized in the treatment of obesity. For over a year, she had been treating on a weekly basis Mr. L., a man in his thirties, for his problems with overeating.

Although Nicole Orr, as part of the clinic's procedure, took a rather detailed history on Mr. L., she hardly used any of it in her treatment. Rather, she rewarded him with praise when he lost weight and punished him with silence when he gained weight. Although Nicole empathically listened to Mr. L.'s many complaints about his "cold, ungiving, castrating wife," she did not at any point in the treatment remind Mr. L. that the description he gave of his wife was almost identical with the description he gave at intake of his mother. Furthermore, although on many occasions Nicole pointed out to Mr. L. that he seemed to overeat the most when he did not receive the recognition on the job that he very much desired, she did not link this important dynamic sequence to another crucial time in Mr. L.'s childhood. Mr. L. had told

Nicole several times that he began to overeat at the age of four when his sister was born, a time when he felt very emotionally neglected.

Recognizing that her behavior modification approach yielded very limited therapeutic result, Nicole brought the case for consultation to a clinician whose perspective was a psychodynamic one. As Nicole was helped to sensitize herself to the hungry child inside her client, she was able to change her own therapeutic procedure and help her client to see and to feel how he was reliving his past in his marriage as well as in his work. Eventually, he began to experience Nicole as "a giving mother" and ingested her dynamic formulations with relish!

Many psychoanalysts take the position that if the client talks about the present, the analyst should talk about the past. And, if the client talks about the past, the analyst should talk about the present. Although not an absolute axiom, this point of view has much merit so that when put to use by the therapist, the disjointedness that has taken place in the client's mind between past and present has a chance of being removed. One of the therapist's central jobs is to help the client restore connections in his or her life and break through the sense of isolation and disjointedness (Fine, 1982).

We would like to emphasize again that it should never be assumed that the mere recollection of past events will in itself have therapeutic value. In that connection, Reuben Fine (1972) pointed out:

> What counts is really healing the rupture between present and past, so that the patient can come to have the feeling that his life is all of one piece. Sometimes past material will be relevant, sometimes present, sometimes both. The emphasis should always continue to be put on the way in which the patient's awareness of himself and his life is growing . . . . In greater or lesser degree, the genetic point of view has to be taught to every patient. Some-times it has to be injected almost as a didactic exercise; the patient must be told in so many words: You are this way because you were brought up in such-and-such a manner, not because you are inherently bad . . . .(p. 182)

In trying to help clients cope with their pasts, clinicians should be alert to the type of defensiveness that is utilized by their clients. Some find it very difficult to believe that their parents played a role in their difficulties and refuse to acknowledge hostile feelings toward them. If the therapist shares this kind of defense, the client's past will tend to be ignored. However, if the therapist does not share this kind of defensiveness, he or she should be cautious about being too critical too fast of the client's parents. When clients need to idealize their parents and cannot tolerate aggressive feelings toward them, the therapist's aggressive remarks about the client's parents can provoke the client to attack the therapist and leave treatment. Many clients would rather maintain a punitive superego and keep hoping they will get their parents' love. For this, it is worth it to them to give up their therapy.

There are, as we have noted several times, clients who ascribe most of their current difficulties to their parents. They need to see that although their parents began the process, it is they who continue it (Fine, 1982). For clients to see this, they need therapists who have not remained hypercritical and hostile toward their own parents, but also are not so defensive about them that they cannot tolerate criticisms of them.

OVEREMPHASIS ON REALITY

One of the seeming paradoxes about dynamic psychotherapy is that clients seek out an expert to help them cope better with a problem in reality, and the expert responds to the request by encouraging the client to talk about and examine many issues that seem to have little to do with their realistic problems. For example, if a parent seeks help from an expert in a child guidance clinic because the parent's son or daughter has a school phobia, the therapist might spend considerable time talking with the parent about the latter's own childhood, particularly how the parent felt when he or she left home. Similarly, if a man has difficulty getting along with his boss, obsessing about him all day long and worried that the boss will fire him, the practitioner might very well engage the man in a discussion about his fantasies, dreams, history, as well as his relationship to his father. And if a wife has an aversion to her husband when he initiates sex, the therapist instead of discussing sexual techniques and procedures might help the wife talk about her hatred of her father and brother and her competition with boys and men when she was a child.

It has been noted by many practitioners that those clients who are free to discuss their fantasies, dreams, guilts, and past usually respond quite well to treatment (Strean, 1985/1990). Consequently, we can infer that when clients harp on realistic issues, they are trying to ward off guilt feelings, to ignore their fantasies and dreams, and of most importance, they do not want to take responsibility for their own role in their unhappiness.

Although most therapists recognize that an exclusive discussion of real problems places limits on the effectiveness of the therapy, many of them find themselves drawn into such a discussion. Why?

Very often when a client brings a problem to the therapist, the client feels if the problem is not solved quickly, it appears to be the end of the world. A parent may think that his or her child's school phobia will turn the child into an academic dropout, an imbecile, or an idiot. A conflict with the boss might cause the employee to feel that he is going to be fired tomorrow, be penniless next week, and be doomed to a life of poverty. The wife who has an aversion to sex with her husband might worry about the termination of her marriage and the possibility that she will never be loved by a man again.

Inasmuch as many clients fear that their realistic problems might bring death, abandonment, lovelessness, castration, or social ostracism, they want an immediate solution. If the therapist identifies strongly with the client's desperation and does not see that the client has regressed and is suffering from an anxiety that befits a child, such as separation anxiety, castration anxiety, or loss of love, the therapist will want to give realistic appraisals and realistic solutions to the client as soon as possible.

In addition to overidentifying with the client's plight, therapists have other reasons for joining clients in their exclusive discussion of reality concerns. Just as an over-emphasis on reality by clients can help them defend against looking at guilt feelings, examining fantasies, exploring dreams, and assuming some responsibility for their lives, therapists can employ the same defense for the same purpose. As we noted in earlier chapters of this book, if a practitioner is angry at his or her spouse, therapist, or child and wishes to sustain the anger, the practitioner will be inclined to collude with his or her client and both client and therapist will tacitly concur that the client's "significant others" or current environment are to blame for the client's maladies.

Upon recognizing their own guilt, therapists like clients feel a pressure to modify their immature behavior. However, it is much easier most of the time to hate a spouse, boss, or a colleague than to face one's childish wishes and try to love rather than hate. Many therapists, like many clients, see loving as a humiliation and would rather find realistic justification to sustain their hatred.

Finally, when therapists confront their fantasies and dreams, like clients, they feel more pressure on themselves to see that, indeed, they do write their own neurotic scripts. Often, it is easier to obsess about a realistic problem than to take responsibility for one's self-destructiveness and masochism.

Linda Norton, a psychiatrist in private practice, was treating Mr. M., a man in his forties, on a twice-weekly basis. The main reason that Mr. M. came into treatment was because he was constantly sexually impotent in his relationships with women. Whether it was a steady relationship or a brief one, Mr. M. could never achieve an erection. In addition to his sexual problems, he felt very ill at ease with women. Just as he could not initiate sex, he could not initiate conversations—he would be "tongue-tied."

During Mr. M.'s third month of treatment, he confided to Linda that he had a problem all of his life that he had never discussed with anyone else. Even though he had seen other therapists in the past, he never felt comfortable to "raise" the issue. According to Mr. M., what very much embarrassed him was that he had a small penis. He was quite sure that his small penis was a factor in his impotence, and because a small penis was something he "could do nothing about," he doubted if he could ever become sexually potent.

It was reasonable to infer that Mr. M. was having sexual fantasies toward Linda when he wanted to "raise" the issue, despite the fact that he was implying that feeling sexual toward Linda was terrifying to him as he "could do nothing about it." However, Linda responded to Mr. M. as if the size of his penis was really his exclusive problem; she asked him directly about the size of his penis and when he told her "four inches," Linda told him that was only "slightly smaller than most men." Regardless of Linda's reassurances that the size of his penis was acceptable, Mr. M. fought her help, much the same way he fought getting together with women sexually. The situation became more desperate for both client and therapist and finally Linda arranged for Mr. M. to have testosterone shots.

As often happens when the therapist offers help outside the treatment relationship, the client takes it as a sign of their joint weakness and that psychotherapy can't help. Furthermore, from Mr. M.'s response to the male doctor who administered the shots, it was clear that he experienced the testosterone injections as homosexual seductions, which intimidated him. He referred to the physician as "overbearing, intrusive, and sadistic."

The testosterone shots did not free Mr. M. from his impotence. They made him feel worse. Not only could he not "get anywhere" with his woman therapist, Linda Norton, but he felt "nobody and nothing can help me." Therefore, he left treatment despite Linda's strong attempts to convince him to stay with her.

When Linda discussed her work with a senior colleague, she eventually realized that by focusing exclusively on her client's realistic problem, she avoided helping him face his sexual fantasies, sexual wishes, sexual dreams, and his many anxieties. Linda also became aware of the fact that one of the main reasons she was overly absorbed with the reality of Mr. M.'s small penis was because she feared imagining it as big and erect. This, of course, was Mr. M.'s major fear and without consciously being aware of it, Linda was reinforcing her client's sexual inhibitions. On further reflection, Linda realized that she was afraid of her sexual fantasies toward her handsome client and was afraid of hearing his sexual fantasies toward her.

By focusing on Mr. M.'s small penis, Linda was also subtly revealing her own resistance to having a close relationship with her client. And, when she referred him for medical help, she was perhaps not so subtly rejecting him as a client. Feeling rejected, the client rejected the therapist.

The case of Linda Norton and Mr. M. also suggests that when practitioners refer clients to other professionals, for example, group therapists, family therapists, or medical doctors, many clients experience the referral as an attempt by the practitioner to get rid of the client and/or diminish the intensity of the treatment relationship. Sometimes what clients experience is also an accurate perception of the therapist's motives—to dilute the therapeutic relationship or end it entirely.

UNDEREMPHASIS ON REALITY

If clients are frightened to examine upsetting realities in marriage, on the job, or elsewhere, their anxiety about these realities can be somewhat reduced by focusing exclusively on their internal lives. In effect, they can change the subject. For example, a client who cannot tolerate anger toward a boss may bring to therapy sessions many dreams that deal with punitive father figures, but the client may not be able to associate the dreams with the real job conflict that is being experienced. Similarly, a woman may be having real conflicts with her husband, but because she experiences much pain in facing these conflicts, she may fill her treatment sessions with fantasies of the perfect man and not be aware of the connection of these fantasies to her real conflicts (Strean, 1985/1990).

If practitioners are particularly intrigued with dreams and fantasies, they will be inclined to overlook the possibility that dreams and fantasies can be used by the client as a resistance. Fenichel (1945) gave an illustration of this in his report of a man in psychoanalytic treatment who described many dreams that involved his drinking milk. Questions, confrontations, clarifications, and interpretations by the analyst were to no avail, because an important reality in the man's life was being avoided in the treatment. The patient was giving practically all of his money to his analyst; thus, he was truly economically impoverished. Yet, he could not feel free to discuss his destitute condition with the analyst. His resistance took the form of dreaming every night about milk, but suffering daily because his real hunger was not being satisfied.

When a client constantly presents the therapist with dreams and fantasies that contain the same theme, but have no pertinent references to the realities of the client's life, the therapist should try to establish a link between the dreams and fantasies on one hand, and what is transpiring in the client's day-to-day life on the other. If the therapist does not establish this link, he or she is usually too preoccupied with the client's dreams and fantasies or too uninterested in the client's external life.

As the reader is aware, when a therapist overlooks something pertinent in the client's real life, in most cases the therapist does not want to face something in his or her own life. If clients focus exclusively on something, for example, dreams, fantasies, the past, or the transference, the practitioner can usually be safe in inferring that the client does not want to face a particular issue in his or her life. But, when practitioners find themselves going along with the client's exclusive focus, that is, the client's subtle resistance, practitioners should ask themselves, "What am I avoiding looking at in my own life?"

Jacques Montague, a social worker in private practice, had been treating Ms. N., a 33-year-old married woman, for about six months, twice a week. When he realized that his client spent almost all of her treatment sessions relating dreams about her mother, he realized something was amiss. Although the dreams were rich in content, with Ms. N. displaying a great deal of ambivalence toward her mother, it occurred to Jacques Montague to ask Ms. N. what was actually transpiring between Ms. N. and her mother in their day-to-day relationship.

In response to Jacques's question, Ms. N. told him that she was embarrassed to tell him something. But with Jacques's accepting and nonjudgmental approach having a positive impact on her, Ms. N. could eventually tell him that she was missing her mother who had moved to another part of the country after having lived in the same city as Ms. N. for many years. Although Jacques was helpful to Ms. N. in enabling her to talk about her resistance in revealing her separation anxiety, he had to ask himself, "Why did I let the client's real relationship with her mother elude us for so long?"

In reflecting on his own question, Jacques realized that ever since he was planning to have his own mother placed in a residential home for senior citizens, he had been remiss in attending to the reality problems that his clients were having with their parents. Unable to face his own guilt and separation anxiety vis-à-vis his mother, he could not and would not help his clients face similar issues in their treatment.

Another reality that is often defended against by both clients and therapists, to which we have referred in previous chapters, is the realistic behavior of the therapist in the treatment situation. Clients and therapists can resist confronting issues such as the therapist's latenesses, cancellations, sleeping, and other blatant counterresistances. However, very often the therapist shows less obvious counterresistances, which nonetheless affect the treatment relationship but are not discussed in sessions. For example, as we pointed out in Chapter 5, the client's reactions to an extratherapeutic contact might be exclusively attributed to a "father transference," because both client and therapist resist facing how they felt about meeting each other at the theatre, for example. Or, a woman therapist might be wearing sexy clothes, and although both client and therapist have feelings about it, the realistically sexy attire is dismissed in the therapy.

Wanda Leibkind, a psychologist in private practice, was treating Ms. O., a single woman of 30. Ms. O. sought treatment because she was very depressed, was not moving ahead in her career as a nurse, and found her relationships with men very unfulfilling.

After being in psychoanalytic treatment on the couch four times a week for about one year, Ms. O. brought up a problem that had been bothering her but which she could not discuss until this time. What upset Ms. O. was the fact that Wanda always had three cats in her consultation room, running around incessantly, sometimes crawling on the couch and getting on top of Ms. O. After being unable to talk about the situation for so long, Ms. O. let go one day and blurted out angrily, "I find these cats of yours very distracting.

They interfere with my treatment and I'd like you to get rid of them. They are a hindrance and I don't see why you need them here. I should be the only person here."

Wanda, who obviously needed her cats in her consultation room but did not want to face what their presence did for her, responded, "Let's see why you need me all to yourself and cannot share me." Wanda's response, although manifestly "analytic," did not take into consideration the realistic disruption of the cats, nor did it permit the client to have any responses other than those Wanda wanted to hear. Although Ms. O. may have had problems in sharing, she first had to be given the opportunity to vent her anger about the cats. If she were listened to empathically, rather than questioned, the client may have been willing later to analyze her discomfort.

Therapists, as we know, are more than transference figures. They show *real* behaviors that need to be acknowledged by them. Frequently, when practitioners do not acknowledge real characteristics about themselves or their offices, certain realities in their lives are too painful for them to face.

NOT GRASPING THE MEANING OF REMARKS

The dialogue between client and therapist is never a completely rational one. As we know, clients always experience their therapists' remarks through the lens of their current transference state. If they feel positively toward the therapist, they will use the remarks constructively. If they are in a negative transference, they will be inclined to disagree with their therapists' comments and oppose working on them.

What pertains to clients applies to therapists as well. Therapists can have difficulty understanding what clients are saying, despite persistent efforts by both parties. Sometimes a therapist tries very hard to listen to the client's descriptions of events and reactions to people but finds his or her mind wandering. Even when the therapist asks the client to repeat the statement or the story, he or she fails to grasp the meaning of the client's material.

Very often client and therapist both fail to grasp the meaning of each other's remarks. What is not being faced, however, is that they are in a negative transference-countertransference situation.

Ben Kingsley, a psychiatrist in a mental health clinic, was treating Mr. P., a 25-year-old man who came for help because he was a chronic gambler. Seen in twice-weekly therapy, Mr. P. initially liked coming to see Ben Kingsley and shared many of his problems with Ben. They looked together at Mr. P.'s depression, insomnia, angry outbursts, and sexual impotence. Within four months, Mr. P. felt considerably better and functioned in a more adaptive manner.

During the fifth month of treatment, client and therapist began to probe the meaning of Mr. P.'s chronic gambling. At this point in their relationship, their communication deteriorated. Mr. P. would try to explain some of his feelings prior to gambling, during the gambling, and afterwards. However, each time Mr. P. talked, Ben could not grasp the meaning of his client's remarks. Ben could not make connections and would mentally wander away from Mr. P. Despite his best intentions, he was not emotionally present in the interviews.

Ben tried everything to keep focused on his client's material but nothing seemed to work. When he brought the case to a supervisory seminar, one of his peers asked him if he had ever told the client that the client was difficult to follow. As Ben was feeling that the client would experience this comment as an attack, another member of the seminar asked, "Are several of your patients difficult to follow or is Mr. P. the only one?" Ben was aware that Mr. P. was the only one he was experiencing this problem with, but he felt very wary about commenting to his client on his being difficult to understand. With more help from his peers, and more self-examination, Ben realized that he had a great deal of hostility toward Mr. P. for his gambling habit. Ben's father had gambled and disrupted the harmony of their family. Never fully resolving his anger toward his father, Ben, without realizing it, was punishing Mr. P. by not understanding him. If he could not understand him, he could not help him.

Although some clients consciously or unconsciously arrange not to be understood, the matter of not grasping the meaning of the client's remarks is usually a two-way process, with client and therapist participating in the communication failure.

Direct communication between client and therapist is something to be strived for throughout the therapeutic process. When it is achieved and sustained, treatment usually succeeds. When client and therapist mutually agree that the treatment has been successful, they are ready to consider termination, the subject of Chapter 7, our concluding chapter.

7

Termination

Termination is an inevitable phase of most therapies; yet, there are only a small number of writers who have discussed termination as a realistic goal of psychotherapy. Even fewer have dealt with some of the technical procedures that are applicable to the termination process.

When there is limited discussion in the clinical literature on such a salient issue as termination, it seems reasonable to hypothesize that many counterresistances are aroused in the practitioner during the termination phase, some of which are shrouded in secrecy. However, just as the termination phase conjures up painful associations for the client, it also arouses similar responses in the therapist. Memories of past rejections, abandonments, and losses are some. As Fox, Nelson, and Bolman (1969) suggested, the gap in the literature appears to be a reflection of the therapist's defensive processes against the affects involved in termination—a sort of "institutionalized repression."

Consonant with the conceptual framework utilized throughout this book, in this chapter we focus primarily on the practitioner's counterresistances that emerge during the termination process and that affect the outcome of therapy.

CRITERIA FOR TERMINATING PSYCHOTHERAPY: SUBJECTIVE ISSUES

The difficulties in establishing criteria for the termination of psychotherapy include the divergent expectations of client and therapist. For example, as Nunberg (1954) pointed out, most clients are quite satisfied with symptom change alone; their therapists, on the other hand, would like to see them achieve major changes in character organization and in ego functioning. Very often therapists are so skeptical of symptom changes in their clients that they ascribe pejorative labels to these changes, such as "transference cures" (Fenichel, 1945; Macalpine, 1950) or "flights into health" (Robbins, 1937). According to Firestein (1978), "flight into health" refers "to prompt subsidence of symptoms—whatever the underlying dynamics—not explainable on the basis of therapeutic interaction of *long enough duration*" (p. 225). "Transference cure," a label applied to the same observed changes, "may be based on transference wishes" (e.g., to please the therapist), "transference fears" (of emotional entanglement with the therapist), and "identification with the idealized [therapist]" (presumed to be a paragon of mental health). "The literature is sketchy about these symptomatic improvements" (p. 225).

Although the tension between clients and practitioners around the theme of termination more often involves the client wanting to end the treatment after certain symptoms have been eradicated while the therapist has more lofty ambitions, the reverse is occasionally true. Sometimes the client would like to achieve more changes while the therapist would like to terminate the treatment.

Reasons for the discrepancy in expectations between clients and therapists are many. For practitioners in private practice who make their living exclusively from conducting therapy, it is not a pleasant thought to consider the loss of income that is a necessary part of ending a therapeutic relationship. Unless waiting lists are long, which in the 1990s is the exception rather than the rule for most private practitioners, a client's farewell frequently implies a loss of income. Many therapists, consciously and unconsciously, can place a higher priority on their own financial security than on their client's economic and even psychological welfare. In addition, the more times per week a given patient is seen, the higher percentage of the therapist's income will be "lost" when that patient terminates.

When clients are in treatment with private practitioners, their therapy frequently involves paying a large portion of their income. Although insurance and other forms of third-party payments help clients lower the cost of their psychotherapy, treatment is often a heavy expense for most of them. Frequently, clients who expend money have strong desires to terminate an experience that is costly, in contrast to their therapists who earn the money.

Clients have psychological reactions to paying fees to their therapists, often viewing the obligation as if they were children putting out for their demanding parents. Therefore, one of the major reasons given by clients for wanting to quit treatment is that they "are going broke." They feel they are giving their "all" to a parent who wants too much.

In sum, many therapists want the therapy to continue because it is their "bread and butter," which they need, while many clients want the therapy to discontinue because "it is the shit that [they] resent producing."

Of course, money is not the only issue that influences the discrepancy between therapists and clients on their outlook about termination. In most therapeutic situations, it is the client who reveals a great deal as the therapist listens and reveals very little. It is the client who exposes his or her major vulnerabilities, neuroses, character flaws, and deficiencies, while the therapist comments on the client's limitations and keeps his or her own problems a private matter most of the time. It is the therapist who is usually considered the expert, the teacher, and the authority, while the client is usually the one who is considered the layman, the nonexpert, and the one who frequently feels in the subordinate position. These discrepancies in role-sets certainly can provoke many clients to want to quit the therapy, while their counterparts want it to continue.

Even in clinics and social agencies, there are tensions between clients and therapists around termination because of noneconomic factors such as those just mentioned. As indicated previously, the "success" of treatment may be defined very differently by a therapist and client. For example, "success" for many clinicians is when the client stays in therapy for "a long enough duration" (Firestein, 1978) and improves in ego functioning. For a client, "success" may mean getting rid of symptoms quickly and leaving treatment in record time. As was suggested earlier in this chapter, therapists tend to devalue this kind of behavior and call it "a flight into health" or a "transference cure."

In most human dyads, when one party suggests that the relationship should end, the other person may feel quite upset regardless of the reason. Both clients and therapists may feel unloved, rejected, or even hated, when their counterparts suggest the possibility of terminating treatment.

Although therapists are often viewed by clients and by themselves as "parental figures," a client's wish to terminate treatment can induce a reversal of roles (A. Freud, 1946), whereby the therapist feels like a misunderstood child and views the client as a callous and cold parent. Of course, when therapists initiate the idea of termination, the client may feel misunderstood and mistreated by a callous and cold parental figure, as well.

Termination is also influenced by the respective parties' attitudes toward perfection and their similarities or differences in their ambitiousness. Schmideberg (1938) cautioned against clinicians being influenced in their judgment concerning termination by idiosyncratic notions of "perfect results" to be awaited or achieved through unending work. She took the position that if the treatment lasted longer than six years, the client could become estranged from reality.

Ginsburg (1950) suggested that although the clinician's views should not be permitted to run to perfectionistic extremes, he or she must decide, in collaboration with the client, what constitutes a remainder of "tolerable conflict."

If either therapist or client is much more perfectionistic and ambitious than the other, there will be the strong possibility of tension between them, with each party trying to convince the other that one position is superior to the other. Of course, if sharp discrepancies like these exist, they should have been noted before the termination phase was begun. However, it is important to keep in mind that issues such as ambitiousness, dependency, and autonomy that have not appeared—during the course of treatment—or have only partially appeared often emerge in full blast at termination (Fine, 1982; Firestein, 1978; Reich, 1950; Strean, 1985/1990).

When therapist and client take leave of each other, in most cases never to see each other again, termination can be "a last chance" to show and tell what has been held back. Consequently, emerging from both client and therapist at termination can be certain id wishes that have been repressed and suppressed, superego injunctions and ego ideals that have been denied, and subtle resistances and counterresistances that have been unexamined. New or partially new material that is exposed can affect the termination process for better or for worse.

Another subjective factor influencing termination is how "troublesome" or "agreeable" client and therapist have found each other (Lechat, 1954). Interminable treatment situations often ensue when client and therapist find each other "agreeable." Also, therapies of short duration, as we have seen from vignettes in earlier chapters, often occur when at least one member of the therapy dyad finds the other "troublesome." Of course, clients and therapists can defend against unacceptable affects so that it is possible for a dyad who harbor hostile feelings toward each other to deny or repress their affects and prolong the therapy.

If client and therapist have had a good working alliance, with honesty and openness being constant components of their communication, there will be, in all likelihood, a mutual decision regarding the time to end the treatment. Greenson (1966) suggested that a good way to assess the correctness of the timing of termination is to take careful note of the client's and the therapist's affective responses to the idea of termination. In Greenson's experience, if either party is surprised when the prospect of termination is broached, this means that something is amiss.

CRITERIA FOR TERMINATION: OBJECTIVE FACTORS

Now that we have considered some of the subjective issues that affect the decision to terminate therapy, the objective factors mentioned by leading clinicians and scholars seem to pale in comparison. For example, in one of the "Introductory Lectures on Psychoanalysis" (1917), Freud referred to the neurotic individual's return to health in terms of "whether the subject is left with a sufficient amount of capacity for enjoyment and of efficiency" (p. 457). This statement seems to have heralded the origin of the familiar maxim for assessing mental health according to the client's capacity "to love and to work." The implication of the maxim is that a client is ready to leave treatment when he or she can love consistently and work productively (Firestein, 1978).

Although few clinicians would dispute Freud's criteria for termination of treatment, "to love and to work" are global concepts and lack sufficient specificity. In addition, we know that Freud, too, was influenced by subjective factors in arranging for the termination of his patients' treatment. In the case of Dora, it appears that he was quite irritated by her and the treatment ended prematurely after three months. In contrast, the Wolf Man, whom Freud seemed to have loved, was in therapy with him for five years (Fine, 1972). It is questionable whether Freud's maxim for assessing mental health was the most crucial variable in deciding termination for either Dora or the Wolf Man.

What we have said about Freud's coping with terminating Dora and the Wolf Man is probably true of many, if not most, therapists much of the time. Whether we talk about where "id was, there shall ego be" (Nunberg, 1928, 1931) or whether we assert that now "there is an ability to distinguish between fantasy and reality" (Firestein, 1978) or that "a healthy person must have the capacity to suffer and to be depressed" (Hartmann, 1939, p. 6), transference and countertransference issues, resistances, and counterresistances govern the termination process, we believe, much more than the objective criteria that we reviewed.

Indeed, Glover (1955), after researching the subject of termination quite carefully through the use of lengthy questionnaires, which he distributed to many psychoanalysts in England, emphasized "intuition" as a frequent criterion for termination. Held (1955) wondered whether the clinician's intuition about readiness for termination was related to some variety of telepathic communication from the client. Other writers have ventured similar hypotheses (Atkin, 1966; Nacht, Bouvet, & Benassy, 1954).

Although they are also influenced by subjective factors, we believe that an ideal time for therapist and client to consider termination is when they are in agreement that the client has come as close as he or she can to fulfilling "the analytic ideal" (Fine, 1982). Therefore, the client must be able to love more and hate less, seek pleasure, have sexual gratification, have a feeling for life yet one which is guided by reason, have an adequate role in the family, have a sense of identity, be constructive, work, be creative, have a role in the social order, be able to communicate, and be reasonably free of neurotic symptoms.

As we have suggested, this is an "ideal" that is rarely if ever achieved, but it is something for therapist and client to aim for. However, as we have implied thoughout this book, various counterresistances during the course of the treatment process can interfere with the attainment of "the analytic ideal." Although factors in the client's personality and living situation play a role too, interfering with the attainment of treatment goals, in this book we have emphasized the therapist's role. Consequently, in the remaining part of this chapter, we discuss several common counterresistances that appear or can appear during the termination phase of treatment.

PREMATURE TERMINATION

Although we have given several examples throughout the book of premature terminations, in this section we will concentrate on one form of premature termina-

tion: when the therapist sets a termination date before the client is psychologically ready to depart from the therapist.

"Premature termination" arranged by the practitioner occurs when he or she wants to get rid of the client for one reason or another. The client may be paying a low fee and the therapist would like to replace him or her with a better paying client. The client may be boring, demanding, or irritating. The client may arouse fantasies in the practitioner that create anxiety such as murderous fantasies or lustful wishes; by getting rid of this client, the therapist can get rid of intolerable anxiety. The client may be making limited or no progress and the therapist feels very guilty about this. Consequently, the therapist ends the treatment and does not have to be reminded of being a failure or of being inadequate. In some cases, the therapist who feels that no progress has been made might refer the client to another practitioner—maybe to a colleague the therapist thinks can do better with the client or perhaps to a colleague who will also fail and therefore help the therapist not suffer alone!

The therapist's narcissistic need for success affects the decision to terminate and can take a variety of forms. As we will discuss in the next section, this desire can manifest itself in a wish to prolong the treatment and to try to make the results as perfect as possible. However, there are therapists who are so anxious about the treatment outcome, and so apprehensive about facing therapeutic results that are less than perfect, that they discharge their clients prematurely (Firestein, 1978; Held, 1955). These practitioners are similar to students who do not study for their examinations and therefore do not get good results. They are frightened to study because they might have to face the possibility of achieving less than good academic results after they have expended considerable effort, and this feels worse to them.

Philip Jarvis, a therapist in private practice, had treated a man in his late sixties for over a year. Mr. Q. had sought treatment because he was very ambivalent about retiring from his job of over 40 years. He was an insurance broker. Feeling somewhat depressed about his waning energy, which affected not only his work but his marriage, particularly his sexual relationship with his wife, Mr. Q. was hopeful that psychotherapy would help him feel less depressed and more enthusiastic and would be helpful to him in making the right decision about retiring.

In the first few months of the once-a-week treatment, Philip Jarvis and Mr. Q. communicated very well. Philip was experienced by his client as "an affable, kind man."

Mr. Q.'s spirits were lifted by the therapy, but his sexual relationship with his wife did not change very much nor did his ambivalence about retiring recede. Noting this lack of change during the ninth month of treatment, Philip began to be more confrontational in the therapy sessions. He told Mr.

Q. that he was not facing his passivity, that he was too often turning his aggression inward, and that he was deriving much secondary gain from his symptoms.

Inasmuch as all of the statements by Philip were correct, Mr. Q. could not have opposed them anyway; according to the client, "the therapist is always right." Said Mr. Q., "I cannot dispute the truth of your statements, but I just can't help myself." What Phillip did not see was the client's latent wish to oppose him and the therapy.

Because of his overactive therapeutic ambitiousness, Philip "gave up" after one year of treatment. He told Mr. Q. that by the time someone reaches his late sixties, there was limited possibility of change and that he would have "to live with his problems." Being overtly compliant, Mr. Q. accepted Philip Jarvis's assessment and terminated therapy.

When therapists have high therapeutic aspirations for themselves, there is a danger that they will impose their goals on their clients and overlook crucial dimensions of their clients' transference reactions and resistances. Therefore, their clients do not improve. Ambitious therapists can then become angry at their clients and berate them with confrontations and interpretations. Usually clients react to admonishments with anger and/or depression. They rarely respond with therapeutic improvement.

What overambitious therapists also tend to overlook is the fact that when their clients are berated, they tend to want to defy. One way of defying the therapist is to get worse and, more often than not, this is what occurs.

PROLONGED TREATMENT AND TERMINATION

As we already pointed out, there are many reasons why therapy can be unduly prolonged. These range all the way from the therapist's need for economic enhancement to strong symbiotic fantasies that both client and therapist share and wish to gratify in their relationship with each other.

One cause of prolonged treatment that we wish to discuss in this section is the therapist's narcissistic need for success. Many individuals who become psychotherapists are people who have had emotionally troubled lives. Like parents who experienced unhappiness in their own childhoods and want their sons and daughters to have happier lives than they experienced, clinicians can feel the same way. If the clinician has suffered from problems such as sibling rivalry, oedipal competition, or latent homosexuality, he or she may work overtime to insure that the client carefully and painstakingly works through these problems. If therapists want to relive their own lives vicariously through their clients every time a residue of one of their own conflicts emerges, they prolong the treatment by trying very hard to achieve

the success they wanted for themselves by pressuring their clients to achieve it for them.

Darryl Ivey was a social worker in a mental health center treating a teenager, Cindy R. The 16-year-old came for help because she was depressed as a result of being scapegoated by her peers. Cindy felt that one of the reasons she was picked on was because she was Afro-American, and the majority of the students in her school were White and didn't like anyone different from them.

Darryl, who was Afro-American himself, felt very identified with Cindy. He could empathize with how angry and depressed she felt when she was slighted or ostracized. But Darryl's philosophy, shared by many members of minority groups, was that "you have to work twice as hard to get ahead and you have to be better than" the others. Darryl, an experienced professional for over five years, knew that it would be antibtherapeutic to overtly impose his ambitions on Cindy. Nonetheless, he pushed hard to make her a treatment success. Not only did Darryl want to make Cindy into his own ego ideal, but he also tried to replicate his own personal therapy in his clinical work with her. He saw her twice a week, which was the frequency of his own therapy. He also adhered to several of the same practices his therapist utilized with him, such as greeting the client in a prescribed way, charging one half of the fee for a missed session, and offering certain self-disclosures to his client.

Cindy benefitted a great deal from her treatment with Darryl. She learned how to cope better with racism, spent more time constructively studying, worried less, accepted more of her own aggression, felt less guilty, and raised her self-esteem. Her grades went up and she had more friends. After a year of treatment, Cindy felt that she could "try it alone" without Darryl.

When Cindy suggested she could end treatment the day before she graduated from high school, Darryl was against it and said so. They had not discussed much about going to college yet, and Cindy needed more help with this as far as Darryl was concerned. Therapist and client then got involved in a power struggle, both arguing the merits of their respective positions. Cindy wanted independence and autonomy. Darryl wanted Cindy to stay in treatment and use his help so that she could do well in college.

In response to Darryl's argumentative stance, Cindy began to arrive late for sessions and cancelled several. Finally, despite Darryl's strong position, Cindy quit treatment without telling her therapist what her plans were for the future.

Darryl Ivey's experience with Cindy R. is very instructive for many reasons. First, it affirms the fact that whenever practitioners argue with their clients, though they may win the argument, they usually lose the case. Few clients respond well to a therapist who argues. They feel demeaned and unappreciated and rarely respect the therapist for losing his or her composure. Second, a client's wishes regarding termination, or any other issue, should always be given an empathetic ear. As we have stressed throughout this book, when clients have their wishes respected and listened to carefully, they feel supported, and then most of them can go on to actively consider other alternatives than the one they proposed. Third, a client's judgment of what is "enough treatment" cannot and should not be dismissed by the practitioner. Although the therapist may not agree, many clients feel more comfortable about stopping treatment at one point in their lives and then resuming it later. Particularly when the client has made a lot of progress, as did Cindy in the case above, his or her ideas about when to terminate should be respected.

Too often, practitioners use their own lifestyles and their own personal therapy as paradigms for their clients. When they do this, they fail to individualize their clients, disrespect their clients' values, defenses, and lifestyles, and instead turn them into clones. Being a clone of a psychotherapist never particularly enhances a client's mental health. Furthermore, when a therapist constantly wants to duplicate his or her own therapy with clients, the therapist has not sufficiently separated from his or her own therapist. Otherwise the therapist would not have to resurrect his or her own therapy experience.

SEPARATION ANXIETY

In psychoanalytic usage, separation refers to one of the intrapsychic processes involved in separation-individuation, specifically those whereby the individual gains a sense of the self as a distinct entity functioning separately from the object (Moore & Fine, 1990). This ability is an essential part of human growth and development and the capacity to tolerate separation is one indicator of that developmental achievement (Mahler, Pine, & Bergman, 1975).

Many clients in psychotherapy have experienced untimely, sudden, or abrupt separations which contribute heavily to the difficulties they bring to treatment (Bowlby, 1980). Thus, termination revives for clients the anxiety associated with traumatic and other upsetting separations. Inasmuch as therapists' backgrounds are similar to their clients', they, too, can suffer much separation anxiety around termination. This can take the form of depression, feelings of worthlessness, and even thoughts of suicide at the time that termination of therapy takes place.

Because many people, due to the continuing influence of "the child" in us, experience separation as a sign of being unloved, many clients are quite convinced that termination would not be taking place if they were really loved by the therapist. If the therapist cannot understand that the client is feeling like an abandoned child, the therapist may try to reassure the client rather than to help the client discuss the painful feelings that have been revived from the past.

Theresa Hannigan, a psychiatrist in a mental health clinic, had achieved excellent therapeutic results with Mr. S., a man of 30, who had sexual and interpersonal problems. Mr. S., who could only take limited initiative in dating women, was extremely shy on dates and was totally unable to be sexually potent with virtually any of his female companions. Through his twice-weekly therapy sessions, which lasted a little over a year, Mr. S. began to date women regularly, could enjoy sex with them, and improved his self-esteem and self-image enormously.

Noting Mr. S.'s excellent progress, Theresa suggested that they consider termination. Although Mr. S. initially responded positively to the idea of termination, within two weeks he became depressed and his symptoms of impotence and social anxiety returned. Inasmuch as there was a good working alliance between therapist and client, it did not take long for them to agree that Mr. S. was reacting to the idea of ending the therapy.

Said Mr. S., "I feel you are saying you have had enough of me. You really are bored by me and you would like to get rid of me." Since Mr. S.'s perception of the therapist's motives were far different from what Theresa Hannigan intended them to be, she was shocked at his reaction. Not monitoring her countertransference responses, she blurted out, "Nothing could be further from the truth! I think you have made a lot of progress and I want you to feel like a successful graduate."

Although Mr. S. was mildly reassured by Theresa's comment, his self-confidence and sexual freedom did not return. The more he noticed the resurgence of his disabling symptoms, the more he was convinced that he was a failure as a client and unlovable as a man. The more anxiety he manifested, the more Theresa tried to reassure him. The more reassurance he received from her, the more he distrusted Theresa.

As Theresa noted the rather acute regression that took place in her client and saw for herself the futility of her reassuring remarks, she began to explore with the aid of a senior colleague the nature of her client's resistance and of her own counterresistances.

Examining her counterresistances first, Theresa had to face the fact that the return of her client's symptoms made her feel like a failure as a therapist. Reassuring her client of his lovableness was really an indirect way of reassuring herself of her own competence. To Theresa, Mr. S.'s impotence as a sexual man meant that as a clinician she was impotent to help him in a major way.

Feeling caught up in protecting herself interfered with Theresa's ability to recognize how angry her client was at her wanting to say good-bye to him. Because Theresa was unable to help Mr. S. discharge his anger toward her, he turned it against himself and became depressed.

As we have observed in preceding chapters, when the practitioner faces his or her own counterresistances and courageously confronts their causes, he or she is more sensitive to the client's resistances and their causes. This is what occurred with Theresa. After facing her own impotent feelings, she could help her client better understand his own. After accepting her own anger at her client for not pleasing her, Theresa could then help Mr. S. voice his displeasure with her.

Separation often stirs up the most primitive of emotions. When someone suggests that he or she might leave us, or in fact does, it can appear like a death sentence to us. Many therapists and clients have enormous difficulty with termination because they experience themselves as either being killed or killing, depending on who initiates the idea of termination.

As we saw in the case above, separation also conjures up associations of being unlovable, incompetent, defective, castrated, and hated. To ward off these very painful affects in themselves, therapists often obstruct the termination process.

> After having been in treatment for four years three times a week, Ms. T. suggested to her therapist, May Garvey, that they consider termination. Ms. T., a woman in her late twenties who came into treatment after a divorce, was now dating men and enjoying herself with them. She had completed her graduate work as a social psychologist and she was on much better terms with her parents, with whom she had feuded a great deal prior to beginning therapy.
>
> As Ms. T. discussed the possibility of terminating treatment, she brought out much gratitude toward May Garvey and told her how accepted she felt regardless of what she was feeling and thinking.
>
> Despite the client's positive transference and good working alliance with her therapist, May felt rejected by her client's wish to terminate. In contrast to her consistent stance of careful listening and her disciplined manner of conducting herself in the sessions, after listening for two sessions to the client's thoughts about ending treatment, May blurted out with sarcasm, "If you love me so much, why do you want to leave me?" Ms. T. was startled by May's question but seemed more composed than her therapist and said, "I love you and I assume you love me. I think that when people love each other, they want the best for each other. I think it's best for me to move on. Maybe what you are telling me is that it's not the best thing *for you* if I end treatment."
>
> May found Ms. T.'s response to her question as upsetting as she found her request to end treatment. May realized that what her client said was an accurate rendition of May's position on termination. Yet, May found termination of her work with Ms. T. unacceptable because it frustrated her own wishes to continue her relationship with her client. To May, as long as she was actively treating her client, she felt very much alive and worthwhile. To May, terminating treatment had the meaning of making her a "nobody," worthless and virtually dead.
>
> May learned through her own personal therapy and experiences with other

clients that termination of her therapeutic work activated memories for her in which she was valued only if she performed a specific chore for a family member. Therefore, to stop taking care of others brought much wrath, scorn, and rejection from her parents. Her superego, of course, internalized these critical voices and May, in effect, wiped herself out when she was not actively taking care of somebody.

Understanding the dynamics of her counterresistances to termination helped May become much less angry and hurt when clients initiated termination of treatment. She learned later in discussions with colleagues that the voices of her punitive superego that pressured her to take care of others were also voices that resonated in the superegos of many of her peers. They, too, found it difficult to like themselves unless they were taking care of others.

COPING WITH THE CLIENT'S REGRESSION

As the reader is now very much aware, because termination of treatment conjures up painful emotions, many clients regress and manifest the very symptoms and maladaptive behaviors that brought them into treatment in the first place. By reverting to the old symptoms and the old pathology, and presenting themselves as they were when treatment began, clients are frequently expressing, albeit unconsciously, a wish to begin treatment all over again, rather than ending it. A. Reich (1950) observed that the revived symptomatology is very often the client's reaction to his or her awareness that childish wishes (e.g., wishes for a perfect parent) for a gratifying symbiosis or to be eternally omnipotent are not going to be gratified by the practitioner. Saul (1958) suggested that the reappearance of old symptoms is an expression of revenge. The client is indirectly saying, "Look, you have had no effect on me!"

It would appear that under the impact of separation, with all of the anxiety that it induces, clients are crying out for a loving parent to comfort them by unconsciously returning to the psychological state that existed at the beginning of treatment (Kohut, 1971).

In many ways, the separation anxiety that clients experience at termination can be viewed as quite similar to the way infants feel at weaning, or toddlers at toilet training. The young child, having been the recipient of consistent tender love, care, and nurturing, is reluctant to give it up. Adult clients, no different in many ways from young children, are reluctant to take on frustrations and to take care of themselves. Termination induces in most clients the helpless, angry, disorganized state of a child who feels tortured on being told to "go it alone."

As we have already seen, when confronted by the client's wish to regress and by the revival of his or her symptoms, therapists can feel quite disillusioned. They wonder about their competence and worry about their impact on the client. If they are beginning therapists, they may wonder whether psychotherapy can help anyone.

Although each therapist has his or her own idiosyncratic response to termination and separation, it is important to bear in mind that many, if not most, clients are often secretly wishing that the therapist will become upset and disorganized by their regressive behavior. In the therapist's panic, the client hopes, the therapist may prolong the therapy and forget about termination. Or, if the therapist becomes visibly upset when the client regresses, the client can feel a sense of triumph and a feeling of revenge for being mistreated.

Although it is the major thesis of this book that therapists must always pay strict attention to their counterresistances at every phase of treatment, this thesis is extremely important to keep in mind at a time when the client regresses and reverts to old symptoms and maladaptive behavior. At termination, when the therapist has said that treatment has been successful and is now ready to bid farewell to the client, it can be humiliating to witness a client deteriorating when we think we have "cured" him or her. This is when therapists can falsely reassure their clients, respond to them with anger, or do something that is antitherapeutic.

A psychologist in private practice, Alan Feder had treated Mr. U. once a week for a little over a year. Mr. U., a man in his late twenties, came to see Alan Feder because he had a gambling addiction. Although Mr. U. made a good living as a book salesman, on many occasions, he would use up all of his earnings and go heavily into debt.

As Mr. U. was helped by Alan to understand and to master many of his grandiose fantasies within three to four months after therapy began, Mr. U. stopped gambling. Further, his work habits got much better, he made more money, and saved some. Soon he formed a close and mutually enjoyable relationship with a woman and they planned to get married.

Inasmuch as Mr. U. had sustained his therapeutic gains for several months, Alan introduced the idea of termination toward the end of the eleventh month of treatment. Mr. U. seemed to agree with idea, but he missed his next appointment and started coming late for others. In addition, he began to relate to Alan with indifference and apathy.

Alan commented to Mr. U., "Ever since we discussed the possibility of ending our work, you seem to be upset." Mr. U. denied any feelings and merely stated, "When something is over, it's over!" As Mr. U. became more and more reluctant to confront his behavior and to face some of his feelings toward his therapist, Alan became more frustrated and tried harder to get his client to talk about termination and all that it meant to him. The harder Alan tried, the more resistant Mr. U. became and, of course, Alan tried even harder. Eventually there was a real power struggle taking place between therapist and client. A latent irritation became more manifest and in one interview, after a month of struggling, Alan said to Mr. U., "You are stubborn!" Angry, but eager to frustrate his therapist and act out some revenge, Mr. U. tried his best to appear very calm and said, "I think you are having more difficulties than I am!" This was a real blow to Alan's narcissism and he became exasperated and said furiously, "You are trying your best to make my life very difficult!" To this Mr. U. stated, "On the contrary. I'm trying to make it easier. That's why I haven't told you that I started to gamble again. I thought it would hurt your feelings and I didn't want to do that. So, you are wrong!"

As Alan Feder certainly realized, it is very difficult to maintain one's composure, equilibrium, objectivity, and empathy when, after struggling hard to help a client and then finally achieving something, the client wants to defeat you. Soon therapy can become two people seeking revenge on each other for hurting each other.

What is often difficult for practitioners to recognize is that even when therapy is successful and a great deal has been achieved, the client is still very angry about ending. Sometimes therapists do not realize the enormous gratification clients derive when they can be themselves over a long period of time, receive an empathetic response almost always, and rarely be judged negatively or harshly. To be asked to give this up feels like a slap in the face, a rejection, and an abandonment. Therefore, clients at this time try to make their therapists feel as they do—angry, hurt, and resourceless.

When therapists feel angry, hurt, and resourceless at termination, it is not only helpful to recognize that this is what their clients want them to feel, and then use this information to give to clients at the appropriate time, but it is also helpful to understand their own anger, hurt, and resourcelessness as well as possible. Usually therapists are feeling like hurt and incompetent children at this time but do not want to face it. Most of the time therapists have an inordinate need to feel and appear like mature parents. Consequently, they are too apt to make interpretations about the child in their clients, rather than face the child in themselves who feels abandoned at termination. When they face the child in themselves and give the child a hearing, they are more enabled to become mature therapists.

DENIAL OF AFFECT

Just as Mr. U. in the above illustration tended to deny his strong affects that were precipitated by the termination of treatment, therapists can do the same. One way of coping with an event that is painful is to pretend that it does not exist. This is often what many people do when a loved one dies. Kubler-Ross (1972) pointed out that one of the first defenses utilized when we mourn is denial. So difficult and painful is the reality of the death that all of us tend to behave at first as if nothing occurred—the loss is too great.

When therapists find that they are not feeling very much at termination, they should ask themselves, "Why not?" If they are honest with themselves, they will usually find that the termination process is reminding them of a real death in their lives at a time when they did not face their own feelings. Another reason accounting for why the practitioner is exempt from affect is that the client may be reminding the practitioner of an important loved one who is alive—and the possibility of thinking of that loved one dying is just too overwhelming.

> Realizing that she had little emotion during the termination process with her client, Mr. V., whom she had been treating for three years twice a week, Keiko Etoshi, a social worker in private practice, began to reflect on her absence of affect. Actually it was her client who brought her lack of affect at termination to her attention.
>
> Mr. V. reminded Keiko of her younger brother of whom she was very fond. She realized that it was this positive countertransference that enabled her to be very empathetic with and therapeutically helpful to Mr. V. To say good-bye to her "brother" forever was too painful for Keiko to contemplate, so she denied and repressed her feelings about termination with him.

Just as the termination phase can stir up unresolved problems of the client's, so too can termination bring to the surface old and new problems of the therapist's. In Keiko Etoshi's case, she had never faced the end of a relationship with her brother. Before she could assist Mr. V. to end treatment, she had to come to grips with some aspects of her attachment to her brother.

Usually when practitioners initiate seeing their clients after termination, either in the consultation room and/or socially, the client remains a transference object (a brother, mother, father, sister, or good friend) from whom the therapist cannot take leave. Just as it has often been suggested that major transference issues of the client's should be resolved before termination can take place, major countertransference issues of the therapist should be resolved as well. If the practitioner is deluged with fantasies about seeing the client in different contexts after treatment is over, or in fact initiates such contact, usually, if not always, major countertransference problems have not been resolved.

Weinshel (1984) suggested that during most of the treatment process, and particularly during the termination phase, the therapist is trying to help the client slowly come to grips with the fact that there is no such thing as magic. In order to do this, the therapist should have mastered his or her wishes to be a magician. In accepting that they are not magicians, therapists can be more accepting of their own imperfections. Consequently, they can help their clients deal with life in an imperfect world and help them realize that bliss is momentary and pain and frustration are inevitable.

As the client's wishes and fantasies of omnipotence are toned down because the therapist has mastered his or her grandiose desires, as the client's resistances to termination are essentially resolved because the therapist's counterresistances to termination are essentially resolved, client and therapist are ready to part company. They do so usually with mixed feelings—sad at the farewell which denotes loss, happy with the results attained, angry that many good things must come to an end. But, they part with the hope that the cooperative effort in which they both intensely participated will continue to pay dividends for both of them. Client and therapist usually agree with Shakespeare's notion that "Parting is such sweet sorrow!"

References

Abend, S. (1982). Serious illness in the analyst: Countertransference considerations. *Journal of the American Psychoanalytic Association, 30*, 365–380.

Abend, S. (1986). Countertransference, empathy, and the analytic ideal: The impact of life stresses on analytic capability." *The Psychoanalytic Quarterly, 55*, 536–575.

Abend, S. (1989). Countertransference and psychoanalytic technique. *The Psychoanalytic Quarterly, 58*, 374–395.

Abraham, K. (1919). A particular form of neurotic resistance against the psychoanalytic method. In K. Abraham (Ed.), *Selected papers on psychoanalysis*. New York: Basic Books.

Ackerman, N. (1958). *The psychodynamics of family life*. New York: Basic Books.

Adler, K. (1967). Adler's individual psychology. In B. Wolman (Ed.), *Psychoanalytic technique*. New York: Basic Books.

Aichorn, A. (1925). *Wayward youth*. New York: Viking Press.

Alexander, F., & French, T. M. (1946). *Psychoanalytic therapy: Principles and applications*. New York: Ronald Press.

Alexander, F., & Ross, H. (1952). *Dynamic psychiatry*. Chicago, IL: The University of Chicago Press.

Allphin, C. (1982). Envy in the transference and countertransference. *Clinical Social Work, 10*, 151–164.

Applebaum, A. (1988). Psychoanalysis during pregnancy: The effect of a sibling constellation. *Psychoanalytic Inquiry, 8*, 177–196.

Arlow, J. (1985). Some technical problems of countertransference. *The Psychoanalytic Quarterly, 54*, 164–174.

Atkin, S. (1966). Discussion. In R. E. Litman (Ed.), *Psychoanalysis in the Americas* (pp. 240–246). New York: International Universities Press.

Aull, G., & Strean, H. (1967). The analyst's silence. *The Psychoanalytic Forum, 2*, 72–87.

Baranger, M., Branger, W., & Thom, J. (1983). Process and non-process in analytic work. *International Journal of Psychoanalysis, 64*, 1–15.

Barbara, D. (1958). *The art of listening*. Springfield, IL: Charles C Thomas.

Benjamin, A. (1974). *The helping interview* (2nd ed.). Boston: Houghton Mifflin.

Bergler, E. (1969). *Selected papers of Edmund Bergler*. New York: Grune & Stratton.

Bernstein, A. (1972). The fear of compassion. In B. Wolman (Ed.), *Success and failure in psychoanalysis and psychotherapy*. New York: The Macmillan Company.

Blanck, G., & Blanck, R. (1979). *Ego psychology II. Psychoanalytic developmental psychology.* New York: Columbia University Press.

Blum, H. (1981). The forbidden quest and the analytic ideal: The superego and insight. *The Psychoanalytic Quarterly, 50,* 535–556.

Blum, H. (1983). The position and value of extratransference interpretation. *Journal of the American Psychoanalytic Association, 31,* 587–618.

Boesky, D. (1990). The psychoanalytic process and its components. *The Psychoanalytic Quarterly, 59,* 550–584.

Bowlby, J. (1980). *Attachment and loss* (Vol 3). New York: Basic Books.

Brenner, C. (1982). *The mind in conflict.* New York: International Universities Press.

Brenner, C. (1985). Countertransference as compromise formation. *The Psychoanalytic Quarterly, 54,* 155–163.

Breuer, J., & Freud, S. (1893-1895). Studies in hysteria. In J. Strachey (Ed. & Trans.), *The standard edition of the complete psychological works of Sigmund Freud* (Vol. 3, pp. 1–252). London: Hogarth Press.

Bruch, H. (1984). *Eating disorders: Obesity, anorexia nervosa, and the person within.* New York: Basic Books.

Burton, A. (1972). *Twelve therapists.* San Francisco, CA: Jossey-Bass.

Chasseguet-Smirgel, J. (1985). *The ego ideal: A psychoanalytic essay on the malady of the ideal.* New York: W. W. Norton.

Cohen, J. (1983). Psychotherapists preparing for death: Denial and action. *American Journal of Psychotherapy, 37,* 222–226.

Compton, A. (1988). *COPE study group discussion of the psychoanalytic process.* Unpublished.

Compton, A. (1990). Psychoanalytic process. *The Psychoanalytic Quarterly, 59,* 585–598.

Compton, B., & Galaway, D. (1975). *Social work processes.* Homewood, IL: The Dorsey Press.

Dahlberg, C. (1970). Sex contact between patient and therapist. *Contemporary Psychoanalysis, 6,* 107–124.

Dewald, P. (1982). Serious illness in the analyst: Transference, countertransference and reality responses. *Journal of American Psychoanalytic Association, 30,* 347–363.

Dewey, J. (1939). *Intelligence in the modern world. John Dewey's philosophy.* New York: Random House Library.

Eissler, K. (1974). On some theoretical and technical problems regarding the payment of fees for psychoanalytic treatment. *International Review of Psychoanalysis, l,* 73–101.

Eissler, K. (1975). On the possible effects of aging on the practice of psychoanalysis: An essay. *Journal of the Philadelphia Association for Psychoanalysis, 2,* 138–152.

Epstein, L. (1979). The therapeutic function of hate in the countertransference. In L. Epstein & A. Feiner (Eds.), *Countertransference: The therapist's contribution to the therapeutic situation.* New York: Jason Aronson.

Epstein, L., & Feiner, A. (1979). *The therapist's contribution to the therapeutic situation.* New York: Jason Aronson.

Erikson, E. (1950). *Childhood and society.* New York: W. W. Norton.

Feldman, Y. (1958). A casework approach toward understanding parents of emotionally disturbed children. *Social Work,* 3, 23–29. (Also in H. Strean [Ed.] [1970]. *New approaches in child guidance.* Metuchen, NJ: Scarecrow Press)

Fenichel, O. (1945). *The psychoanalytic theory of neurosis.* New York: W. W. Norton.

Fenichel, O. (1954). *The collected papers of Otto Fenichel.* H. Fenichel & D. Rapaport (Eds.) (2nd series). New York: W. W. Norton.

Ferenczi, S. (1950). *Sex in psychoanalysis* (Ernest Jones, Trans.). New York: Basic Books.

Fine, R. (1972). *The healing of the mind* (1st ed.). New York: David McKay Company, Inc.

Fine, R. (1979). *The history of psychoanalysis.* New York: Columbia University Press.

Fine, R. (1982). *The healing of the mind* (2nd ed.). New York: The Free Press.

Fine, R. (1985). Countertransference and the pleasures of being an analyst. *Current Issues in Psychoanalytic Practice,* 2, 3–19.

Finell, J. (1984). Projective identification: Mystery and fragmentation. *Current Issues in Psychoanalytic Practice,* 1, 47–62.

Finell, J. (1985). Narcissistic problems in analysts. *International Journal of Psychoanalysis,* 66, 433–445.

Firestein, S. (1978). *Termination in psychoanalysis.* New York: International Universities Press.

Fox, E., Nelson, M., & Bolman, W. (1969). The termination process: A neglected dimension in social work. *Social Work,* 14, 53–63.

Freeman, L., & Strean, H. (1981). *Freud and women.* New York: Ungar.

Freud, A. (1946). *The ego and the mechanisms of defense.* New York: International Universities Press.

Freud, S. (1910). Wild analysis. In J. Strachey (Ed. & Trans.), *The standard edition of the complete psychological works of Sigmund Freud* (Vol. 11, pp. 141–151). London: Hogarth Press.

Freud, S. (1912). The dynamics of transference. In J. Strachey (Ed. & Trans.), *The standard edition of the complete psychological works of Sigmund Freud* (Vol. 12, pp. 97–108). London: Hogarth Press.

Freud, S. (1913). On beginning the treatment. In J. Strachey (Ed. & Trans.), *The standard edition of the complete works of Sigmund Freud* (Vol. 12, pp. 121–144). London: Hogarth Press.

Freud, S. (1914a). Remembering, repeating and working through. In J. Strachey (Ed. & Trans.), *The standard edition of the complete works of Sigmund Freud* (Vol. 12, pp. 145–156). London: Hogarth Press.

Freud, S. (1914b). On narcissism. In J. Strachey (Ed. & Trans.), *The standard edition of the complete works of Sigmund Freud* (Vol. 12, pp. 67–104). London: Hogarth Press.

Freud, S. (1915). Observations on transference love. In J. Strachey (Ed. & Trans.), *The standard edition of the complete works of Sigmund Freud.* (Vol. 12, pp. 157–171). London: Hogarth Press.

Freud, S. (1916). Some character types met with in psychoanalytic work. In J. Strachey (Ed.

& Trans.), *The standard edition of the complete works of Sigmund Freud*. (Vol. 14, pp. 309–333). London: Hogarth Press.

Freud, S. (1917). Analytic therapy. In J. Strachey (Ed. & Trans.), *The standard edition of the complete works of Sigmund Freud*. (Vol. 16, pp. 448–463). London: Hogarth Press.

Freud, S. (1919). Lines of advance in psychoanalytic therapy. In J. Strachey (Ed. & Trans.), *The standard edition of the complete works of Sigmund Freud*. (Vol. 17, pp. 139–168). London: Hogarth Press.

Freud, S. (1926). Inhibitions, symptoms, and anxiety. In J. Strachey (Ed. & Trans.), *The standard edition of the complete works of Sigmund Freud*. (Vol. 20, pp. 77–174). London: Hogarth Press.

Freud, S. (1937). Analysis terminable and interminable. In J. Strachey (Ed. & Trans.), *The standard edition of the complete works of Sigmund Freud*. (Vol. 23, pp. 209–253). London: Hogarth Press.

Freud, S., & Jung, C. (1974). *Letters*. Princeton, NJ: Princeton University Press.

Garfield, D. (1990). Manifestations of grief and grievance: A therapist's response to his analyst's death. In H. Schwartz & A. Silver (Eds.), *Illness in the analyst: Implications for the treatment relationship*. New York: International Universities Press.

Garrett, A. (1951). *Interviewing: Its principles and methods*. New York: Family Service Association of America.

Gill, M. (1954). Psychoanalysis and exploratory psychotherapy. *Journal of the American Psychoanalytic Association, 2*, 771–797.

Gill, M. (1982). *Analysis of transference. Vol. 1*. New York: International Universities Press.

Ginsburg, S. (1950). Values and the psychiatrist. *American Journal of Orthopsychiatry, 20*, 460–478.

Glover, E. (1949). *Psychoanalysis*. London, England: Staples Press.

Glover, E. (1955). *The technique of psychoanalysis*. New York: International Universities Press.

Goldberger, M. (1991). Pregnancy during analysis. *The Psychoanalytic Quarterly, 60*, 207–226.

Greenacre, P. (1966). Problems of overidealization of the analyst and analysis. *Psychoanalytic Study of the Child, 21*, 193–212. New Haven, CT: Yale University Press.

Greenacre, P. (1971). *Emotional growth*. New York: International Universities Press.

Greenson, R. (1966). Discussion. In E. Litman (Ed.), *Psychoanalysis in the Americas* (pp. 263–266). New York: International Universities Press.

Greenson, R. (1967). *The technique and practice of psychoanalysis*. New York: International Universities Press.

Greenson, R. (1978). *Explorations in psychoanalysis*. New York: International Universities Press.

Grotjahn, M. (1952). A psychoanalyst passes a small stone with big troubles. In M. Pinnar & B. Miller (Eds.), *When doctors are patients*. New York: W. W. Norton.

Grunebaum, H., & Christ, J. (1976). *Contemporary marriage: Structure, dynamics, and therapy*. Boston: Little, Brown.

Guibert, H. (1991). *To the friend who did not save my life*. New York: Athenum.

Hamilton, G. (1951). *Theory and practice of social casework*. New York: Columbia University Press.

Hartmann, H. (1939). Psychoanalysis and the concept of health. In *Essays on ego psychology* (pp. 3–18). New York: International Universities Press (1964).

Hartmann, H. (1958). *Ego psychology and the problem of adaptation*. New York: International Universities Press.

Heimann, P. (1950). On countertransference. *International Journal of Psychoanalysis, 31*, 81–84.

Held, R. (1955). Les criteres de la fin du traitement psychanalytique. *Review Francais Psychanalytique, 19*, 603–614.

Hollis, F. (1964). *Casework: A psychosocial therapy*. New York: Random House.

Hurwitz, M. (1986). The analyst, his theory, and the psychoanalytic process. *The Psychoanalytic Study of the Child, 41*, 439–466. New Haven, CT: Yale University Press.

Issacharoff, A. (1976). Barriers to knowing. In L. Epstein & A. Feiner (Eds.), *Countertransference: The therapist's contribution to the therapeutic situation*. New York: Jason Aronson.

Jaffe, D. (1991). Beyond the what, when, and how of the transference: A consideration of the why. *Journal of the American Psychoanalytic Association, 39*, 491–512.

Jones, E. (1953). *The life and work of Sigmund Freud: The formative years and the great discoveries* (Vol 1). New York: Basic Books.

Kadushin, A. (1972). *The social work interview*. New York: Columbia University Press.

Kelman, H., & Vollmerhausen, J. (1967). On Horney's psychoanalytic techniques: Developments and perspectives. In B. Wolman (Ed.), *Psychoanalytic techniques*. New York: Basic Books.

Kernberg, O. (1965). Notes on countertransference. *Journal of the American Psychoanalytic Association, 13*, 38–56.

Kernberg, D. (1991). Sadomasochism, sexual excitement, and perversion. *Journal of the American Psychoanalytic Association, 39*, 333–362.

Kesten, J. (1970). Learning through spite. In. H. Strean (Ed.), *New approaches in child guidance*. Metuchen, NJ: Scarecrow Press.

Kohut, H. (1971). *The analysis of the self: A systematic approach to the psychoanalytic treatment of narcissistic personality disorders*. New York: International Universities Press.

Kohut, H. (1984). *How does analysis cure?* Chicago: University of Chicago Press.

Kubler-Ross, E. (1972). On death and dying. *Journal of the American Medical Association, 221*, 174–179.

Kulish, N. (1984). The effect of the sex of the analyst on transference: A review of the literature. *Bulletin of Menninger Clinic, 48*, 95–110.

Kulish, N. (1989). Gender and transference: Conversations with female analysts. *Psychoanalytic Psychology, 6*, 59–71.

Langs, R. (1973). *The technique of psychoanalytic psychotherapy* (Vol 1). New York: Jason Aronson.

Langs, R. (1974). *The technique of psychoanalytic psychotherapy* (Vol 2). New York: Jason Aronson.

Langs, R. (1976). *The Bipersonal field.* New York: Jason Aronson.

Langs, R. (1981). *Resistances and interventions.* New York: Jason Aronson.

Langs, R., & Stone, L. (1980). *The therapeutic experience and its setting.* New York: Jason Aronson.

Lasky, R. (1990). Keeping the analysis intact when the analyst has suffered a catastrophic illness: Clinical considerations. In H. Schwartz & A. Silver (Eds.), *Illness in the analyst: Implications for the treatment relationship.* New York: International Universities Press.

Lax, R. (1969). Some considerations about transference and countertransference manifestations evoked by the analyst's pregnancy. *International Journal of Psychoanalysis, 50,* 363–372.

Lechat, R. (1954). Colloque sur les criteres de la fin du traitement psychanalytique. *Review Francais Psychanalytique, 18,* 355–363.

Little, M. (1951). Countertransference and the patient's response to it. *International Journal of Psychoanalysis, 32,* 32–40.

Little, R. (1967). Transference, countertransference, and survival reactions following an analyst's heart attack. *Psychoanalytic Forum, 2,* 107–126.

Lloyd, R., & Paulson, I. (1972). Projective identification in the marital relationship as a resistance in psychotherapy. *Archives of General Psychiatry, 27,* 410–413.

Macalpine, I. (1950). The development of the transference. *The Psychoanalytic Quarterly, 19,* 501–539.

Mahler, M. S., Pine, F., & Bergman, A. (1975). *The psychological birth of the human infant.* New York: Basic Books.

Malcolm, J. (1981). *Psychoanalysis: The impossible profession.* New York: Knopf.

May, M. (1991). Observations on countertransference, addiction and treatability. In A. Smaldino (Ed.), *Psychoanalytic approaches to addiction.* New York: Brunner/Mazel.

Mayer, E., & deMarneffe, D. (1991). Gender and referral patterns. *The Psychodynamic Letter, 1,* 1-3.

McLaughlin, J. (1981). Transference, psychic reality, and countertransference. *The Psychoanalytic Quarterly, 50,* 539–664.

McLaughlin, J. (1991). Clinical and theoretical aspects of enactment. *Journal of the American Psychoanalytic Association, 39,* 595–614.

Meghnagi, D. (1991). Jewish humour on psychoanalysis. *Review of Psychoanalysis, 18,* 223–228.

Menninger, K. (1958). *Theory of psychoanalytic technique* (1st ed.). New York: Basic Books.

Menninger, K. (1973). *Theory of psychoanalytic technique* (2nd ed.). New York: Basic Books.

Moore, B., & Fine, B. (1990). *Psychoanalytic terms and concepts.* New Haven, CT: Yale University Press.

Nacht, S., Bouvet, M., & Benassy, M. (1954). Colloque sur les criteres de la fin du traitement psychanalytique. *Review Francais Psychanalytique, 18*, 328–335.

Nagelberg, L. (1959). The meaning of help in psychotherapy. *The Psychoanalytic Review, 46*, 50–63.

Naterson, J. (1991). *Beyond countertransference.* Northvale, NJ: Jason Aronson.

Noble, D., & Hamilton, A. (1983). Coping and complying: A challenge to health care. *Social Work, 28*, 462–466.

Novey, R. (1983). Otto Rank: Beginnings, endings and current experience. *Journal of the American Psychoanalytic Association, 31* (4), 985–1002.

Novick, J., & Novick, K. (1991). Some comments on masochism and the delusion of omnipotence from a developmental perspective. *Journal of the American Psychoanalytic Association, 39*, 307–331.

Nunberg, H. (1928). *Problems of therapy.* In H. Nunberg (Ed.), *Practice and theory of psychoanalysis* (pp. 105–119). New York: Nervous and Mental Disease Publishing Co. (1948).

Nunberg, H. (1931). The synthetic function of the ego. In H. Nunberg (Ed.), *Practice and theory of psychoanalysis* (pp. 120 –136). New York: Nervous and Mental Disease Publishing Co. (1948).

Nunberg, H. (1954). Evaluation of the results of psychoanalytic treatment. *International Journal of Psychoanalysis, 35*, 2–7.

Ormont, L., & Strean, H. (1978). *The practice of conjoint therapy.* New York: Human Sciences Press.

Parad, H. (1965). *Crisis intervention.* New York: Family Service Association of America.

Perlman, H. (1968). *Persona: Social role and personality.* Chicago, IL: University of Chicago Press.

Perry, H. (1982). *Psychiatrist of America. The life of Harry Stack Sullivan.* Cambridge, MA: Harvard University Press.

Racker, H. (1953). The countertransference neurosis. *International Journal of Psychoanalysis, 34*, 313–324. Reprinted in H. Racker, *Transference and counter-transference.* New York: International Universities Press (1968).

Racker, H. (1968). *Transference and countertransference.* New York: International Universities Press.

Rangell, L. (1981). Psychoanalysis and dynamic psychotherapy: Similarities and differences twenty-five years later. *The Psychoanalytic Quarterly, 50*, 665–693.

Raphling, D. (1991). Countertransference in the treatment of sexually abused patients. *The Psychodynamic Letter, 1*, 1–3.

Reich, A. (1950). On the termination of analysis. In *Annie Reich: Psychoanalytic contributions* (pp. 121–135). New York: International Universities Press (1973).

Reich, A. (1951). On countertransference. In *Annie Reich: Psychoanalytic contributions* (pp 25–31). New York: International Universities Press (1973).

Reich, W. (1949). *Character analysis* (3rd ed.) New York: Orgone Publishing Press.

Reik, T. (1941). *Masochism in modern man.* New York: Grove Press.

Robbins, B. (1937). Escape into reality. *The Psychoanalytic Quarterly*, 6, 353–364.

Rogers, C. (1951). *Client-centered therapy*. Boston: Houghton Mifflin.

Rosenthal, L. (1958). Some aspects of a triple relationship: Activity group, group therapist, and supervisor. In A. Esman (Ed.), *New frontiers in child guidance*. New York: International Universities Press.

Rothenberg, A. (1988). *The creative process of psychotherapy*. New York: W. W. Norton.

Sandler, J. (1976). Countertransference and role responsiveness. *International Review of Psychoanalysis*, 3, 43–48.

Saul, L. (1958). *Technique and practice of psychoanalysis*. Philadelphia: Lippincott.

Schafer, R. (1983). *The analytic attitude*. New York: Basic Books.

Schmideberg, M. (1938). After the analysis. *The Psychoanalytic Quarterly*, 7, 122–142.

Searles, H. (1978). Psychoanalytic therapy with the borderline adult. In J. Masterson (Ed.), *New perspectives on psychotherapy with the borderline adult*. New York: Brunner/Mazel.

Segraves, R. (1982). *Marital therapy: A combined psychodynamic-behavioral approach*. New York: Plenum.

Sifneos, P. (1987). *Short-term dynamic psychotherapy: Evaluation and treatment*. New York: Plenum.

Sigman, M. (1985). The parallel processing phenomenon in the supervisory relationship: A therapist's view. *Current Issues in Psychoanalytic Practice*, 2, 21–31.

Siporin, M. (1975). *Introduction to social work practice*. New York: Macmillan Publishing Company.

Slakter, E. (1987). *Countertransference*. Northvale, NJ: Jason Aronson.

Smaldino, A. (1991). Substance abuse nightmares and the combat veteran with PTSD: A focus on the mourning process (pp. 28–50). In A. Smaldino (Ed.), *Psychoanalytic approaches to addiction*. New York: Brunner/Mazel.

Socarides, C. (1978). *Homosexuality*. New York: Jason Aronson.

Sonnenberg, S. (1991). The analyst's self-analysis and its impact on clinical work: A comment on the sources and importance of personal insight. *Journal of the American Psychoanalytic Association*, 39, 687–704.

Spotnitz, H. (1976). *Psychotherapy of preoedipal disorders*. New York: Jason Aronson.

Stein, A. (1972). Causes of failure in psychoanalytic psychotherapy. In B. Wolman (Ed.), *Success and failure in psychoanalysis and psychotherapy*. New York: The Macmillan Company.

Stone, L. (1961). *The psychoanalytic situation*. New York: International Universities Press.

Stone, L. (1973). On resistance to the psychoanalytic process. In B. Rubenstein (Ed.), *Psychoanalysis and contemporary science*. New York: The Macmillan Company.

Strean, H. (1978). *Clinical social work*. New York: The Free Press.

Strean, H. (1979). *Psychoanalytic theory and social work practice*. New York: The Free Press.

Strean, H. (1981). Extra-analytic contacts: Theoretical and clinical considerations. *The Psychoanalytic Quarterly*, 50, 238–259. (Also in H. Strean [Ed.], *Controversy in psychotherapy*. Metuchen, NJ: The Scarecrow Press)

Strean, H. (1985). *Resolving marital conflicts*. New York: Wiley and Sons.

Strean, H. (1988). *Behind the couch*. New York: Wiley and Sons. (Also in paperback, New York: Continuum [1990])

Strean, H. (1990). *Resolving resistances in psychotherapy*. New York: Brunner/Mazel. (Original work published 1985)

Strean, H., & Blatt, A. (1976). Some psychodynamics in referring a patient for psychotherapy. In H. Strean (Ed.), *Crucial issues in psychotherapy*. Metuchen, NJ: The Scarecrow Press.

Strean, H., & Freeman, L. (1991). *Our wish to kill: The murder in all of our hearts*. New York: St. Martin's Press.

Sullivan, H. (1953). *The interpersonal theory of psychiatry*. New York: W. W. Norton.

Szasz, T. (1957). On the experiences of the analyst in the psychoanalytic situation: A contribution to the theory of psychoanalytic treatment. *Journal of the American Psychoanalytic Association, 4*, 197–223.

Tarachow, S. (1963). *An introduction to psychotherapy*. New York: International Universities Press.

Tarnower, W. (1966). Extra-analytic contacts between the psychoanalyst and the patient. *The Psychoanalytic Quarterly, 35*, 399–413.

Teitelbaum, S. (1991). Countertransference and its potential for abuse. *Clinical Social Work, 19*, 267–277.

Ticho, E. A. (1972). Termination of psychoanalysis: Treatment goals, life goals. *The Psychoanalytic Quarterly, 4l*, 315–333.

Viederman, M. (1991). The real person of the analyst and his role in the process of psychoanalytic cure. *Journal of the American Psychoanalytic Association, 39*, 451–470.

Weinshel, E. (1984). Some observations on the psychoanalytic process. *The Psychoanalytic Quarterly, 52*, 63–92.

Weinshel, E. (1990). Further observations on the psychoanalytic process. *The Psychoanalytic Quarterly, 49*, 629–649.

Winnicott, D. (1949). Hate in the countertransference. *International Journal of Psychoanalysis, 30*, 194–203.

Wolberg, L. (1968). Short-term psychotherapy. In J. Marmor (Ed.), *Modern psychoanalysis*. New York: Basic Books.

Wolman, B. (1972). *Success and failure in psychoanalysis and psychotherapy*. New York: The Macmillan Company.

Wolpe, J. (1958). *Psychotherapy by reciprocal inhibition*. Stanford, CA: Stanford University Press.

Zerbe, K. (1990). Through the storm: Psychoanalytic theory in the psychotherapy of the anxiety disorders. *Bulletin of the Menninger Clinic, 54*, 171–188.

Name Index

Subject Index